EDVANTAGE INTERACTIVE

UTS AP Chemistry

Book 2

MW01712922

Development Team

Authors

Cheri Smith
Yale Secondary
School District 34 Abbotsford

Gary Davidson
School District 22 Vernon

Megan Ryan
Walnut Grove Secondary
School District 35 Langley

Chris Toth
St. Thomas More Collegiate
Burnaby, British Columbia

Program Consultant
Lionel Sandner
Edvantage Interactive

Customization by
Jennifer Pitt-Lainsbury
UTS, Toronto

COPIES OF THIS BOOK MAY BE OBTAINED BY CONTACTING:

Edvantage Interactive

E-MAIL:
info@edvantageinteractive.com

TOLL-FREE FAX:
866.275.0564

TOLL-FREE CALL:
866.422.7310

EDVANTAGE INTERACTIVE

UTS AP Chemistry – Book 2

ISBN 978-1-77249-437-2
University of Toronto Schools – 2016 Version

Vice-President of Marketing: *Don Franklin*
Director of Publishing: *Yvonne Van Ruskenveld*
Design and Production: *Donna Lindenberg*
Proofreading: *Eva van Emden*
Editorial Assistance: *Rhys Sandner*
Index: *Noeline Bridge*
Photos: *p. 33, K. Jung; p. 34, Bureau international des poids et mesures (BIPM)*

The AP Big Ideas at the beginning of each chapter are quoted from AP Chemistry: Course and Exam Description, revised edition, effective Fall 2013, published by the College Board, New York, NY. Advanced Placement, AP and College Board are registered trademarks of the College Board.

QR Code — What Is This?
The image to the right is called a QR code. It's similar to bar codes on various products and contains information that can be useful to you. Each QR code in this book provides you with online support to help you learn the course material. For example, find a question with a QR code beside it. If you scan that code, you'll see the answer to the question explained in a video created by an author of this book.
You can scan a QR code using an Internet-enabled mobile device. The program to scan QR codes is free and available at your phone's app store. Scanning the QR code above will give you a short overview of how to use the codes in the book to help you study.
Note: We recommend that you scan QR codes only when your phone is connected to a WiFi network. Depending on your mobile data plan, charges may apply if you access the information over the cellular network. If you are not sure how to do this, please contact your phone provider or us at info@edvantageinteractive.com

Contents

UTS AP Chemistry
Book 2

EDVANTAGE INTERACTIVE

3 and 4
Energy Changes and Rates of Reaction

Big Ideas

- ☐ Energy changes and rates of chemical reactions can be described quantitatively.
- ☐ Efficiency of chemical reactions can be improved by applying optimal conditions.
- ☐ Technologies that transform energy can have societal and environmental costs and benefits.

Overall Expectations

By the end of this course, students will

- ☐ D1. analyse technologies and chemical processes that are based on energy changes, and evaluate them in terms of their efficiency and their effects on the environment;
- ☐ D2. investigate and analyse energy changes and rates of reaction in physical and chemical processes, and solve related problems;
- ☐ D3. demonstrate an understanding of energy changes and rates of reaction.

Learning Goals	**Success Criteria**
Relating Science to Technology, Society and the Environment	*Relating Science to Technology, Society and the Environment*
☐ Analyse some conventional and alternative energy technologies	☐ I can evaluate the efficiency and impact on the environment of conventional and alternative energy technologies (e.g. fossil fuel-burning power plants, hydro-powered generators, solar panels, wind turbines, fuel cells)
☐ Analyse the conditions required to maximize the efficiency of some common natural or industrial chemical reactions	☐ I can identify several common natural and industrial chemical reactions and explain how to improve the efficiency of the reactions ☐ I can optimize the efficiency of chemical process while maximizing environmental sustainability
Developing Skills of Investigation and Communication	*Developing Skills of Investigation and Communication*
☐ Articulate and understand Thermodynamic and Kinetic terminology	☐ I can describe and correct use the concepts the terms enthalpy, entropy, Gibbs Free Energy, activation energy, endothermic, exothermic, potential energy, specific heat capacity, calorimetry, spontaneous, non-spontaneous, state-function, intrinsic, extrinsic
☐ Write thermochemical equations	☐ I can write correct thermochemical equations, indicating states, ΔH as a value or as a heat term in an equation ☐ I can modify the thermochemical equation to demonstrate the extrinsic nature of enthalpy

☐ Solve problems involving analysis of heat transfer in a chemical reaction	☐ I can use the equations $Q = mc\Delta T$, $C = Q/\Delta T$, $\Delta H = Q/n$ and heat lost + heat gained = 0 (the Law of Conservation of Energy) to calculate the heat ☐ In an isolated environment composed of a system and the surroundings, I understand that energy is transferred between the system and the surroundings through heat transfer or through work transfer ☐ transferred between the system and the surroundings in a chemical reaction or a physical process
☐ Plan and conduct an inquiry to calculate, using a calorimeter, the heat of reaction of a substance	☐ I can design an experiment to calculate the experimental heat of reaction or heat of solution of a chemical process using a calorimeter ☐ I understand that calorimetry is an experimental technique used to determine the heat transferred between a system and the surroundings ☐ I can calculate the theoretical heat of reaction or heat of solution and compare the theoretical value to my experimental value to evaluate the percent error in my experiment ☐ I can suggest several sources of error in calorimetry reactions ☐ I can optimize the experimental design to minimize error
☐ Solve problems related to energy changes in a chemical reaction, using Hess's law	☐ I can combine a series of thermochemical reactions and manipulate them to calculate the enthalpy of an overall reaction using Hess's Law
☐ Conduct an inquiry to test Hess's law	☐ I can experimentally determine the enthalpy of an overall reaction using Hess's Law by combining the data collected from a series of reactions that can easily be completed in the lab ☐ I understand why it is often difficult to determine the enthalpy of an overall reaction with just one reaction in a laboratory experiment
☐ Calculate the heat of reaction for a formation reaction, using a Table of Standard Enthalpies of formation and applying Hess's law	☐ I can correctly use a Table of Standard Enthalpies to determine the Heat of Formation for a reaction ☐ If the Heat of Formation for a chemical species is not directly available from a Table of Standard Enthalpies, I can use Hess's Law and combine several Heat of Formation thermochemical equations to determine an overall Heat of Formation thermochemical equation
☐ Calculate the concentration of reactants or products at a specific point in a reaction using the Integrated Rate Law for zeroth, first and second order reactions (AP)	☐ I can use the Integrated Rate Law for an equation given time and concentration data to determine if a reaction is zeroth, first or second order with respect to a reactant (AP) ☐ I can sketch graph for the linear relationships between concentration of reactant and time for zeroth, first and second order reactions (AP) ☐ I can write the linear relationship between concentration and time for zeroth, first and second order reactions (AP) ☐ I can use the linear relationships for zeroth, first and second order reactions to calculate the concentration of a reactant at a specific time in the reaction (AP)

☐ Calculate the half-life of a zeroth, first and second order reaction using the integrated rate law (AP)	☐ I can use the integrated rate law, time and concentration data to calculate the half-life of a reaction with respect to a reactant (AP) ☐ I can rearrange the integrated rate law into an expression for the half-life of a reactant according to of zeroth, first and second order rate laws (AP) ☐ I can determine the relationship between the half-life and the concentration of a reactant for zeroth, first and second order reactions and calculate unknown half-life and concentration values (AP)
☐ Plan and conduct an inquiry to determine how various factors affect the rate of a chemical reaction	☐ I can design an experiment to increase and decrease the rate of a chemical reaction using my knowledge of the factors that affect the rate of a reaction ☐ I can collect concentration and time data to determine the Rate Law of a chemical reaction (AP)
Understanding Basic Concepts	*Understanding Basic Concepts*
☐ Compare the energy changes resulting from physical change, chemical reactions and nuclear reactions	☐ I can distinguish between endothermic and exothermic physical, chemical and nuclear changes ☐ I can describe the reasons why heat is released or absorbed from a system ☐ I understand that chemical processes can be distinguished from physical processes because I understand the difference between chemical bonds and intermolecular attractions
☐ Compare the energy change from a reaction in which bonds are formed to one in which bonds are broken, and explain these changes in terms of endothermic and exothermic reactions	☐ I can determine whether a reaction is exothermic or endothermic by comparing the bond energies of the reactants and products quantitatively ☐ I understand that the net energy change during a reaction is the sum of the energy required to break the bonds in the reactant molecules and the energy released in forming the bonds of the product molecules
☐ Explain how mass, heat capacity, and change in temperature of a substance determine the amount of heat gained or lost by the substance	☐ I understand that temperature is a measure of the average kinetic energy of atoms and molecules ☐ I understand that systems and surroundings can gain or lose heat and that heat is transferred from one to the other according to the First Law of Thermodynamics ☐ I understand how to calculate the enthalpy of a reaction per mole reaction
☐ State Hess's law, and explain, using examples, how it is applied to find the enthalpy changes of a reaction	☐ I can articulate Hess's Law clearly and explain its importance in calculating the enthalpy of a reaction using examples ☐ I can write a system of chemical reactions to clearly demonstrate Hess's Law
☐ Explain what entropy is and how changes in entropy affect the spontaneity of a reaction (AP)	☐ I can describe what entropy is in terms of microstates and energy dispersal (AP) ☐ I can assess whether the change in entropy of a given chemical reaction or physical process is thermodynamically favourable or not and explain why a negative change in entropy is thermodynamically unfavourable while a positive change in entropy is thermodynamically favourable (AP) ☐ I can state the Second and Third Laws of Thermodynamics and understand how they apply to assessing the spontaneity of chemical and physical processes (AP)

☐ Explain what Gibbs Free Energy is and how it can be used to assess the thermodynamics of a chemical or physical process (AP)	☐ I understand that when the change in Gibbs Free Energy ΔG is < 0, a chemical or physical process is thermodynamically favoured and when $\Delta G > 0$ a process is thermodynamically unfavourable (AP) ☐ I understand how to calculate the ΔG of a process using $\Delta G = \Delta H - T\Delta S$ (AP) ☐ I understand how to calculate ΔG using the standard Gibbs Free Energy of formation tables (AP) ☐ I understand that the magnitude of ΔG provides information about the about the thermodynamic favourability of a process (AP) ☐ I understand that although a process may be thermodynamically favourable, the rate of the reaction is determined by other factors as well (AP)
☐ Explain, using collision theory and potential energy diagrams, how factors such as temperature, the surface area of the reactants, the nature of the reactants, the addition of catalysts, and the concentration of the solution control the rate of a chemical reaction	☐ I can state the factors which affect the rate of a reaction (reactant concentration, presence of a catalyst, surface area, nature of reactants, temperature) ☐ I can explain how each factor affects the rate of a reaction using collision and transition state theory ☐ I can explain how the rate of a reaction is influenced by the concentration or pressure of reactants, the phase of reactants and environmental factors such as temperature or solvent, affect the rate of a reaction ☐ I can use collision theory, potential energy diagrams and activation energy to explain why all reactant collisions do not produce products and how to optimize reaction conditions to increase the rate of reaction ☐ I can explain how a Maxwell-Bolzmann distribution depicts the relationship between temperature and the fraction of effective collisions in a reaction ☐ I can differentiate between a homogeneous and a heterogenous catalyst and explain, in general terms how a catalyst acts to lower the activation energy of a reaction ☐ I can calculate the Rate Law of a reaction given concentration and rate of reaction reactants that are zeroth, first and second order with respect to a reaction ☐ I can determine the rate constant for the Rate Law of an equation, including the units of the rate constant, given concentration of reaction and rate of reaction data
☐ Describe simple potential energy diagrams of chemical reactions	☐ I can sketch the potential energy profile of endothermic and exothermic reactions given the enthalpy and the activation energy of the forward or the reverse reaction ☐ I can label the potential energy of the reactants and products, the enthalpy of the forward and reverse reactions, the activation energy of the forward and reverse reactions on a potential energy diagram ☐ I can depict how the presence of a catalyst will affect the potential energy profile of a reaction ☐ I can depict and label intermediates on a potential energy diagram

☐ Understand the magnitude and temperature dependence of the rate of reaction is quantitatively related to the rate constant and the magnitude of the activation energy (AP)	☐ I can explain how the temperature dependence of reaction rates is contained in the temperature dependence of the magnitude of the rate constant (AP) ☐ I understand how the Arrhenius equation can be used to summarize experiments on the temperature dependence in terms of activation energy needed to reach a transition state (AP)
☐ Explain, with reference to a simple chemical reaction, how the rate of a reaction is determined by the series of elementary steps that make up the overall reaction mechanism	☐ I can identify the rate determining step in a reaction mechanism ☐ I can use the rate determining step to assess the credibility of a proposed Rate Law for a reaction ☐ I can identify intermediates, reactants, products and catalysts in a reaction mechanism ☐ I understand how the elementary steps of a reaction mechanism combine to give the overall chemical reaction ☐ I can determine the Rate Law for a reaction given a reaction mechanism (AP) ☐ I can sketch a Potential energy diagram to illustrate the relative activation energies of the elementary steps and illustrate the overall enthalpy of the reaction ☐ I can determine the molecularity of an elementary step

In the AP curriculum, these topics relate to AP Big Idea 4: Rates of chemical reactions are determined by details of the molecular collisions and Big Idea 5: The Laws of Thermodynamics describe the essential role of energy and explain and predict the direction of changes in matter.

3 Thermodynamics

Chapter 3 Prep Questions

1. Indicate whether each of the following changes is endothermic or exothermic:
   (a) Barbecuing a steak

   (b) Freezing a tray full of water to make ice

   (c) Neutralizing an acid spill with baking soda

   (d) Making a grilled cheese sandwich

   (e) Lighting a barbecue igniter

   (f) Condensing water on a mirror

2. Convert the following ΔH notation equations into thermochemical equations using the smallest whole number coefficients possible:
   (a) $\frac{1}{2}\, C_3H_8(g) \rightarrow \frac{1}{2}\, C_3H_8(l)$ $\Delta H = -175$ kJ/mol

   (b) $Li(s) + \frac{1}{2}\, CaCl_2(aq) \rightarrow LiCl(aq) + \frac{1}{2}\, Ca(s)$ $\Delta H = -362$ kJ/mol

   (c) $2\, B(s) + 3\, H_2O(g) \rightarrow B_2H_6(g) + 3/2\, O_2(g)$ $\Delta H = 762$ kJ/mol

   (d) $\frac{1}{2}\, P_4(s) + 3\, Cl_2(g) \rightarrow 2\, PCl_3(s)$ $\Delta H = -613$ kJ/mol

   (e) $NH_3(g) + 3/2\, N_2O(g) \rightarrow 2\, N_2(g) + 3/2\, H_2O(l)$ $\Delta H = -505$ kJ/mol

   (f) $\frac{1}{2}\, Fe_3O_4(s) + \frac{1}{2}\, CO(g) \rightarrow 3/2\, FeO(s) + \frac{1}{2}\, CO_2(g)$ $\Delta H = 9$ kJ/mol

3. Convert the following thermochemical equations into ΔH notation using the smallest whole number coefficients possible.
   (a) $C(s) + 2\, H_2(g) + \frac{1}{2}\, O_2(g) \rightarrow CH_3OH(l) + 201$ kJ/mol

   (b) $\frac{1}{2}\, Cu(s) + \frac{1}{2}\, H_2(g) + \frac{1}{2}\, O_2(g) \rightarrow \frac{1}{2}\, Cu(OH)_2(s) + 225$ kJ/mol

   (c) 389 kJ/mol $+ \frac{1}{2}\, Sb_4O_6(s) + 3\, C(s) \rightarrow 2\, Sb(s) + 3\, CO(g)$

   (d) 56 kJ/mol $+ NO_2(g) \rightarrow NO(g) + \frac{1}{2}\, O_2(g)$

(e) $PCl_3(g) + \frac{1}{2} O_2(g) \rightarrow Cl_3PO(g) + 286$ kJ/mol

(f) $F_2(s) + \frac{1}{2} O_2(g) \rightarrow OF_2(g) + 22$ kJ/mol

4. Use the equations in question 3 to answer the following questions:
   (a) How much energy would be released during the formation of 4 mol of methanol?

   (b) How many moles of nitrogen dioxide could be decomposed through the use of 168 kJ of energy?

   (c) Is more energy absorbed or released during the formation of Cl_3PO gas from PCl_3 and O_2 gas?

   (d) What is the ΔH value for the decomposition of OF_2 gas into its elements?

   (e) How much energy is required to decompose 1 mol of copper(II) hydroxide?

5. Does the following potential energy diagram represent an endothermic or an exothermic reaction? What is ΔH for this reaction?

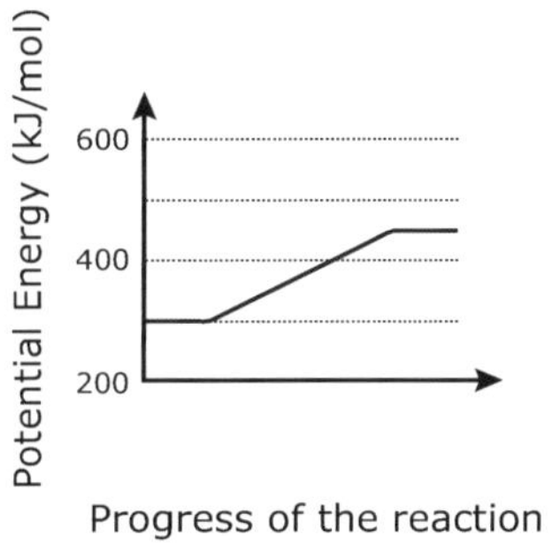

6. What is ΔH for this reaction?

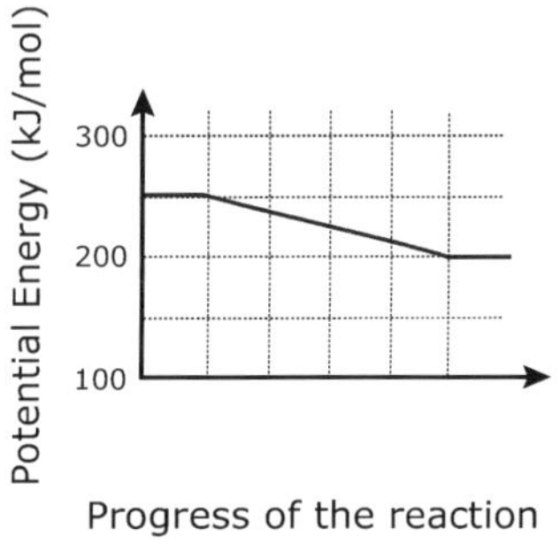

3.1 Law of Thermodynamics and Calorimetry

Warm Up: Calorimetry – The Measurement of Heat Transfer

The apparatus shown here is used to collect data that produces the graph shown. The hot plate supplies kinetic energy to the water sample the entire time. As heat is absorbed, the temperature rises. What is that energy being used for in each labeled region on the graph? Approximately how much energy was used for each change to the water? (Region A is completed as a sample.)

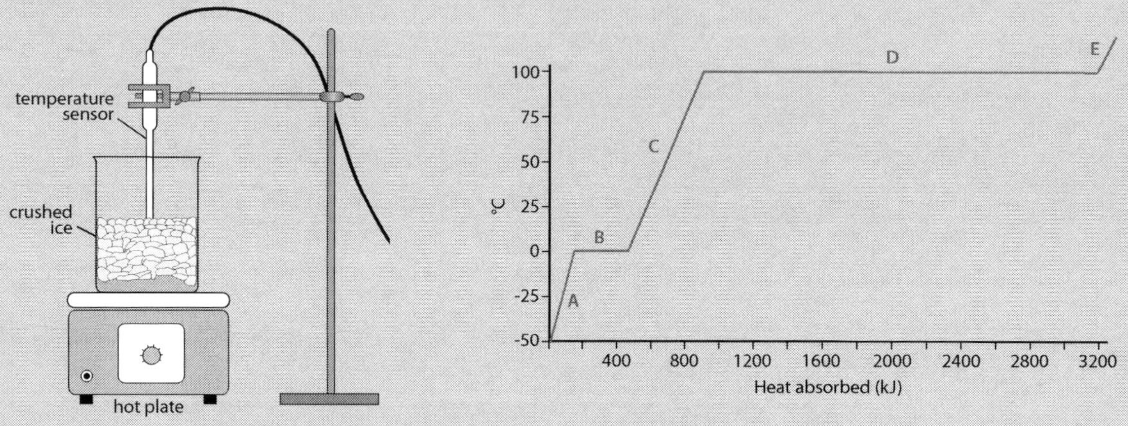

Region	Energy is used to...	Energy required
A	Heat solid water from –50 to 0°C	Approximately 180 kJ of energy
B		
C		
D		
E		

Study regions A, C, and E. What three things might cause the energy required to differ?

1.
2.
3.

Study regions B and D. What two things might cause the energy required to differ?

1.

2.

Internal Energy, State Functions, and Conventions of Thermochemistry

Chemical energy is one of our most important energy sources. It can be converted into the heat, mechanical, and electrical energy we all use to operate a myriad of devices every day. The origin of this chemical energy lies in the position and motion of atoms, molecules, and subatomic particles. The various types of energies that combine to give the total **internal energy, *E***, of a sample of matter include the following:

- *electronic* — kinetic energy of moving electrons and most significantly, potential energy due to electron-nuclei interactions
- *rotational* — kinetic energy due to rotation of a molecule about its center of mass
- *vibrational* — kinetic energy due to vibrations of atoms within the molecule
- *translational* — kinetic energy associated with gas molecules as they move linearly from one place to another

Many physics textbooks use the symbol *U* for internal energy.

Thermodynamics is the study of energy changes and the laws governing the conversion of heat into other forms of energy. Thermodynamics is primarily concerned with *macroscopic properties,* those you can see or measure such as temperature, pressure and volume, so a detailed analysis of the of the sources of internal energy is not necessary in this discussion. The mathematical study required is better covered in a university physical chemistry course. The reaction or physical system we are studying will be called the **system** and the rest of the universe will be called the **surroundings**. Additionally, we will refer to certain quantities as *state properties or functions.*

A **state function** or *state variable* is a property that depends on the current "state" of a system. These are conditions such as its volume, temperature, pressure and composition. State functions are independent of the pathway taken to reach the state. Common state functions include internal energy and enthalpy changes. ΔE does not depend on how a change in internal energy takes place, but on the difference between the initial and final internal energy of the system. Entropy and free energy are state functions you can look forward to encountering later in your AP Chemistry career.

Functions that do depend on the pathway taken to reach the current state may be referred to as **pathway dependent functions** or *process quantities*. Conditions such as work and heat are examples.

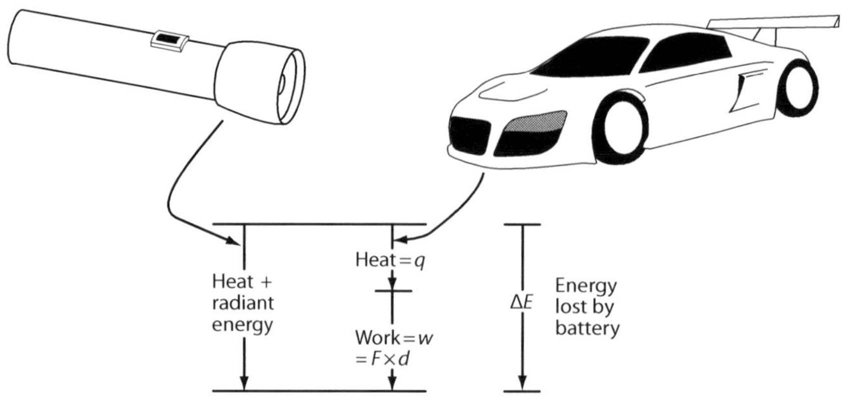

Figure 3.1.1 *A flashlight (left) and a remote control car (right) are operated using the same two D-cell batteries. The total change in internal energy is the same. However, the work done and heat and radiant energy released differ. This indicates that ΔE (internal energ equal to q + w) is a state function while q (heat) and w (work) are not.*

Sign conventions apply to most state functions. Energy leaving or produced by the system has a negative sign. Energy entering the system from the surroundings has a positive sign. If the volume of a system decreases, ΔV will be negative. If the volume of a system increases or expands, ΔV will be positive. When work involves gases being formed or consumed in a chemical reaction, the change in the number of moles of gas, Δn, should be shown as negative if the total number of moles of gas decrease and positive if they increase.

The **First Law of Thermodynamics**, a restatement of, Antoine Lavoisier's **Law of Conservation of Mass**.

Energy cannot be created or destroyed. It can be converted from one form to another.

$$\Delta E_{universe} = \Delta E_{system} + \Delta E_{surroundings} = 0$$

Two common methods for transferring energy between a system and its surroundings are heat, q, and work, w. The first law is sometimes expressed by defining internal energy as the sum of heat and work.

Although there are many different types of work, we will discuss primarily electrical work in our unit on electrochemistry and the work done by expanding gases. Work done by expanding gases is called, **pressure-volume work** and is equal to the product of the constant external pressure, P, exerted on the expanding gas and the change in volume, ΔV. Work can be converted to the familiar unit of energy, the joule, with the conversion factor 101.3 J equivalent to 1 litre-atmosphere.

$$\Delta E = q + w \text{ and } w = -P\Delta V$$

Sample Problem — Internal Energy, Heat, and Work Relationships

A potato cannon propels a piece of potato using the energy from a combusted fuel. The fuel performs 948 J of work on the potato and heats the cannon with 1355 J of heat. Calculate ΔE for the combustion process.

What to Think about	How to Do It
1. Determine the q and w values. 2. Assign the appropriate signs.	The cannon gets *hot*; therefore the reaction is exothermic. So $q = -1355\text{ J}$ Work is done BY the system; therefore the reaction is exergonic. So $w = -948\text{ J}$
3. Use $\Delta E = q + w$ to determine the answer.	$\Delta E = -1355\text{ J} + (-)948\text{ J} = \mathbf{-2303\text{ J}}$

Practice Problems — Internal Energy, Heat, and Work Relationships

1. A system absorbs 392 J of heat while the surroundings do 234 J of work on the system. What is the change in internal energy for the system?

2. A system releases 475 J of heat as it performs 524 J of work on the surroundings. Calculate ΔE for the system.

3. A system released 64 kJ of energy as its internal energy increased by 43 kJ. Did the system do work on the surroundings or was work done on the system? How much work was involved?

The ideal gas law, $PV = nRT$, can be rearranged to show that the ratio of the product of a gas sample's pressure and volume to the product of the gas sample's number of moles, n, and Kelvin temperature, is a constant. That ratio, R, only changes with the units of pressure selected. It may be 0.0821 L•atm/mol•K or 62.4 L•mmHg/mol•K for example. Multiplication of the first value by 101.3 J/L•atm gives 8.31 J/L•atm. The ideal gas law will be used extensively in the chapter on gases. It can also be used in the following derivation for pressure-volume work situations.

$$\Delta E = q - P\Delta V \text{ and since } PV = nRT \text{ then } \Delta E = q - \Delta nRT$$

When heat is absorbed or released from a chemical system and the external pressure is constant, the heat released or absorbed is equal to the enthalpy change of the process, $q_p = \Delta H$. For reactions that do not involve gases or a change in the number of moles of gas, the pressure-volume work done is zero, the $P\Delta V$ term becomes zero and $\Delta H = \Delta E$.

Sample Problem — Enthalpy vs. Internal Energy at Constant Pressure

Consider the following reaction occurring in an open container.

$$CaCO_3(s) \rightarrow CaO(s) + CO_2(g) \quad \Delta H° = 571 \text{ kJ/mol}_{rxn}$$

(i) How do q and ΔH compare under these conditions?
(ii) Calculate the change in internal energy.
(iii) How would ΔE and ΔH compare if both values were given to two significant figures?

What to Think About	How to Do It
1. Consider external pressure conditions. In this case, external pressure is constant and is equal to atmospheric pressure.	Under these conditions, $q_p = \Delta H$
2. $\Delta E = q + w$ where $q_p = \Delta H$ and $w = -P\Delta V = -\Delta nRT$ $\Delta E = \Delta H - \Delta nRT$ where $\Delta n = +1$ mole of gas	$\Delta E = 571 \text{ kJ/mol}_{rxn} - \left(\frac{1 \text{ mol}}{\text{mol}_{rxn}}\right)\left(\frac{0.00831 \text{ kJ}}{\text{mol K}}\right)(298 \text{ K})$ $= 571 \text{ kJ/mol}_{rxn} - 2.48 \text{ kJ/mol}_{rxn}$ $= 569 \text{ kJ/mol}_{rxn}$
3. Round the given ΔH and calculate ΔE to two significant figures.	$\Delta E = \Delta H = 570 \text{ kJ/mol}_{rxn}$ Note: There is only 2.48 kJ difference per mole of gas formed (or consumed). To two significant figures, the values are virtually the same.

Practice Problems — Enthalpy vs. Internal Energy at Constant Pressure

1. Consider the imaginary reaction: $A(s) + 2\,B_2C_3(aq) \rightarrow 4\,D(g) + 3\,EF_4(g)$
   The reaction's ΔE value is measured as 442.26 kJ/mol$_{rxn}$. What is $\Delta H°$?

2. A cylinder equipped with a piston expands against an external pressure of 1.04 atm. A combusted fuel causes an expansion from 0.243 L to 1.650 L with the emission of 1.553 kJ of heat. What is ΔE for this process? Note: Be sure to include the conversion factor 101.3 J/L•atm where necessary.

3. To inflate a weather balloon you must increase its volume from 0.58 L (nearly empty for a weather balloon) to a full volume against an external pressure of 1 atm exactly. The process requires 22.632 kJ of work. What is the volume of the balloon?

Specific Heat, Heat Capacity, Heat of Fusion, and Heat of Vaporization

Recall that heat is the exchange of thermal energy between a system and its surroundings. This exchange is caused by a temperature difference and the energy always moves from a region of high temperature to a region of lower temperature.

Temperature is a measure of the average *thermal energy* in a sample of matter.

Heat is the energy *transferred* from one body to another because of a difference in temperature.

The quantity of energy required to change the temperature of a particular sample of material is the sample's **heat capacity**. It is symbolized by an upper case letter **C**. Heat capacity is generally measured in units of **J/°C**. For the most part in chemistry, it is much more useful to consider a material's **specific heat capacity**, sometimes simply referred to as **specific heat.** This is represented by a lower case letter ***c***.

Substance	J/g°C
Elemental Solids	
Aluminum	0.900
Beryllium	1.830
Cadmium	0.230
Copper	0.387
Germanium	0.322
Gold	0.129
Iron	0.448
Lead	0.128
Silicon	0.703
Silver	0.234
Other Solids	
Brass	0.380
Glass	0.837
Ice (–5°C)	2.090
Marble	0.860
Wood	1.700

Substance	J/g°C
Liquids	
Alcohol (ethyl)	2.400
Mercury	0.140
Water (15°C)	4.180
Gas	
Steam (100°C)	2.010

Table 3.1.1 *Specific heat capacity values for common substances*

Specific heat capacity, *c*, is the quantity of *heat* required to raise the temperature of a *specific quantity* of a substance by *one degree celsius.*

For water, $c = 4.180$ J/g°C = 1 cal/g °C

Quick Check

Examine Table 3.1.1.

1. How do the specific heat capacities of metals compare to that of liquid water?

2. If equal masses of water and iron were exposed to the same heat source, which one would reach the temperature of 100°C first?

3. Consider equal masses of iron and water at 100°C. Which would cool to room temperature more quickly?

Regions A, C, and E of the Warm Up graph indicate that not only does the identity of a substance influence its specific heat capacity, but so does the state. Comparing regions A and C of the graph in the Warm Up, we can see that for a 50°C increase in temperature, ice required about 100 kJ but liquid water required about 200 kJ over the same temperature increment. Liquid water took two times the energy required to warm the same amount of ice. As indicated in Table 3.1.1, liquid water's specific heat capacity c = 4.18 J/g °C, while solid water, or **ice has c = 2.09 J/g°C**. Interestingly, gaseous water or **steam has c = 2.01 J/g°C,** which is close to that of ice. The high heat capacity of liquid water is responsible for the relatively constant temperatures of coastal and island cities such as Vancouver, San Francisco, Honolulu, and Shanghai.

Changes of State

Frozen water molecules vibrate but can't change places.

Water molecules in a liquid state slide over each other.

Water molecules in a gaseous state move randomly throughout their container.

Figure 3.1.2 *The states of matter*

Regions B and D of the Warm Up graph indicate the significant amount of energy required to change the state of matter without raising its temperature. This energy is required to overcome the attractive forces holding the substance's molecules together in the solid or liquid state. These attractive forces are generally referred to as **intermolecular forces (IMFs**). There are three types, increasing in strength for a particular substance:

- **London dispersion forces** — a weak force that involves instantaneous induced poles of opposite charge on the molecules
- **dipole-dipole forces** — a slightly stronger force caused by permanent poles of opposite charge produced by differences in atoms' electronegativity at the opposite ends of bonds in a molecule
- **hydrogen bonds** — the strongest IMF is due to very strong dipoles produced by bonds where hydrogen is attached to one of the three smallest diameter, largest electronegativity elements – N, O, or F

As water melts and evaporates (or boils), its weak London dispersions forces and its strong dipole-dipole/hydrogen bonds must be overcome to allow freedom of motion as the water changes state.

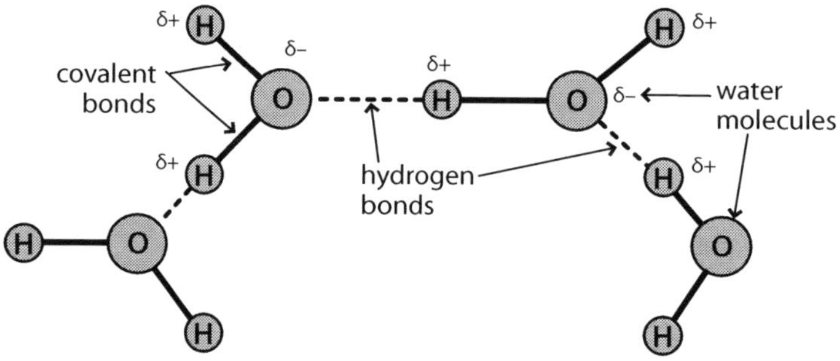

Figure 3.1.3 *Hydrogen bonds form between the slightly negative partial charges on oxygen atoms on one water molecule and the slightly positive partial charges on hydrogen atoms on another water molecule. The partial charges, indicated with a lower case delta (δ), are due to the higher electron density on the side of the covalent bond closest to the more electronegative oxygen atom and the lower electron density on the hydrogen side of the bond in the water molecule. Note the difference between intermolecular H-bonds and intramolecular covalent bonds.*

The energy required to overcome these intermolecular forces is called the **heat of fusion** or **heat of vaporization** depending on whether the substance is undergoing melting or evaporation.

> The **heat of fusion** is the quantity of *heat* required to change a particular *quantity* of a pure solid *at its melting point* into a *liquid.*
>
> H_{fusion} of water = 334 J/g

The **heat of vaporization** is the quantity of *heat* required to change a particular *quantity* of a pure liquid *at its boiling point* into a gas.

$$H_{vaporization} \text{ of water} = 2250 \text{ J/g}$$

Note that regions B and D in the Warm Up graph indicate the difference between H_{fusion} and H_{vap} for water. The heats of fusion and vaporization are independent of the temperature change as there is no temperature change. The temperature remains constant during a change of state. This is because all energy is being used to overcome the intermolecular forces between the particles. During cooling, heat is released as intermolecular forces are formed. The magnitude of energy needed for the change is the same, but the value of the energy is given a negative number to indicate that energy is released. The energy required for the phase change from gas to liquid is called **heat of condensation** and energy required for the phase change from liquid to gas is **the heat of solidification**. A heat change that occurs at constant temperature is referred to as **latent heat**.

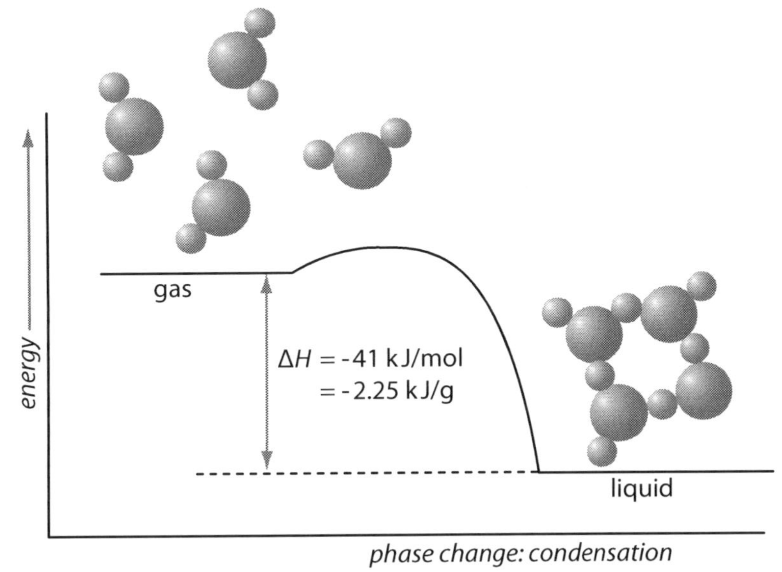

Figure 3.1.4 *Hydrogen bonds form as gaseous water condenses to become liquid. Note that $H_{vap} = -H_{cond}$ and the magnitude of the energy is the same, but the sign is reversed and the value may be expressed in units of kJ/mol or kJ/g. There will be a difference of 18.01 times when comparing the value in kJ/mol to that in kJ/g as this is the mass of one mole of water.*

The amount of heat absorbed or released during a cooling or heating process can be calculated by considering the specific heat capacity, the mass, and the temperature change. Where a state change is included, only the mass and the heat of vaporization and/or fusion need be considered. Heat is represented by *q*.

For a temperature change: $\boldsymbol{q = mc\Delta T}$

For a state change: $\boldsymbol{q = H_{fus}m}$ or $\boldsymbol{q = H_{vap}m}$

For these calculations, the system is assumed to be entirely insulated from the surroundings so that no heat can enter or leave the system from or to any outside heat source or sink.

Sample Problem — Calculation of Heat Changes

Calculate the heat required to change 50.0 g of water at 25.0°C into steam at 120.0°C.

What to Think About

1. It is helpful to represent the energy changes with a sketch.
2. Apply the appropriate equations to each portion of the problem.
3. Calculate the heat required to accomplish each change. *Take care* with substitution into the equations. It is easy to confuse the *c* values for different states and the *H* values for fusion and vaporization.
4. Sum the *q* values for each portion. Take care with significant figures and units, rounding only at the end and ensuring all of the energy values have the same units before adding them together
5. Remember that when summing or subtracting the final answer is rounded to the *least precise place value*.

How To Do It

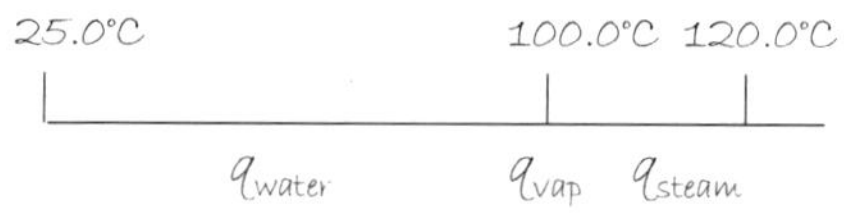

$q_{water} = mc_{water}\Delta T$
$q_{vap} = H_{vap}m$
$q_{steam} = mc_{steam}\Delta T$

$q_{water} = 50.0\ \text{g} \times \dfrac{4.18\ \text{J}}{\text{g}\,°\text{C}} \times 75.0\ °\text{C}$

$q_{water} = 15\,675\ \text{J}$ (3 sig figs)

$q_{vap} = \dfrac{2250\ \text{J}}{\text{g}} \times 50.0\ \text{g} = 112\,500\ \text{J}$ (3 sf)

$q_{steam} = 50.0\ \text{g} \times \dfrac{2.01\ \text{J}}{\text{g}\,°\text{C}} \times 20.0\ °\text{C} = 2010\ \text{J}$ (3 sf)

Note: All ΔT values are treated as (+).

$15\,675\ \text{J} + 112\,500\ \text{J} + 2010\ \text{J}$

$130\,185\ \text{J} = 1.30 \times 10^5\ \text{J} = 130.\ \text{kJ}$

(In this case, the thousands place is the least precise.)

Practice Problems — Calculation of Heat Changes

1. Aluminum metal is commonly used to determine the temperature of different portions of a Bunsen burner flame. Calculate the heat required to completely melt a 0.325 g piece of aluminum wire beginning at a room temperature of 22.5°C. The melting point of aluminum is 660.3°C and its heat of fusion is 398 J/g. Refer to Table 3.1.1 for the specific heat capacity.

2. A piece of iron metal initially at a room temperature of 21.5°C is left on the window ledge in the lab on a sunny day. It absorbs 862.4 J of heat and warms to 32.5°C. What is the mass of the iron? See Table 3.1.1.

3. A 75.45 g sample of silicon initially at 20.5°C absorbs 1326 J of heat. What is the final temperature of the sample? See Table 3.1.1.

4. Calculate the heat required to change a 55.00 g ice cube at –15.0°C into steam at 125.0°C. (Hint: There should be five different *q* values in your calculation.)

The First Law of Thermodynamics – Energy is Always Conserved

Heat calculations involving physical processes which consider the system and the surroundings, for example, where something hot is added to something cold, require a generalized version of the First Law of Thermodynamics expressed simply as the Law of Conservation of Energy.

> heat lost + heat gained = 0
>
> or
>
> (–) heat lost = heat gained
>
> Where *heat lost* is the *total* heat lost by the hotter substance and *heat gained* is the *total* heat gained by the colder substance.

As with the previous calculations, we are assuming the interacting systems are thermally insulated from the rest of the universe.

Sample Problem — Calculating Heat Changes in Systems Combining Hot and Cold

If 50.0 g of water at 15.0°C is added to 40.0 g of water at 85.0°C, what is the final temperature of the system?

What to Think About	How To Do It
1. A sketch along the lines of the one shown in the previous sample problem is helpful; however, the final temperature is represented by a variable such as *T*. Again, *remember* to consider all ΔT values to be positive.	15.0°C T°C 85.0°C |————————————| 50.0 g q_{cold} q_{hot} 40.0 g
2. Apply the appropriate equations to each portion of the problem. Note that for simplification, we are working with the absolute values of q_{hot} and q_{cold}.	Since $q_{cold} = q_{hot}$, then $mc\Delta T_{cold} = mc\Delta T_{hot}$ and $m_{cold}c_{water}(T - 15.0)$ $= m_{hot}c_{water}(85.0 - T)$
3. Calculate the heat required to cause each change. *Take care* with substitution into the equations. In addition to different temperature values, there are different masses to keep track of.	$50.0\text{ g} \times 4.18\text{ J/g°C} \times (T - 15.0) =$ $40.0\text{ g} \times 4.18\text{ J/g°C} \times (85.0 - T)$ So,
4. A bit of algebra, involving first, distribution through the brackets…then collection of like terms…and finally solving for *T*…provides an answer.	$= 209T - 3135 = 14\,212 - 167.2T$ $\therefore 376.2T = 17\,347$
5. Notice the answer *makes sense* as it is between the two initial temperatures and closer to the cold one as the cold mass was greater.	$\therefore\ T = 17\,347/376.2 =$ **46.1°C** Note: The significant figures in the final answer are based on the original problem rather than each step in the algebra. Sig figs apply to measurements, not algebra.

Practice Problems — Calculating Heat Changes in Systems Combining Hot and Cold

1. A 29.65 g solid gold earring at 33.5°C falls from your ear into a thermally isolated 245.0 mL cup of 65.5°C coffee. Use information from the Table 3.1.1 to determine the final temperature of the earring and the coffee when they reach the same temperature (*thermal equilibrium*). Assume the specific heat capacity and the density of the coffee is the same as those of water and that the final temperature will be between the initial temperatures.

2. A brass ball bearing with an initial temperature of 95.55°C is placed in a thermally insulated beaker containing 125.0 mL of water (assume d_{water} = 1 g/mL exactly) at 20.50°C. When the two substances reach thermal equilibrium, their final temperature is 26.55°C. What is the mass of the brass ball bearing?

3. What is the final temperature when a 348.00 g block of ice at –44.5°C is added to 95.00 g of steam at 125.5°C in an insulated system? Assume the final result will be liquid water.

Coffee Cup Calorimetry

Most people are familiar with the Calorie unit of heat measurement in the context of the labels of virtually all prepared foods we purchase in supermarkets today. Government regulations have required nutrition facts labels on all prepared foods since 1994 in the United States and since 2003 in Canada (see Fig 3.1.6).

The caloric content on these labels is in Calories (Cal) or "big C" calories. A food calorie reported on Nutrition Facts labels is actually equivalent to 1000 cal or 1 kcal.

1 Cal = 1000 cal = 1 kcal = 4.184 kJ
= the energy to warm 1 g of water by 1 Celsius degree
(or 1 Kelvin degree as the *change* is the same)

Where does the information on the caloric content of foods values come from? How is it measured? The caloric content is measured with a device called a **calorimeter**. The first calorimeter was designed and used by Antoine Lavoisier and Pierre Laplace in the early 1780s. They used the mass of ice melted by a chemical change as a measure of the amount of heat produced during the change. In laboratories everywhere, we now use the temperature change produced in a given mass of water as a measure of the amount of heat produced or absorbed during a physical or chemical change occurring in the calorimeter. If the change is exothermic, energy is released and the temperature increases; if it is endothermic, energy is absorbed from the water and the temperature decreases.

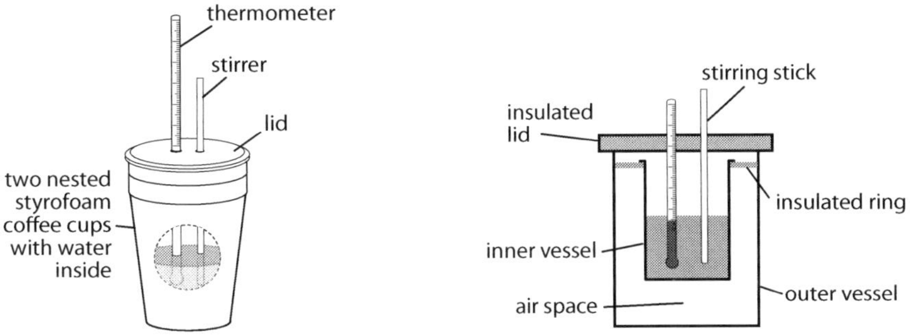

Figure 3.1.5 *Calorimeters. The nesting of two cups, one inside the other, provides reasonable insulation in a coffee cup calorimeter. A thermos with a sealed thermometer and stirrer is similar but slightly more sophisticated. A layer of air provides excellent insulation.*

The principle behind the calorimeter is once again, the law of conservation of energy, a simplified expression of the first law of thermodynamics.

> heat lost + heat gained = 0
>
> Hence, heat lost, or gained, by the physical or chemical change in the calorimeter *equals* heat gained, or lost, by the system—usually an aqueous solution—inside the calorimeter.

Simple calorimeters may be used to collect data for the situations in the practice problems in the first half of this section. Additionally, they may be used to determine heats of reaction and heats of solution.

Sample Problem — Determining the Enthalpy Change of an Aqueous Solution

A neutralization reaction between 50.0 mL of 1.00 mol/L HCl and 50.0 mL of 1.00 mol/L NaOH is performed with constant stirring at a room temperature of 20.50°C. The temperature rises to 27.13°C. Assume the solution volumes are additive and that the density and specific heat capacity of the final solution is the same as those values for water. Assume also that only a negligible amount of heat is absorbed or released from or to the surroundings. Calculate the molar enthalpy change (ΔH_{neut}) for this reaction.

What to Think About

1. Determine a balanced chemical equation for the process. As the reactants are present in "equimolar" quantities, neither is in excess, so we can assume both will be consumed completely.
2. Calculate the heat absorbed by the 100.0 mL of resulting solution. Remember to treat all temperature changes as positive values.
3. Since *heat lost* = *heat gained*, the heat absorbed by the solution must equal the heat released by the neutralization reaction.

How To Do It

HCl(aq) + NaOH(aq)® NaCl(aq) + $H_2O(l)$

$50.0\ \cancel{mL} \times \frac{1.00\ mol}{1000\ \cancel{mL}} = 0.0500$ mol each of HCl and NaOH will be completely converted to 0.0500 mol of NaCl dissolved in water.

Since $q = mc\Delta T$,

$$q = \left(100.0\ \cancel{mL} \times \frac{1\ g}{\cancel{mL}}\right) \times \frac{4.18\ J}{°C} \times (27.13°C - 20.50°C)$$

$$= 100.0\ \cancel{g} \times \frac{4.18\ J}{\cancel{g°C}} \times 6.63\cancel{°C}$$

$$= 2770\ J$$

Continued on next page

Sample Problem — *Continued*

What to Think About

4. Finally, relate the heat released to the quantity of reactant neutralized. Since the reaction takes place at constant pressure, $q = \Delta H$.

5. Once the magnitude has been calculated, check the *sign*. In this case, heat was *released* from the neutralization to the solution, thus the reaction must be *exothermic* and so a *negative* sign is appropriate.

How To Do It

$q_{solution} = q_{neutralization} = 2770 \text{ J}$

$\Delta H = \dfrac{2770 \text{ J}}{0.0500 \text{ mol}} \times \dfrac{1 \text{ kJ}}{1000 \text{ J}} = 55.4 \text{ kJ/mol}$

$\Delta H_{neutralization} = -55.4 \text{ kJ/mol}$

Practice Problems — Determining the Enthalpy Change of an Aqueous Solution

1. When 500.0 mL of 2.00 mol/L $Ba(NO_3)_2$ solution at 22.50°C is combined in a coffee cup calorimeter with 500.0 mL of 2.00 mol/L Na_2SO_4 solution also at 22.50°C, a white precipitate forms and the temperature of the mixture rises to 25.60°C. Assume the calorimeter materials absorb only a negligible quantity of heat and the final solution's density and specific heat capacity are identical to those of water. Calculate the molar enthalpy of precipitation of $BaSO_4(s)$.

2. A coffee cup calorimeter contains 50.00 g of water at 20.73°C. When 2.13 g of NH_4NO_3 pellets are stirred into the water, the temperature falls to 17.41°C. Assume the heat capacity of the resulting solution is the same as that of water and that no energy is absorbed or released from or to the surroundings. Calculate the molar enthalpy of dissolution of ammonium nitrate, a chemical commonly used in the production of cold packs.

3. Given: $2\ HCl(aq) + Ba(OH)_2(aq) \rightarrow BaCl_2(aq) + 2\ H_2O(l) + 118 \text{ kJ/mol}_{rxn}$. Calculate the heat released when 300.0 mL of 0.500 mol/L hydrochloric acid is combined with 100.0 mL of 1.00 mol/L of barium hydroxide. Assume that the temperature of both solutions is initially 21.55°C. The final mixture has a mass of 400.0 g and a heat capacity the same as that of water with negligible heat "leakage" to or from the system. What is the final temperature of the mixture?

Constant Volume Calorimetry — The Bomb Calorimeter

A bomb calorimeter is more sophisticated than a coffee cup or even a thermos-type calorimeter. It is often used to determine the heat change involved in a chemical reaction, including reactions that do not occur in solution such as combustion reactions. The reaction chamber is surrounded by a metal jacket that sits inside a known mass of water at a known temperature. The prototype bomb calorimeters had extremely precise thermometers extended from inside the bomb with a sliding magnifying lens to assist in reading the temperature to the third decimal place. Modern calorimeters provide the temperature as a digital read out.

A known quantity of reacting substance is placed into the bomb and the bomb is sealed inside the calorimeter. A spark or electric current from a DC source supplies the activation energy to initiate the reaction. The maximum temperature of the system is recorded. As in the coffee cup or thermos calorimeter, it is assumed that no energy is lost or gained by the system apart from the energy produced or required by the reaction.

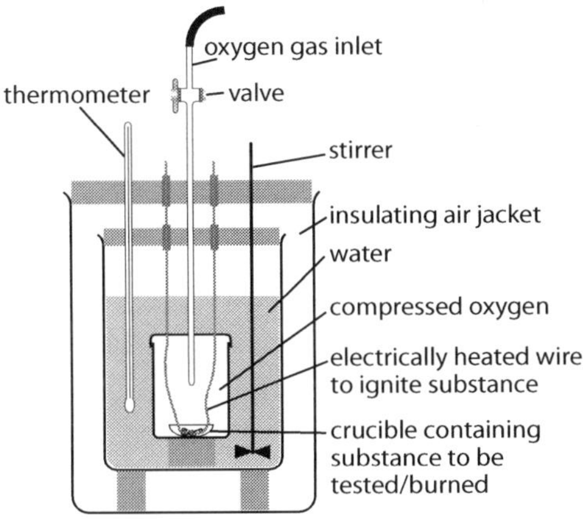

Figure 3.1.6 *A bomb calorimeter measures the heat released at constant volume, q_v or ΔE, which is extremely close to ΔH.*

Sometimes calculations involving bomb calorimeters require an overall q or ΔH value to be determined by calculating a value for the water inside the calorimeter *and* a value for the metal jacket using the specific heat capacities and the masses of each. These may be added together.

Other times, an overall *heat capacity* in units of J/°C may simply be used for the entire calorimeter and all of its components. Some references call this value a **calorimeter constant**. It indicates the number of joules the entire calorimeter must absorb or release in order to change its temperature by one Celsius (or one Kelvin since it is a *change*) degree.

Nutrition Facts

Serving Size 1 piece (219g)
Servings per container 6

Amount per serving	
Calories 520	Calories from Fat 240
	% Daily Value *
Total Fat 27g	41%
Saturated Fat 12g	61%
Cholesterol 255mg	86%
Sodium 1110mg	46%
Total Carbohydrates 29g	10%
Dietary Fiber 1g	5%
Sugars 1g	
Protein 39g	
Vitamin A 20% •	Vitamin C 4%
Calcium 15% •	Iron 25%

* Percent Daily Values are based on a 2,000 calorie diet. Your daily values may be higher or lower depending on your calorie needs:

	Calories	2,000	2,500
Total Fat	Less than	65g	80g
Saturated Fat	Less than	20g	25g
Cholesterol	Less than	300mg	300mg
Sodium	Less than	2,400mg	2,400mg
Total Carbohydrates		300g	375g
Dietary Fiber		25g	30g

Calories per gram:
Fat 9 • Carbohydrates 4 • Protein 4

Figure 3.1.7 *Nutrition Facts label for half a dozen "breakfast muffins" — not exactly a healthy way to start the day.*

Sample Problem — Calculating the Heat of a Combustion Reaction with a Bomb

Anthracene is a unique aromatic compound composed of three fused benzene rings. It is a component of coal tar and can be used to make several different anthroquinone dyes. A 5.12 g sample of anthracene, $C_{14}H_{10}$, was burned in an iron "bomb" having a mass of 1896 g. The bomb was immersed in 2.900 L of water inside a calorimeter. The initial temperature of all parts of the system was 20.80°C and the final temperature was 36.60°C. Calculate the molar heat of combustion of anthracene.

What To Think About	How To Do It
1. First find the heat absorbed by the calorimeter bomb *and* the water. Specific heat capacities of iron and water may be found in Table 3.1.1. Since water has a density of 1 g/mL, 2.900 L has a mass of 2.900 kg or 2900. g.	$q_{Fe\ Bomb} = mc_{Fe}\Delta T = 1896\ g \times \frac{0.448\ J}{g°C} \times (36.60°C - 20.80°C)$ $= 13\ 421\ J = 13.4\ kJ$
2. Assuming no heat loss to the surroundings, the total heat given off by the combustion must equal the sum of the heat absorbed by the water and the heat absorbed by the calorimeter jacket.	$q_{water} = mc_{water}\Delta T = 2900.\ g \times \frac{4.18\ J}{g°C} \times (36.60°C - 20.80°C)$ $= 191\ 528\ J = 192\ kJ$
3. Since $q_{lost} = -q_{gained}$, a negative sign is required.	$q_{total} = q_{calorimeter} + q_{water}$
4. The molar heat of combustion is q/n as dictated by unit analysis.	$q_{gained\ by\ calorimeter\ +\ water} = 192 + 13.4 = 205\ kJ$ $q_{combustion} = q_{lost\ by\ reaction\ system} = -q_{gained}$
5. The negative value is consistent with a combustion reaction.	$= -205\ kJ$ $\frac{205\ kJ}{5.12\ g} \times \frac{178.0\ g}{1\ mol} = 7130\ kJ/mol$

Sample Problem — Using the Calorimeter Constant

The brand new treat Chemical Candies contains only 12.0 Calories per serving according to the Nutrition Facts label. The Chemical Candies are tested by placing one serving in a bomb calorimeter like the one in Figure 3.1.5 and burning them in $O_2(g)$. The temperature rises from 21.431°C to 27.079°C. The heat capacity of the calorimeter is 8.808 kJ/°C. What is the actual caloric content?

What To Think About	How To Do It
1. Determine the amount of energy required to increase the temperature of the calorimeter by the stated amount.	$(27.079°C - 21.431°C) \times \frac{8.808\ kJ}{°C}$ $= 49.75\ kJ$
2. Convert the energy unit from kJ to Calories where 1 Cal = 1 kcal = 4.184 kJ.	$49.75\ kJ \times \frac{1\ Cal}{4.184\ kJ} = 11.89\ Cal$

Practice Problems — Calculating the Heat of a Combustion Reaction

1. A 3.00 g chunk of coal, C(*s*), was burned entirely to produce $CO_2(g)$ in a copper bomb. The mass of the bomb was 2.000 kg and the mass of water in which the copper bomb was immersed was 2.778 kg. The initial temperature of the system was 21.00°C and the final temperature was 29.30°C. Calculate the heat of formation of $CO_2(g)$. See Table 3.1.1 for the specific heat capacity of copper.

2. Toluene, C_7H_8 may be tri-substituted with nitro groups, $-NO_2$, to form the explosive, trinitrotoluene or TNT. A 750.0 mg sample of toluene liquid was placed in a bomb calorimeter with excess oxygen. The heat capacity of the calorimeter was 22.53 kJ/°C. When the calorimeter was fired, the combustion of the toluene caused the temperature to increase from 23.002°C to 24.415°C. Calculate ΔH for the reaction:
$C_7H_8(l) + 9\ O_2(g) \rightarrow 7\ CO_2(g) + 4\ H_2O(l)$.

3. (a) A standard calibration reaction is used to determine the heat capacity, C, of a bomb calorimeter. The temperature increases 1.275°C because of the input of 14 580 J of energy. What is the heat capacity of the calorimeter?

   (b) Use the data in the table of Standard Enthalpy of Formation (in section 3.2) to calculate the $\Delta H_{combustion}$ of methane, $CH_4\ (g)$.

   (c) A sample of 1.754 g of methane is combusted in the calorimeter calibrated in part (b). If the initial temperature of the calorimeter is 20.754°C, what final temperature should be attained?

Energy, Our Environment, and the Future

Fossil fuels have many advantages as an energy source. They are convenient to use, are found in many countries in the world, and are reasonably portable to areas that need them. On the other hand, they are non-renewable and they produce pollution. Despite the problems associated with fossil fuels, we show little inclination to give them up or reduce their use any time soon.

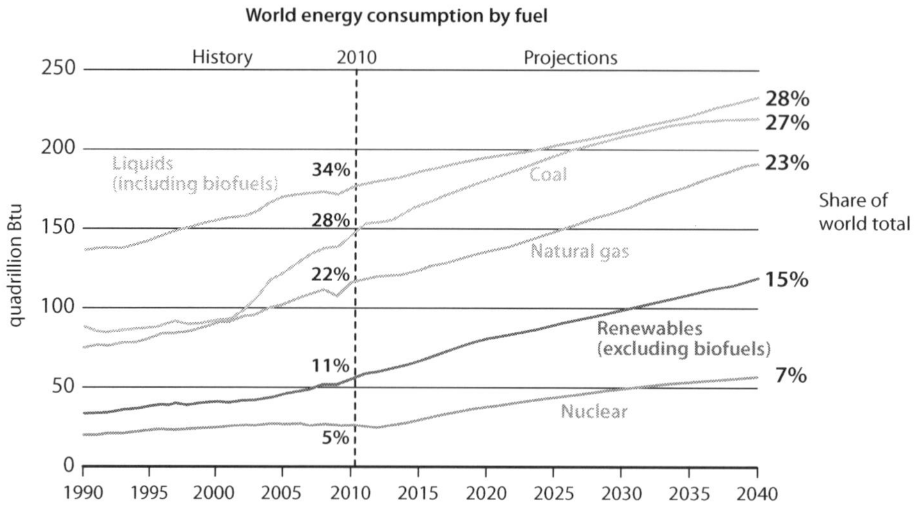

Figure 3.1.8 *Past and projected world energy consumption by fuel type*

Nuclear energy has shown promise, but comes, of course, with many dangers of its own. The 2011 event in Fukushima, Japan, is only the most recent of several major nuclear accidents that have occurred in the past few decades (Figure 3.1.8). Even when nuclear reactors function successfully, there is still the problem of storage for radioactive by-products. The fallout from nuclear accidents can be long lasting and widespread.

Figure 3.1.9 *Map of distribution of nuclear fallout from the Fukushima, Japan, reactor accident in March of 2011.*

Renewable energy sources and biofuels show some of the best promise for the future. Wind power, hydro, and solar energy are some of the least polluting forms of energy production. Later we will spend an entire chapter studying the application of electrochemical reactions to the production of energy in batteries and fuel cells.

As we move further into the 21st century the chemistry students of today may be responsible for changing the shape of the graph in Figure 3.1.8 completely. Maybe you will be responsible for some of the changes!

3.1 Review Questions

1. Complete the following table about symbols and sign conventions in the equation, $\Delta E = q + w$.

Symbol	Description	Sign	Meaning	Sign	Meaning
			System gains thermal energy		
	Work				Done by the system
ΔE		+			

2. Indicate whether each of the following is a state function or is pathway dependent:
   (a) A plane's total mileage meter
   (b) A plane's altimeter (indicates altitude)
   (c) Work
   (d) ΔH
   (e) Your monthly cell phone bill

3. Calculate the change in internal energy for a gas that absorbs 28.5 J of heat and then performs 16.4 J of work.

4. A gas expands from a volume of 1.4 L to 6.7 L against an external pressure of 1.00 atm. During this process, 565 J of heat is transferred from the surroundings to the gas.
   (a) How much work has been done?
   (b) What is the change in internal energy of the system?

5. Though we are unaware of it at rest, breathing requires work. A 70 kg man likely has an "empty" lung volume of 2210 mL.
   (a) If 50.7 J of work is required to take a single breath against a constant external atmospheric pressure of 1.00 atm, what is the man's "full" lung volume?
   (b) During exercise, the elastic lungs expand to a "full" volume of 5250 mL. How much work is required to take a single breath during exercise?

6. The following is a molecular representation of a state change occurring inside a piston-cylinder assembly against a constant external pressure of 1.05 atm.

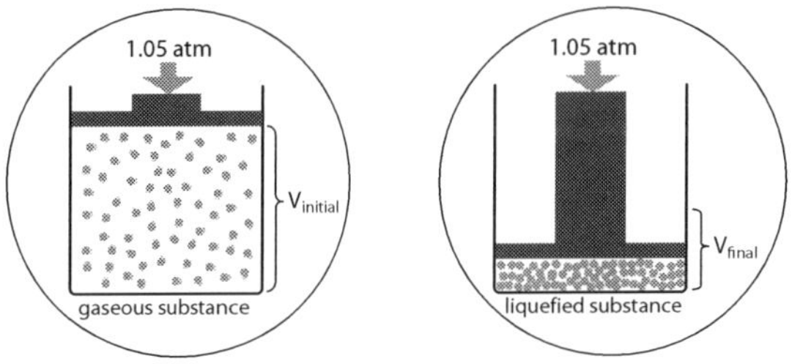

Indicate whether each of the following is (+), (–), 0 or impossible to determine.
Justify your answer in each case.
(a) w_{system}
(b) q_{system}
(c) ΔE_{system}

7. The diagram shows one mole each of the metals copper, iron, zinc, and aluminum. The quarter is included for size comparison only.

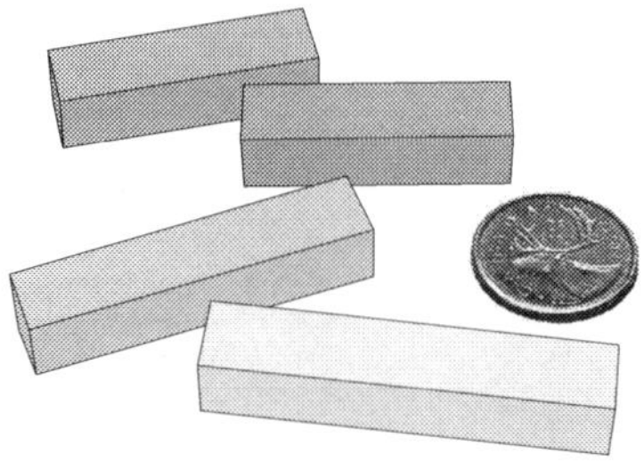

   (a) Use the pictures and a table of molar masses to rank the samples from heaviest to lightest.

   (b) Each bar is placed in boiling water for half an hour and then removed. Given the data in Table 3.1.1 and the heat capacity of zinc is 390. J/kg°C, rank the bars in order from most to least time required to cool to room temperature.

8. What mass of glass can be heated from room temperature (20.0°C) to 75.5°C if 1550 J of heat is added? See data in Table 3.1.1.

9. A restaurant worker places a 1 kg plastic jug full of water into the industrial fridge in the kitchen. At the same time, he places an empty 1 kg aluminum jug into the same fridge. One hour later one of the objects is much colder than the other. Which is colder and why?

10. In biology class, students sometimes hear of "high energy phosphate bonds." In general, how do phosphate bonds produce energy?

11. Copper can just be melted at the tip of the outer blue cone in a Bunsen burner flame where the temperature is 1085°C. How much energy is required to completely melt a 250.0 mg piece of copper wire? Assume the initial temperature of the wire was 22.5°C and the heat of fusion of copper is 205 J/g.

12. When combusted, 5.00 g of anthracite coal gives off 153 kJ of energy. What mass of coal is needed to heat a cauldron of 50.0 L water from 26.5°C until it just boils away, so that all the water vaporizes, but none of the steam is heated above 100.0°C?

13. Determine the final temperature when 145.0 g of ice at −17.5°C is placed into 335.0 g of water at 72.5°C in an insulated system. Assume everything is liquid water when the final temperature is reached.

14. A 45.05 g sample of a metal of unknown identity at 96.5°C is placed into 81.5 mL of water in an insulated container at a room temperature of 19.5°C. If the final temperature of the system is 34.5°C, what is the specific heat capacity of the metal? Use Table 3.1.1 to identify the metal.

15. A 45.0 g piece of silver metal at 15.5°C was placed into an insulated 0.345 g sample of steam at 106.0°C. The steam immediately condensed and coated the piece of silver metal with water. What is the final equilibrium temperature of the system?

16. (a) The following samples, both at 21.00°C, are mixed in a coffee cup calorimeter: 100.0 mL of 2.00 mol/L sodium hydroxide and 100.0 mL of 3.00 mol/L hydrochloric acid. After the reaction, the final solution's temperature rises to 34.40°C. Assuming no loss of heat to the surroundings and/or the calorimeter and a density and specific heat capacity for the final solution equal to those of water, calculate the molar enthalpy of neutralization for the reaction. (Hint: The acid and base are *not* in equimolar quantities.)

(b) Suppose the process in (a) were repeated with double the molarity of sodium hydroxide used.

(i) How would this affect the change in temperature (be specific)?

(ii) How would this affect the amount of heat, q, produced? Explain.

(iii) How would this affect the molar enthalpy of neutralization for the reaction? Explain your answer.

17. The enthalpy of dissolution of cesium hydroxide may be communicated as follows:
$CsOH(s) \rightarrow Cs^{+}(aq) + OH^{-}(aq)$ $\Delta H = -71.55$ kJ/mol. A 15.00 g sample of CsOH is dissolved in 110.0 g of water with both substances at 21.50°C. Calculate the final temperature of the solution, assuming the system is perfectly insulated and has a heat capacity equal to that of water.

18. A combustion experiment performed in a bomb calorimeter produced the following data:

heat capacity of bomb calorimeter = 9.35 kJ/°C
mass of methyl propane burned = 751 mg
initial temperature of calorimeter = 20.415°C
final temperature of calorimeter = 24.435°C

Calculate the molar enthalpy of combustion of methylpropane, which is used as lighter fluid.

19. Octane produces a tremendous amount of energy when combusted in gasoline. The following data were collected from a combustion experiment performed in a bomb calorimeter:

$\Delta H_{combustion} = -5074$ kJ/mol C_8H_{18}
heat capacity of bomb calorimeter = 10.45 kJ/°C
initial temperature of calorimeter = 21.002°C
final temperature of calorimeter = 27.014°C

Determine the mass of the sample of octane combusted in the calorimeter.

20. (a) Use the data in the table of Standard Enthalpy of Formation to calculate ΔH_{rxn} for the combustion of methanol, $CH_3OH(l)$.

(b) A 525.0 mg sample of methanol was used to calibrate a calorimeter. Combustion of the sample caused the calorimeter's temperature to rise from 21.057°C to 22.425°C. What is the heat capacity of the calorimeter? (Express *C* in units of kJ/°C.)

3.2 Enthalpy

Warm Up

Examine the following series of reactions and their associated enthalpy changes.

$CH_4(g) + 2\,O_2(g) \rightarrow CO_2(g) + 2\,H_2O(l) \quad \Delta H^o_{combustion} = -891\ kJ/mol$

$C(s) + O_2(g) \rightarrow CO_2(g) \quad \Delta H^o_f = -394\ kJ/mol$

$H_2(g) + \frac{1}{2}\,O_2(g) \rightarrow H_2O(l) \quad \Delta H^o_f = -286\ kJ/mol$

Using the principles developed in Section 4.4, rearrange the reactions and combine them to give this overall reaction.

Rx 1:

Rx 2:

Rx 3:

$C(s) + 2\,H_2(g) \rightarrow CH_4(g)$

Determine the enthalpy change associated with the overall reaction.

The Use of Bond Energy

A third way to calculate enthalpy changes is to use bond energy values. Bond energy is the *energy required to break a bond.* Bond energy values are frequently presented in tables. Most AP Chemistry texts list bond energies as positive values in units of kJ/mole. Such values represent the amount of energy that must be input into the system to break the bond. To represent the value of the energy released when product bonds form, a negative sign must precede the value given in Table 3.2.1.

Bond energy is the *enthalpy change* required to *break* a *given bond* in *one mole* of *gaseous molecules.* Bond energy is *always positive* and is expressed in units of kJ/mole.

The bond energy of a particular bond between two atoms, for example C-C, will vary depending on the "chemical environment" the bond is in, what other bonds are adjacent to it, and what lone pairs and bonding pairs of electrons are nearby. The bond energy for H-Cl, determined from hydrogen chloride gas, HCl, will differ from that determined within the PVC precursor, C_2H_5Cl, even when it is gasified. This means the bond energies typically reported in tables are really *average bond energies* gathered for each bond in a large variety of different compounds.

Table 3.2.1 *Average Bond Energy (KJ/mol)*

Bond	Energy	Bond	Energy	Bond	Energy	Bond	Energy
Single Bonds							
H–H	432	N–H	391	Si–H	323	S–H	347
H–F	565	N–N	160	Si–Si	226	S–S	266
H–Cl	427	N–P	209	Si–O	368	S–F	327
H–Br	363	N–O	201	Si–S	226	S–Cl	271
H–I	295	N–F	272	Si–F	565	S–Br	218
		N–Cl	200	Si–Cl	381	S–I	~170
C–H	413	N–Br	243	Si–Br	310		
C–C	347	N–I	159	Si–I	234	F–F	159
C–Si	301					F–Cl	193
C–N	305	O–H	467	P–H	320	F–Br	212
C–O	358	O–P	351	P–Si	213	F–I	263
C–P	264	O–O	204	P–P	200	Cl-Cl	243
C–S	259	O–S	265	P–F	490	Cl-Br	215
C–F	453	O–F	190	P–Cl	331	Cl-I	208
C–Cl	339	O–Cl	203	P–Br	272	Br–Br	193
C–Br	276	O–Br	234	P–I	184	Br–I	175
C–I	216	O–I	234			I–I	151
Multiple Bonds							
C=C	614	N=N	418	C≡C	839	N≡N	945
C=N	615	N=O	607	C≡N	891		
C=O	745 (799 in CO_2)	O_2	498	C≡O	1070		

When you examine a number of different average bond energies, such as those represented in this table, several patterns are noticeable. Consider the bond between hydrogen and members of the halogen family, for example. Because the highest energy bond is more difficult to break, HF behaves as a weak acid, while HCl through HI release their hydrogen ions more easily and so are strong acids.

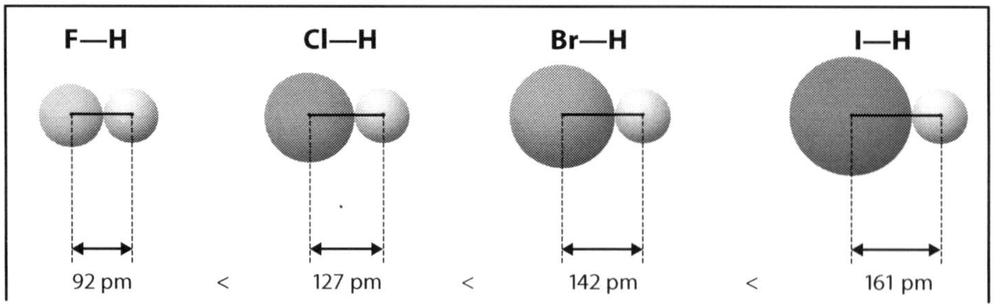

Figure 3.2.1 *Bond length increases with the atomic radius of each atom involved in the bond. Greater bond lengths result in less energetic and thus weaker bonds.*

A second pattern that is obvious is that bond energies depend not only on the elements involved in the bond, but also on whether the bond is single, double, or triple. Triple bonds are the most energetic and hence the strongest, while single bonds are the weakest and least energetic.

Bond energy and strength also relate to bond length. Triple bonds involve more electron energy-level overlap and hence are shorter.

Because bond energies are *averages*, the answer to an enthalpy problem determined using bond energies might not be exactly the same as one calculated using Standard Enthalpy of Formation, but it will closely approximate it. Since bond energy is a state function, there is a simple algorithm available for calculating enthalpy changes using bond energies. It is similar to the one described for the calculation of enthalpy changes.

$$\Delta H_{\text{reaction}} = \sum nB.E._{\text{(bonds broken)}} - \sum nB.E._{\text{(bonds formed)}}$$

Because the reactants and products appear in the opposite order in this equation compared to calculation of enthalpy from Standard Enthalpy of Formation students frequently make errors in the calculation of enthalpy changes using bond energies. The most common incorrect result has the correct magnitude, but the wrong sign. The easiest way to ensure you fully understand how to determine the overall bond energy change is to always remember that:

Bond *breaking requires energy* while bond *forming releases energy*!

Once the structural formulas of all species in a balanced equation are written down, the bonds that are broken and the bonds that are formed can be determined. The broken bonds are assigned *positive* bond energy values and each newly formed bond is assigned a *negative* one. Then the sum of the bond energies is calculated. For example, in the sample problem from the law of Hess,

$$CH_4(g) + 2\,O_2(g) \rightarrow CO_2(g) + 2\,H_2O(g) \qquad \Delta H^\circ_{comb} = -802.7\ \text{kJ/mol}_{rxn}$$

Four C-H bonds and two O=O bonds are broken while two C=O bonds and four O-H bonds are formed. Using tabular bond energy values, we would calculate:

$$\left[\frac{4\ \cancel{\text{mol C-H}}}{\text{mol}_{rxn}}\left(\frac{413\ \text{kJ}}{\cancel{\text{mol C-H}}}\right) \quad \frac{2\ \cancel{\text{mol O=O}}}{\text{mol}_{rxn}}\left(\frac{498\ \text{kJ}}{\cancel{\text{mol O=O}}}\right)\right] +$$

$$\left[\frac{2\ \cancel{\text{mol C=O}}}{\text{mol}_{rxn}}\left(\frac{799\ \text{kJ}}{\cancel{\text{mol C=O}}}\right) - \frac{4\ \cancel{\text{mol O-H}}}{\text{mol}_{rxn}}\left(\frac{467\ \text{kJ}}{\cancel{\text{mol O-H}}}\right)\right] = -818\ \text{kJ/mol}_{rxn}$$

While these two values are not exactly the same, they are both exothermic and are within 2% of each other. For reactions occurring in the gas state, bond energies give very close approximations to the enthalpy changes calculated with standard ΔH°_f values.

Sample Problem — Enthalpy Changes from Average Bond Energy Values

Use Table 3.2.1 to determine the enthalpy change for the Haber process for the production of ammonia:

$$N_2(g) + 3\,H_2(g) \rightarrow 2\,NH_3(g)$$

What to Think About	How To Do It
1. Consider the bonding arrangement of the reactants and products. Structural formulas are very useful.	:N≡N: + 3 H-H → 2 H-N̈-H (with H below N)

Continued on next page

Sample Problem — *Continued*

What to Think About

2. Multiply the bond energies by the appropriate coefficients and apply the correct mathematical symbols according to the convention: (+) for bonds breaking and (–) for bonds forming. Count the number of bonds carefully.

   Note: Should a bond remain intact, there is no need to break and reform it. Simply ignore it in the calculation.
3. Do the math!
4. It's always a good idea to consider the feasibility of your answer.

How To Do It

$$\frac{1\ \text{mol N≡N}}{\text{mol}_{rxn}}\left(\frac{945\ \text{kJ}}{\text{mol}_{N≡N}}\right) + \frac{3\ \text{mol H–H}}{\text{mol}_{rxn}}\left(\frac{432\ \text{kJ}}{\text{mol}_{H–H}}\right) - \frac{6\ \text{mol N–H}}{\text{mol}_{rxn}}\left(\frac{391\ \text{kJ}}{\text{mol}_{N–H}}\right)$$

$= -105\ \text{kJ/mol}_{rxn}$

As we are forming ammonia, an exothermic answer makes sense. The enthalpies of formation table give a ΔH_f as –45.9 kJ/mol of NH_3. The reaction forms two moles of ammonia, so our answer is close enough to be reasonable.

Practice Problems — Enthalpy Changes from Average Bond Energy Values

Use Table 3.2.1 to produce a full *thermochemical equation* for each of the molecular representations below.

1.

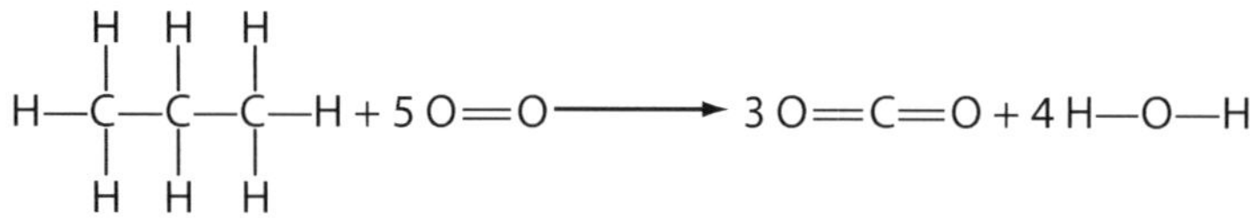

2.

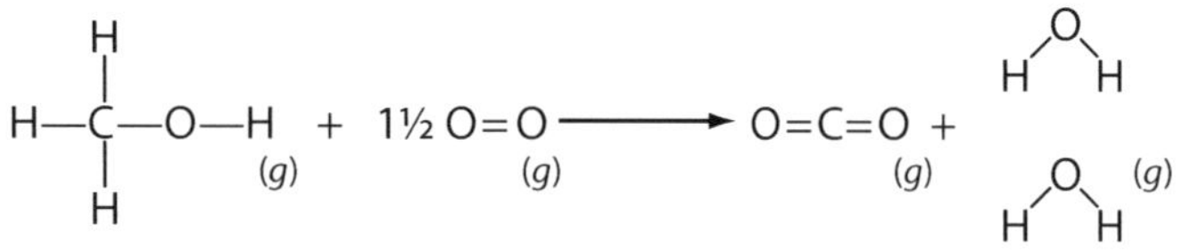

It is comforting to know that there are multiple ways to use tabular data to solve a problem in thermochemistry. But for most chemists, the real joy lies in working in the laboratory to determine the values of the bond energy through calorimetry.

Enthalpy Calculations using Standard Enthalpies (Heats) of Formation

The value of the Enthalpy of Formation for each of the compounds involved in a chemical change may be rearranged to calculate the overall enthalpy change for a process. Using the enthalpies of formation for methane, carbon dioxide, and liquid water we can determine the overall enthalpy change for the combustion of methane as follows:

$$CH_4(g) \rightarrow C(s) + 2\,H_2(g) \qquad \Delta H^\circ = +75\text{ kJ/mol}_{rxn}$$

$$C(s) + O_2(g) \rightarrow CO_2(g) \qquad \Delta H^\circ_f = -394\text{ kJ/mol}_{rxn}$$

$$2\,H_2(g) + O_2(g) \rightarrow 2\,H_2O(l) \qquad \Delta H^\circ_f = -572\text{ kJ/mol}_{rxn}$$

$$CH_4(g) + 2\,O_2(g) \rightarrow CO_2(g) + 2\,H_2O(l) \qquad \Delta H^\circ_{comb} = -891\text{ kJ/mol}_{rxn}$$

The overall enthalpy of a reaction can also be calculated using the formula:

$$\Delta H^\circ_{(overall)} = \sum nH^\circ_{f(products)} - \sum nH^\circ_{f(reactants)}$$

The symbol Σ means "sum of" and n is the coefficient of each species in a balanced equation. It is critical to keep in mind that:

The H°_f for a *pure element* in its standard state is always equal to *zero.*

Observe the state of the species in a balanced chemical equation carefully when using enthalpy values from a table of standard enthalpies of formation , as the state of a substance affects its enthalpy of formation value. The formula above can be used to calculate the overall enthalpy change for the combustion of methane as follows:

$$\Delta H^\circ_{comb} = [1 \times H_{f\,CO_2}(g) + 2 \times H_{fH_2O}(l)] - [1 \times H_{fCH_4}(g) + 2 \times H_{fO_2}(g)]$$

$$\text{thus: } \Delta H^\circ_{comb} = \left[\frac{1\,\cancel{\text{mol CO}_2}}{\text{mol}_{rxn}}\left(\frac{-394\text{ kJ/}}{\cancel{\text{mol CO}_2}}\right) + \frac{2\,\cancel{\text{mol H}_2\text{O}}}{\text{mol}_{rxn}}\left(\frac{-286\text{ kJ/}}{\cancel{\text{mol H}_2\text{O}}}\right)\right] - \left[\frac{1\,\cancel{\text{mol CH}_4}}{\text{mol}_{rxn}}\left(\frac{-75\text{ kJ}}{\cancel{\text{mol CH}_4}}\right) + \frac{2\,\cancel{\text{mol O}_2}}{\text{mol}_{rxn}}\left(\frac{0\text{ kJ}}{\cancel{\text{mol O}_2}}\right)\right] = -891\text{ kJ/mol}_{rxn}$$

As demonstrated, calculating the enthalpy of a reaction using enthalpy values from a table of standard enthalpies of formation will be equivalent to calculating the enthalpy of a reaction using Hess's Law which we will study later.

Table 3.2.2 *Examples of Standard Enthalpy of Formation*

$NH_3(g)$	–45.9 kJ/mol	$NO(g)$	90.3 kJ/mol
$C(s)$ [diamond]	1.896	$NO_2(g)$	33.2
$N_2O_5(g)$	11.0	$C_3H_8(g)$	–105.0
$CO_2(g)$	–393.5	$PF_5(g)$	–1594.4
$C_2H_4Cl_2(g)$	–166.8	$NaHCO_3(s)$	–947.4
$C_2H_5Cl(g)$	–112.2	$Na_2SO_4(aq)$	–1387.1
$C_2H_6(g)$	–84.7	$SO_2(g)$	–296.8
$C_2H_4(g)$	52.5	$SO_3(g)$	–396.0
$HCl(g)$	–92.3	$H_2SO_4(aq)$	–907.5
$H_2S(g)$	–20.2	$H_2O(g)$	–241.8
$CH_4(g)$	–74.9	$H_2O(l)$	–285.8
$CH_3OH(g)$	–238.6	$ZnO(s)$	–348.0

Sample Problem — Standard Enthalpy of Formation

Given the following Standard Enthalpy of Formation, ΔH°_f of $SO_2(g)$ = –296.8 kJ/mol$_f$ and ΔH°_f of $SO_3(g)$ = –396.0 kJ/mol$_f$, what is the enthalpy change for the following reaction: $2\,SO_2(g) + O_2(g) \rightarrow 2\,SO_3(g)$?

What To Think about

1. Determine the ΔH°_f (Standard Enthalpy of Formation) values for each of the species involved in the reaction from a table of standard enthalpies of formation. Remember that the enthalpy of formation for an element in its standard state is zero.
   Note: Generally these values will be found in a *table of standard enthalpies of formation.*
2. Multiply products and reactants by their coefficients and subtract the sum of the products from the sum of the reactants.

How To Do It

ΔH°_f of $SO_2(g)$ = –296.8 kJ/mol and
ΔH°_f of $SO_3(g)$ = –396.0 kJ/mol and
ΔH°_f of O_2 = 0 kJ/mol (pure element)

$$\frac{2\ \text{mol}\ SO_3}{\text{mol}_{rxn}}\left(\frac{-396.0\ \text{kJ}}{\text{mol}\ SO_3}\right) - \left[\frac{2\ \text{mol}\ SO_2}{\text{mol}_{rxn}}\left(\frac{-296.8\ \text{kJ}}{\text{mol}\ SO_2}\right) + \frac{1\ \text{mol}\ O_2}{\text{mol}_{rxn}}\left(\frac{0\ \text{kJ}}{\text{mol}\ O_2}\right)\right]$$

= –198.4 kJ/mol

Practice Problems— Standard Enthalpy of Formation

Use the values in Table 3.2.2 to solve the practice problems below (values are listed alphabetically *by name* in this table):

1. Determine the enthalpy change for each of the following reactions:
   (a) $C_3H_8(g) + H_2(g) \rightarrow C_2H_6(g) + CH_4(g)$

   (b) $2\ H_2S(g) + 3\ O_2(g) \rightarrow 2\ SO_2(g) + 2\ H_2O(l)$

2. Use the following information along with the tabular data to calculate the *molar* enthalpy of ZnS(*s*).
   $2\ ZnS(s) + 3\ O_2(g) \rightarrow 2\ ZnO(s) + 2\ SO_2(g) \qquad \Delta H_f^{\circ} = -878.2\ kJ/mol_{rxn}$

Hess's Law

Enthalpy changes involving an overall *decrease* in potential energy are *exothermic*. The ΔH value for an exothermic change is always a *negative* value as the system is releasing energy. Changes involving an overall *increase* in potential energy are *endothermic* and the ΔH value for such a change is *positive*. Placement of the correct sign in front of ΔH values is an important accounting convention, and the signs must be applied consistently throughout all thermodynamic calculations.

As enthalpy is an *extensive property*, the *magnitude* of an enthalpy change for a chemical reaction *depends on the quantity of material* that reacts. This means if the amount of reacting material in an exothermic reaction is doubled, twice the quantity of heat will be released. Thus for the oxidation of sulfur dioxide gas:

$$SO_2(g) + \tfrac{1}{2}\,O_2(g) \rightarrow SO_3(g) \qquad \Delta H^\circ = -99\ \text{kJ/mol}_{rxn}$$

Doubling the reaction results in:

$$2\,SO_2(g) + O_2(g) \rightarrow 2\,SO_3(g) \qquad \Delta H^\circ = -198\ \text{kJ/mol}_{rxn}$$

A comparison of the absolute enthalpy content of the reactants and products of a reversible reaction makes it evident that the *magnitude* of ΔH for an exothermic reaction *remains the same when it is reversed*. There is merely a *sign change* and the reaction becomes endothermic. Hence if the above reaction were reversed:

$$2\,SO_3(g) \rightarrow 2\,SO_2(g) + O_2(g) \qquad \Delta H^\circ = +198\ \text{kJ/mol}_{rxn}$$

In addition to being an extensive property, enthalpy is also a *state function*. As we just learned, this means an enthalpy change is *completely independent of the pathway followed* to accomplish it. These concepts may be applied to determine the overall enthalpy change for any reaction by manipulation of a series of other reactions. The process is known as **Hess's Law of Heat Summation**. Simply stated:

> The *enthalpy change* of a *reaction* is expressed as the *algebraic sum* of the *enthalpy changes* of a series of other reactions that have been manipulated to produce the overall reaction.

Hess's Law of Heat Summation

In Grade 11, we learned that the enthalpy of a reaction is the result of the chemical potential energy in the bonds of the reactants which is converted into heat absorbed or released as the reactant bonds break and form product bonds.

There are a number of methods for calculating overall enthalpy changes that a chemistry student should be familiar with. The three most common are Hess's Law, the use of tabular Standard Enthalpy of Formation and the use of bond energies.

In addition to being an extensive property, enthalpy is also a state function. Enthalpy change is completely independent of the pathway followed to convert reactants into products. The conversion of reactants into products is often achieved through a series of chemical processes. The overall enthalpy change for any overall reaction is usually calculated by manipulation of a series of reactions that lead to the overall process. The process is known as Hess's Law of heat summation and is defined as:

> The algebraic sum of the enthalpy changes of a series of reactions that produce the overall reaction will equal the overall enthalpy of the reaction.

As indicated in the Warm Up, given the following reactions and their enthalpy changes, it is possible to determine the heat of formation for methane:

$$CH_4(g) + 2\,O_2(g) \rightarrow CO_2(g) + 2\,H_2O(l) \qquad \Delta H^o_{comb} = -891\ kJ/mol_{rxn}$$

$$C(s) + O_2(g) \rightarrow CO_2(g) \qquad \Delta H^o_f = -394\ kJ/mol_{rxn}$$

$$H_2(g) + \tfrac{1}{2}\,O_2(g) \rightarrow H_2O(l) \qquad \Delta H^o_f = -286\ kJ/mol_{rxn}$$

The reaction we are attempting to come up with is:

$$C(s) + 2\,H_2(g) \rightarrow CH_4(g)$$

Begin by *looking for species that appear as reactants and products in the overall reaction.* This will provide a clue as to whether a reaction needs to be reversed or not. Second, *consider the coefficients of species that appear in the overall reaction.* This will help determine whether a reaction needs to be multiplied before the overall summation. Leaving the formation of carbon dioxide reaction as is and doubling the formation of water reaction appears to be a good start in that this will provide the reactants desired. The combustion of methane reaction will need to be reversed to provide the desired number of moles of product. Reorganization of the three equations as described with the accompanying change in their ΔH^o values results in:

$$C(s) + \cancel{O_2(g)} \rightarrow \cancel{CO_2(g)} \qquad \Delta H^o_f = -394\ kJ/mol_{rxn}$$

$$2\,H_2(g) + \cancel{O_2(g)} \rightarrow \cancel{2\,H_2O(l)} \qquad \Delta H^o_f = -572\ kJ/mol_{rxn}$$

$$\cancel{CO_2(g)} + \cancel{2\,H_2O(l)} \rightarrow CH_4(g) + \cancel{2\,O_2(g)} \qquad \Delta H^o_{rxn} = +891\ kJ/mol_{rxn}$$

$$C(s) + 2\,H_2(g) \rightarrow CH_4(g) \qquad \Delta H^o_f = -75\ kJ/mol_{rxn}$$

Sample Problem — Hess's Law

As an alternative to burning coal, the following process, called *methanation,* can be used to produce energy from carbon monoxide, a product of coal combustion. The carbon monoxide is only one component of a mixture called "coal gas." Not only does this reaction produce energy, it also produces methane, itself a valuable component of natural gas that may be further combusted to produce energy.

$$3\,H_2(g) + CO(g) \rightarrow CH_4(g) + H_2O(g)$$

Determine the standard enthalpy change for the methanation reaction using the following series of reactions and their enthalpy changes:

$$2\,H_2(g) + O_2(g) \rightarrow 2\,H_2O(g) \qquad \Delta H^o_f = -483.6\ kJ/mol_{rxn}$$

$$2\,C(s) + O_2(g) \rightarrow 2\,CO(g) \qquad \Delta H^o_f = -221.0\ kJ/mol_{rxn}$$

$$CH_4(g) + 2\,O_2(g) \rightarrow CO_2(g) + 2\,H_2O(g) \qquad \Delta H^o_{comb} = -802.7\ kJ/mol_{rxn}$$

$$C(s) + O_2(g) \rightarrow CO_2(g) \qquad \Delta H^o_f = -393.5\ kJ/mol_{rxn}$$

Continued

What To Think About *continued*	**How To Do It**
1. Hydrogen gas only appears as a reactant in one reaction. So this reaction must be multiplied by 1.5 to give three reactant H_2 molecules.	$(2\,H_2(g) + O_2(g) \rightarrow 2\,H_2O(g) \quad -483.6\ kJ/mol_{rxn})\ x1.5$
2. To make CO a reactant requires reversal of the second reaction. It must be divided by two to give one CO_2 and the sign must be changed.	$(2\,CO(g) \rightarrow 2\,C(s) + O_2(g) \quad +221.0\ kJ/mol_{rxn})\ x\ -0.5$
3. To make methane a product, the third reaction must be reversed and the sign changed.	
4. This leaves one CO_2 to be cancelled, as it does not appear anywhere in the overall reaction. So the last reaction may remain as is.	$(CO_2(g) + 2\,H_2O(g) \rightarrow CH_4(g) + 2\,O_2(g) \quad +802.7\ kJ/mol_{rxn})\ x\ -1$
5. Changing coefficients and altering the enthalpy changes values accordingly.	$(C(s) + O_2(g) \rightarrow CO_2(g) \quad -393.5\ kJ/mol_{rxn})\ x\ 1$
6. Summing the four equations with appropriate algebraic cancelling gives the correct overall equation with the correct ΔH_{rxn} value for the equation as written.	$3\,H_2(g)$ + ~~1.5~~ $O_2(g) \rightarrow 3\,H_2O(g) \quad -725.4\ kJ/mol_{rxn}$ $1\,CO(g) \rightarrow$ ~~1 C(s)~~ + ~~0.5 O₂(g)~~ $\quad +110.5$ ~~CO₂(g)~~ + ~~2 H₂O(g)~~ $\rightarrow CH_4(g)$ + ~~2 O₂(g)~~ $\quad +802.7$ ~~C(s)~~ + ~~O₂(g)~~ → ~~CO₂(g)~~ $\quad -393.5$ ============================== $3\,H_2(g) + CO(g) \rightarrow CH_4(g) + H_2O(g)$ $\Delta H_{rxn} = -205.7\ kJ/mol_{rxn}$

Practice Problems — Hess's Law

1. The complete decomposition of NOCl gas into its elements occurs by the following reaction:

$$2\,NOCl(g) \rightarrow N_2(g) + O_2(g) + Cl_2(g)$$

Use the following two reactions and their enthalpy changes to determine the enthalpy change for the decomposition reaction.

$$\tfrac{1}{2}\,N_2(g) + \tfrac{1}{2}\,O_2(g) \rightarrow NO(g) \qquad \Delta H_f = 90.3\ kJ/mol_f$$

$$NO(g) + \tfrac{1}{2}\,Cl_2(g) \rightarrow NOCl(g) \qquad \Delta H_{rxn} = -38.6\ kJ/mol_{rxn}$$

Continued

Practice Problems — *Continued*

2. Polyvinyl chloride is commonly referred to as PVC. It is a polymer produced from a monomer formed by the addition of ethylene and chlorine gas. Use the following reactions and their enthalpy changes to determine the overall enthalpy change for the PVC monomer reaction:

$H_2(g) + Cl_2(g) \rightarrow 2\,HCl(g)$	$\Delta H_f = -184.6\ \text{kJ/mol}_{rxn}$
$C_2H_4(g) + HCl(g) \rightarrow C_2H_5Cl(l)$	$\Delta H_{rxn} = -65.0\ \text{kJ/mol}_{rxn}$
$C_2H_3Cl(g) + H_2(g) \rightarrow C_2H_5Cl(l)$	$\Delta H_{rxn} = -138.9\ \text{kJ/mol}_{rxn}$
$C_2H_4(g) + Cl_2(g) \rightarrow C_2H_3Cl(l) + HCl(g)$	$\Delta H_{rxn} =$ **(?)**

3. Given the following data (all species are gases):

$2\,O_3 \rightarrow 3\,O_2$	$\Delta H_{diss} = -427\ \text{kJ/mol}_{rxn}$
$O_2 \rightarrow 2\,O$	$\Delta H_{diss} = 495\ \text{kJ/mol}_{rxn}$
$NO + O_3 \rightarrow NO_2 + O_2$	$\Delta H_{rxn} = -199\ \text{kJ/mol}_{rxn}$

Calculate the enthalpy change for the following reaction: $NO + O \rightarrow NO_2$

3.2 Review Questions

1. In the 1970s, scientists became concerned about the depletion of the ozone layer due to the affects of aerosol propellants such as chlorofluorocarbons. Chlorofluorocarbons are now known to absorb high-energy radiation, producing free radical chlorine atoms. These chlorine atoms have a catalytic effect on the removal of ozone from our atmosphere.

   Use the following two reactions and their enthalpy changes to calculate the enthalpy change for the removal of ozone by free radical oxygen. (This is the net equation involved in ozone destruction in the atmosphere.) O atoms (free radicals) are present due to O_2 dissociation by high-energy radiation. All species are gaseous.

   $O_3 + Cl \rightarrow O_2 + ClO$ $\qquad \Delta H° = -126\ kJ/mol_{rxn}$

   $ClO + O \rightarrow Cl + O_2$ $\qquad \Delta H° = -268\ kJ/mol_{rxn}$

   ====================================

2. Determine the enthalpy change for the following reaction:
   $CH_4(g) + 4\ Cl_2(g) \rightarrow CCl_4(l) + 4\ HCl(g)$
   Using the following information:

   $C(s) + 2\ H_2(g) \rightarrow CH_4(g)$ $\qquad \Delta H°_f = -74.6\ kJ/mol_{rxn}$

   $C(s) + 2\ Cl_2(g) \rightarrow CCl_4(g)$ $\qquad \Delta H°_f = -95.7\ kJ/mol_{rxn}$

   $H_2(g) + 2\ Cl_2(g) \rightarrow 2\ HCl(g)$ $\qquad \Delta H°_f = -92.3\ kJ/mol_{rxn}$

3. The **Born-Haber cycle** is a hypothetical series of steps that represent the formation of an ionic compound from its constituent elements. According to Hess's Law, the sum of the enthalpy changes for each step in the series should sum to give the overall enthalpy change for the formation of the ionic compound from its elements in their standard states. The enthalpy change for the formation of an ionic compound from its ions in the gas state is called the **lattice energy** of the compound. Here is the Born-Haber cycle for cesium fluoride.

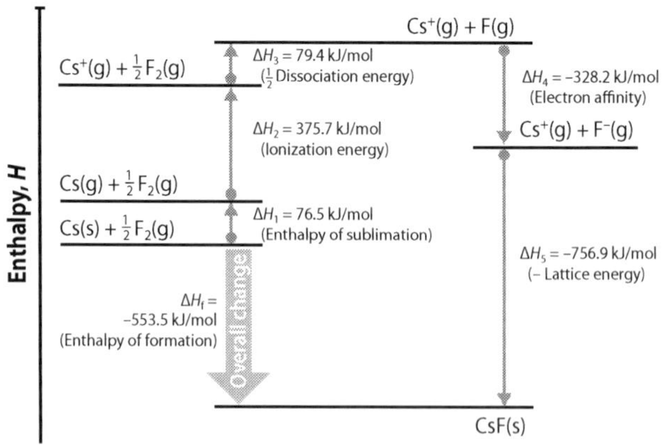

   Use the Born-Haber cycle to show how five equations may be added together using Hess's Law to give the overall enthalpy of formation for cesium fluoride from the following equation: $Cs(s) + ½ F_2(g) \rightarrow CsF(s)$. Label each of the processes involved. Be sure to use *five steps*. The first step is done for you as an example.

Step 1:	$Cs(s) \rightarrow Cs(g)$	$\Delta H_{sub} = 76.5$ kJ/mol$_{Cs}$	sublimation of Cs
Step 2:			
Step 3:			
Step 4:			
Step 5:			
Overall Rxn:	$Cs(s) + ½ F_2(g) \rightarrow CsF(s)$	ΔH_f = **?**	formation of CsF(*s*)

4. The Ostwald process for making nitric acid involves multiple steps, beginning with ammonia reacting with oxygen, forming nitrogen monoxide and water. Determine the ΔH^{o}_{rxn} for this *first step* in the Ostwald process. Begin by writing a *balanced chemical reaction*. Then use the standard enthalpy of formation values.

5. Use the standard enthalpy of formation values to determine the overall enthalpy change for the reaction depicted by the complete combustion of methane depicted below.

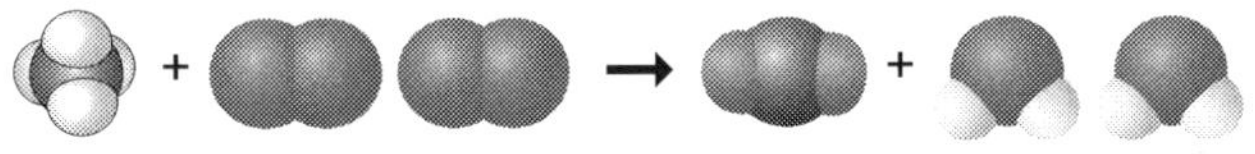

6. Consider the following *unbalanced* molecular representation of an oxidation-reduction reaction. Translate this molecular representation to a balanced formula equation. Then use the table of standard enthalpy of formation values to determine the overall enthalpy change for the balanced molecular equation.

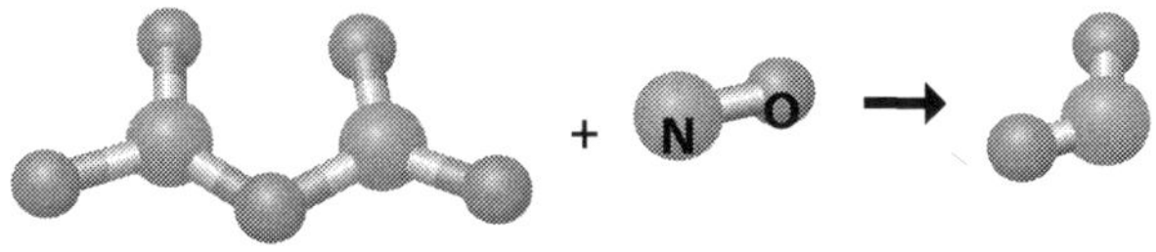

7. Solid baking soda (sodium bicarbonate <u>or</u> sodium hydrogen carbonate) neutralizes sulfuric acid solution spills, producing sodium sulfate, water, and carbon dioxide. Write a complete, balanced *thermochemical* equation for this process.

8. Hess's Law Practice Problem 2 on page 214 involves steps in the production of polyvinylchloride (PVC) plastic. The addition of hydrogen chloride gas, HCl, to ethene, C_2H_4, forms the monomer, $C_2H_5Cl(l)$ which is used to make the polymer, PVC. Given the overall enthalpy change of –65.0 kJ/mol_{rxn} determine the enthalpy of formation for the monomer, $C_2H_5Cl(l)$.

9. Chlorine gas can react in a substitution reaction with the gaseous monomer mentioned in question 8 as follows: $C_2H_5Cl(g) + Cl_2(g) \rightarrow C_2H_4Cl_2(g) + HCl(g)$

(a) Calculate the $\Delta H°$ for the reaction above.

(b) Repeat the calculation done in part (a) using $\Delta H_f°$ values.

(c) Compare the answer to part (a) with part (b). Comment on the comparison.

10. (a) Use a highlighter or some other method to indicate the bonds that break on the reactant side and form on the product side of this reaction. Remember the note in the sample problem about enthalpy changes from average bond energy values in Table 3.2.1 — if a bond remains intact there is no need to break and reform it. Calculate the enthalpy change using the bond energy values.

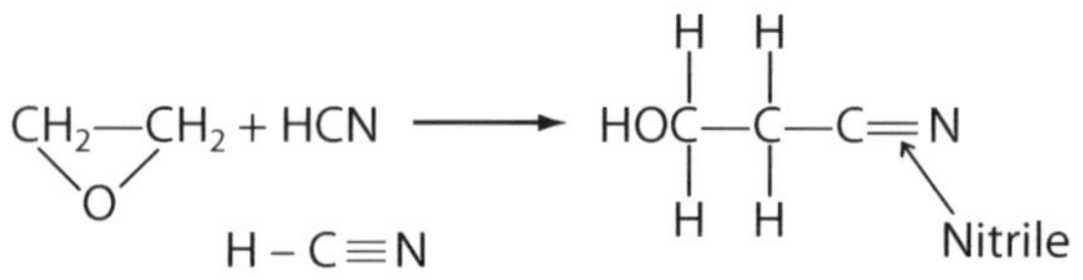

(b) Repeat for this reaction.

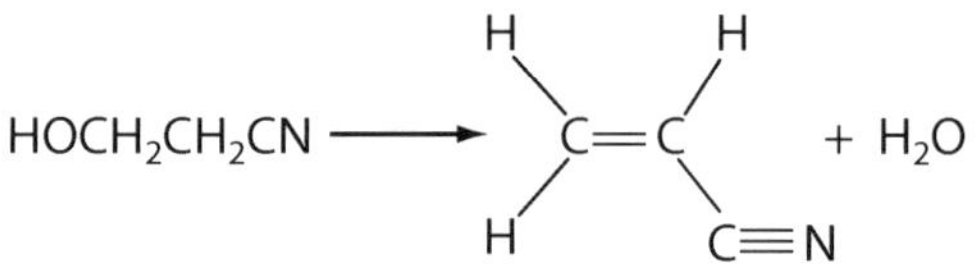

(c) Considering bond energy is a state function, combine steps (a) and (b) into one reaction and calculate the overall enthalpy change.

11. The following shows the structural formulas for the reaction:

$2\ CH_2CHCH_3(g) + 2\ NH_3(g) + 3\ O_2(g) \rightarrow 2\ CH_2CHCN(g) + 6\ H_2O(g)$

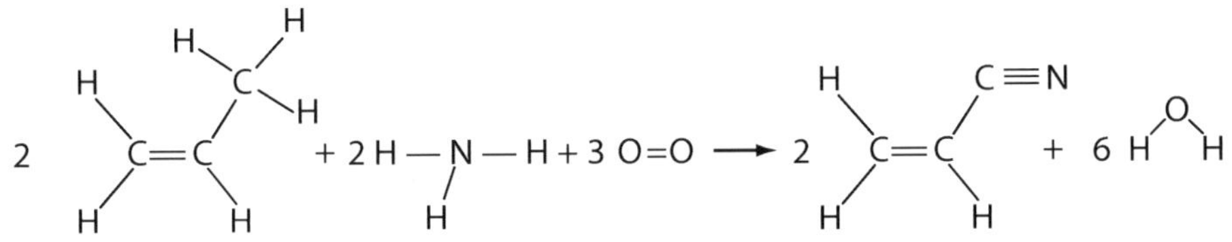

Use the bond energy in Table 3.2.1 to calculate ΔH_{rxn} for the given reaction.

3.3 Potential Energy Diagrams

Warm Up

Complete the following table by placing a checkmark in the appropriate energy change column for each chemical change classification listed.

Reaction Type	Endothermic	Exothermic
Most synthesis (combination) reactions		
Most decomposition reactions		
Neutralization reactions		
Combustion reactions		

Sources of Energy

Fuels such as natural gas, wood, coal, and gasoline provide us with energy. In Grade 11, you learned that most of this energy is stored as chemical potential energy that can be converted into heat. The amount of potential energy available depends upon the position of the subatomic particles making up a chemical sample and the composition of the sample. While the absolute potential energy content of a system is not really important, a change in potential energy content often is. We use conversions of chemical energy to other energy forms to do work for us, such as heating our homes and moving our vehicles. Because chemical energy is most commonly converted to heat, we use the symbol, ΔH to symbolize a change in energy available as heat. The symbol is sometimes read as "delta *H*" or an enthalpy change.

Enthalpy is potential energy that may be evolved (given off) or absorbed as heat.

All sorts of processes, both physical and chemical, have an enthalpy change associated with them. A general change in enthalpy is symbolized as ΔH. Combustion reactions have a large enthalpy change and are frequently used for energy production:

$$C_3H_8(g) + 5\ O_2(g) \rightarrow 3\ CO_2(g) + 4\ H_2O(l) \qquad \Delta H_{combustion} = -2221\ \text{kJ/mol}$$

What causes the enthalpy stored in reactants to differ from that in the products of a physical or chemical change? What exactly is responsible for producing the ΔH value? The answer is the chemical bonds.

The Energy of Chemical Bonds

Suppose your textbook has fallen off your desk to the floor. When you lift it back to the desktop, you give the text potential energy. The gravitational potential energy your text now has in its position on the desktop could easily be converted into mechanical and sound energy should it happen to fall again.

In a similar way, the electrons in the atoms of the molecules of any substance have potential energy. Think of the negative electrons as being pulled away from the positive nucleus of their atom. If it were not for their high velocity, they would certainly rush toward and smash directly into the nucleus of their atom, much like your textbook falling to the floor. By virtue of the position of the negative electrons in an atom relative to the positive nucleus and the other nuclei nearby in a molecule, the electrons (and the protons in the nuclei) have potential energy. This is the chemical potential energy called **bond energy.**

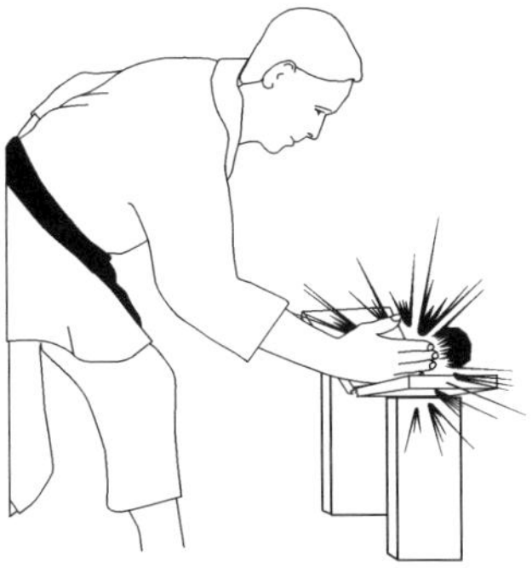

Figure 3.3.1 *Energy is required to break bonds.*

Bond *breaking* requires energy *input*, while bond *forming* results in energy *release*.

It's fairly intuitive that breaking something requires energy. For a karate master to break a board, he must certainly apply energy. Similarly, breaking chemical bonds requires energy. This energy is used to overcome the electrostatic forces that bind atoms or ions together. It should follow from this that bond formation must result in a more stable situation in which energy is released.

If more energy is absorbed as bonds break than is released as bonds form during a chemical change, there will always be a net absorption of energy. As energy is required to break bonds, there will be a gain in enthalpy. Reactions such as these will have a positive ΔH value and are called **endothermic** reactions.

The energy absorbed to break bonds is greater than the energy released during bond formation in an *endothermic* reaction. Therefore, they have *positive* ΔH *values*.

If, on the other hand, more energy is released as bonds are formed than is absorbed as they are broken during a chemical change, there will always be a net release of energy. Hence, there will be a decrease in enthalpy content. Reactions such as these will have a negative ΔH value and are called **exothermic reactions**.

More energy is released during bond formation than is absorbed during bond breaking in an *exothermic* reaction. Therefore, they have *negative* ΔH *values*.

You may recall from Grade 11 there are two ways to express the ΔH value associated with a chemical reaction.

A *thermochemical equation* includes the energy change as an integral part of the chemical equation, while ΔH *notation* requires the energy change to be written after the equation following a "$\Delta H =$" symbol.

Quick Check

Given the following ΔH values, write a balanced thermochemical equation and an equation using ΔH notation with the smallest possible whole number coefficients for each of the following chemical changes. Note: These units imply that the energy released or absorbed is for *1 mol* of the reacting species. The first one is done as an example.

1. $\Delta H_{synthesis}$ of $NH_3(g) = -46.1$ kJ/molNH_3

   Thermochemical equation: $N_2(g) + 3\,H_2(g) \rightarrow 2\,NH_3(g) + 92.2$ kJ/mol$_{rxn}$

   ΔH notation: $N_2(g) + 3\,H_2(g) \rightarrow 2\,NH_3(g)$ $\quad \Delta H = -92.2$ kJ/mol$_{rxn}$

2. $\Delta H_{combustion}$ of $C_2H_6(g) = -1428.5$ kJ/molC_2H_6

3. $\Delta H_{decomposition}$ of $HBr(g) = 36.1$ kJ/molHBr

Transition State Theory

If we could examine reacting molecules coming together in a collision at a molecular level, we would see them slow down as their electron clouds repel one another. At some point, they would collide and then fly apart. If a reaction occurs during a collision, the particles that separate are chemically different from those that collide. When collision geometry is favorable and the colliding molecules have a kinetic energy at least equal to E_a, they interact to a form a high-energy, unstable, transitory configuration of atoms called an **activated complex**. This unstable complex will decompose and form new, lower-energy, more stable products.

As the reacting molecules collide, their electron cloud repulsions cause the reactant bonds to stretch and weaken. As reactant bonds break, kinetic energy is transformed into potential energy. At the same time, new bonds are forming between the atoms of the product. This process evolves energy as the newly formed bonds shorten and strengthen. The activated complex forms when potential energy is at a maximum and kinetic energy is minimized. The energy conversions and mechanics of bond breaking and forming are very complex and occur extremely rapidly (in less than a nanosecond or 10^{-9} s). The easiest way to follow these changes is to use a visual profile of the energy changes that occur during a collision. Figure 3.3.2 shows how the following reactions proceeds:

$$H_2(g) + I_2(g) \rightleftharpoons 2\,HI(g)$$

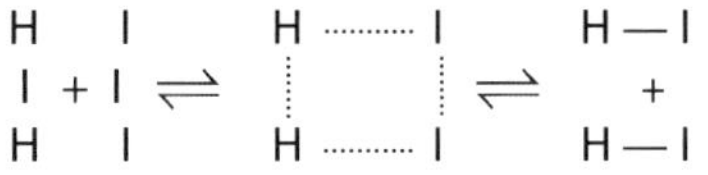

Figure 3.3.2 *H_2 and I_2 bonds break (KE→PE) as HI bonds form (PE→KE). The activated complex H_2I_2 exists for less than a nanosecond between these two processes*

Potential Energy Profiles

A **potential energy diagram** is a graphical representation of the energy changes that take place during a chemical reaction. The enthalpy changes can be followed along the vertical axis, which measures potential energy in kJ/mol. The horizontal axis is called by a variety of names such as the "reaction coordinate" or the "progress of reaction." It is critical to remember it is *not* a time axis. We are simply following the energy profile as the reaction proceeds from reactants to activated complex formation to products. Increasing the rate of the reaction will *not* change the length of this axis.

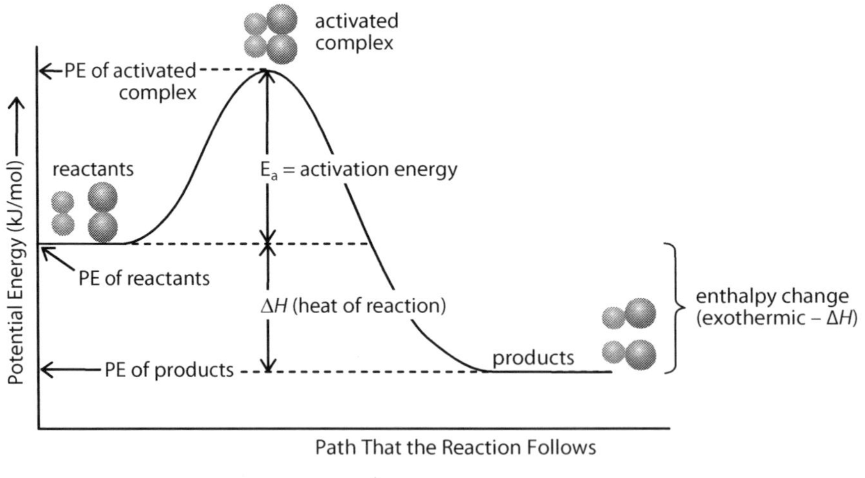

Figure 3.3.3 *A potential energy diagram. The reactants are diatomic elements combining to form an activated complex, which decomposes to form two product molecules.*

The activation energy, E_a, is the difference between the potential energy of the activated complex and the total potential energy of the separated reactant molecules. It represents the amount of energy the reactant molecules must gain to form an activated complex.
Thus $E_a = PE_{\text{activated complex}} - PE_{\text{reactants}}$

It is important to be aware that the net energy evolved or absorbed during the reaction is independent of the activation energy. If the potential energy (enthalpy) of the products is less than that of the reactants, the reaction is exothermic. Such is the case in Figure 3.3.3 above. On the other hand, if the products have more potential energy than the reactants, the reaction must be endothermic.

> The enthalpy change (ΔH) is the difference between the total potential energy of the products and the total potential energy of the reactants.
> Thus $\Delta H = PE_{products} - PE_{reactants}$

While altering factors such as concentration, surface area, or temperature will affect the rate of a chemical reaction, they will *not* affect the appearance of a potential energy diagram. This should make sense if we think of the diagram as a profile of potential bond energies (or enthalpies) per mole. While increasing the concentration of a reactant supplies more bonds, and consequently more bond energy, it also supplies more moles, so the energy *per mole* does not change. Changing temperature changes reaction rate, but it has no effect on the potential energy of the reactant or product bonds.

Sample Problem — Reading an Energy Profile

Read the following potential energy diagram and answer the questions.

1. Is the reaction endothermic or exothermic?
2. What is the activation energy of the reaction?
3. What is the potential energy of the activated complex?
4. What is the ΔH for this reaction?

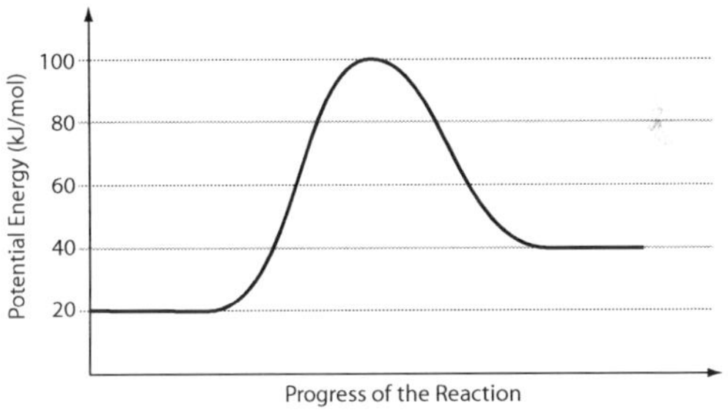

What to Think About	How to Do It
1. Check if the products or the reactants have more PE.	The products have more PE than the reactants. The reaction must be endothermic.
2. Consider the activation energy. The activation energy is the difference between the PE of the activated complex and the reactants.	$E_a = PE_{AC} - PE_{react}$ $= 100 - 20 = 80$ kJ/mol
3. Do not confuse the potential energy of the activated complex with the E_a. Activation energy is *always positive*.	$PE_{AC} = 100$ kJ/mol
4. Note endothermicity or exothermicity to ensure the sign is correct. This is an essential step.	$\Delta H = PE_{prod} - PE_{react}$ $= 40 - 20 = +20$ kJ/mol

Reversible Reactions

Many chemical reactions are reversible under certain conditions. This should be easy to accept if you think about a simple combination reaction being reversed to cause decomposition. The potential energy diagrams for a reaction pair such as these are simply mirror images of one another. Consider the combination of diatomic molecules A_2 and B_2 to form two AB molecules and the decomposition of two AB molecules to form diatomic A_2 and B_2. The potential energy profiles for these reactions would appear as shown in Figure 3.3.4.

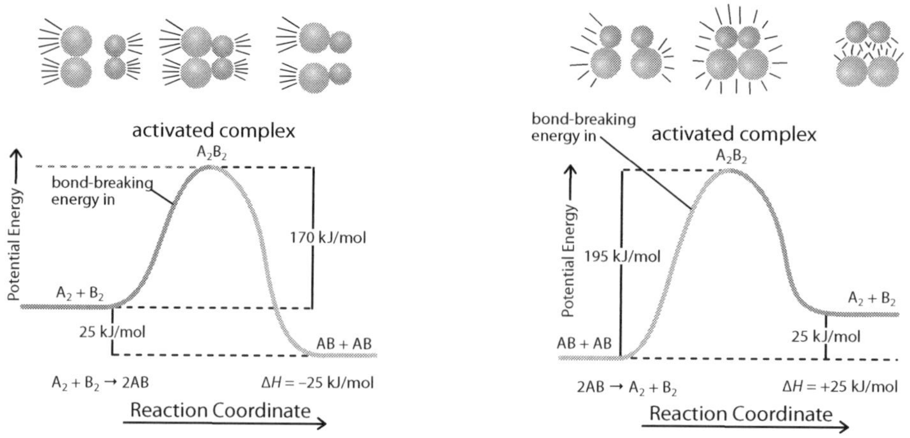

Figure 3.3.4 *The exothermic combination reaction's profile is simply the reverse of that for the endothermic decomposition reaction.*

Notice that the first potential energy diagram could be read in reverse to give the same measurements provided by the second diagram. Whether A_2 and B_2 are reactants or products, their potential bond energy or enthalpy is the same. The same could be said for two AB molecules. As a consequence, the decomposition reaction's ΔH value can be read as +25 kJ/mol from either Figure 3.3.4 or by reading Figure 3.3.3 in reverse (from right to left).

Sample Problem — Reading a Reversible Energy Profile

Read the potential energy diagram for a reversible reaction and answer the questions.

1. Which reaction, forward or reverse, is exothermic?
2. Give ΔH for the forward reaction and the reverse reaction.
3. Give E_a for the forward reaction and the reverse reaction.
4. Give the potential energy for the activated complex. How does this value compare for the forward and reverse reactions? Explain

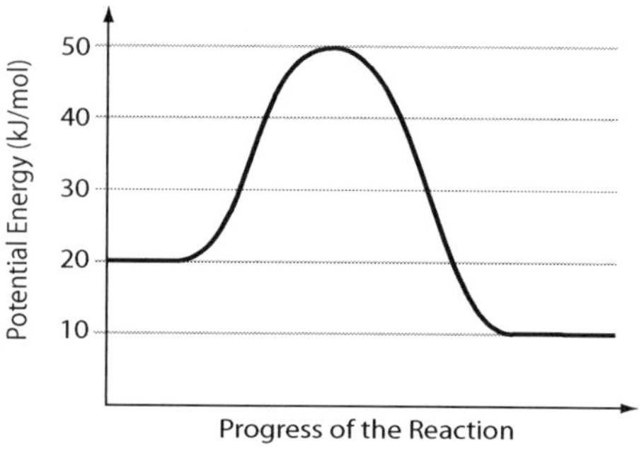

What to Think About	How to Do It
1. Check if the products or the reactants have more PE. Exothermic reactions have $PE_{prod} < PE_{reactants}$.	The forward reaction is exothermic.
2. Identify the sign of the ΔH. We know the forward ΔH is $-\Delta H$ because this is an exothermic reaction. The reverse ΔH must be $+\Delta H$ as the reactants become products and vice versa.	$\Delta H_{forward} = PE_{prod} - PE_{react} = 10 - 20 = -10$ kJ/mol $\Delta H_{reverse} = PE_{prod} - PE_{react} = 20 - 10 = +10$ kJ/mol
3. Recall the definition of E_a. Do not confuse it with the PE of the activated complex. When determining E_a for the reverse reaction, the reactants become the products.	$E_{a(forward)} = PE_{AC} - PE_{react} = 50 - 20 = 30$ kJ/mol $E_{a(reverse)} = PE_{AC} - PE_{react} = 50 - 10 = 40$ kJ/mol
4. Remember that the complex is the same aggregation (collection and arrangement) of atoms whether formed by the reactants or the products.	$PE_{AC} = 50$ kJ/mol for forward and reverse reaction as the same atoms are assembled in the same way and hence have the same potential bond energy (enthalpy) in both cases.

Practice Problems — Reading a Reversible Energy Profile

1. Answer the following questions about this potential energy diagram:

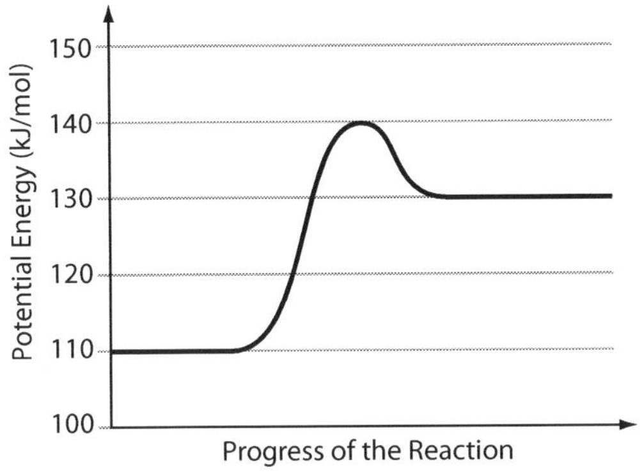

   (a) Is the forward reaction exothermic or endothermic?

   (b) Indicate the following values for the forward reaction:

      (i) activation energy

      (ii) enthalpy change

      (iii) potential energy of the products

      (iv) potential energy of the activated complex

2. Indicate the meaning of each of the measured values, I through IV, on the following potential energy diagram.

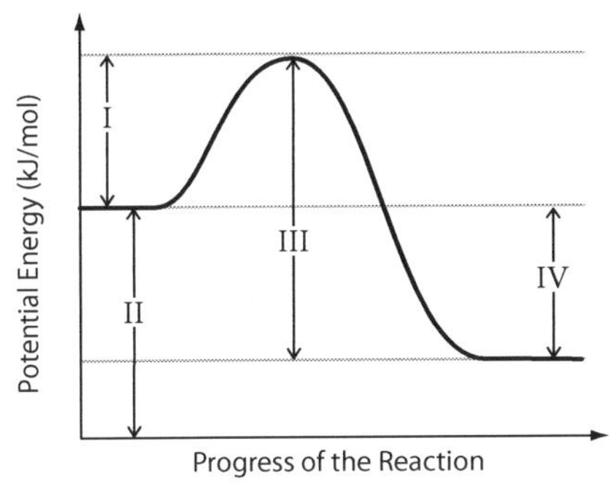

Summary for Reversible Diagrams

In summary, we see that for a reversible potential energy diagram the following points are always true:

- ΔH for the forward and reverse reactions have the *same magnitude* and *opposite signs*.
- E_a is always smaller for the exothermic reaction.
- Altering temperature, pressure, concentration, or surface area will have *no effect* on a potential energy diagram. There is only one thing that will alter a diagram and that is discussed below.

Activation Energy and Catalysis

An increase in temperature or concentration allows many more collisions to attain activation energy and hence react successfully. Increasing temperature may, in some situations, cause the decomposition of reactants before they can react. Increased temperature may also cause the formation of unwanted side products. Fortunately, since the great Swedish chemist Berzelius, scientists have been aware of catalysts that may increase the rate of a reaction without raising the temperature.

In general, catalysts provide an alternate reaction pathway in which a different, lower-energy activated complex can form. Reaction pathways are called *mechanisms*.

Catalysts provide an *additional reaction mechanism* with a *lower activation energy*, which results in an *increased reaction rate*. The catalyst is *neither consumed nor changed* following the reaction.

Catalysts reduce the activation energy to the same extent for both the forward and the reverse reaction in a reversible reaction. Consequently both forward and reverse reaction rates are increased by the same amount.

Catalysts must be consumed in one step of a reaction mechanism and be regenerated in a later step. This is why they are neither consumed, nor changed as a chemical reaction occurs. A consequence of this is that more than one activated complex is formed. This leads to more than one "peak" in the potential energy diagram for most catalyzed reactions. Occasionally textbooks show a single peak in the catalyzed pathway on a potential energy diagram. In those cases, the diagram is simply showing a *net* or *overall* reduced energy pathway produced by the use of the catalyst.

Potential energy profiles for catalyzed reactions will usually involve the formation of more than one activated complex and hence more than one "peak" in the diagram.

The calculation of the activation energy for a multiple peak diagram such as Figure 3.3.5 is simply the difference between the highest energy activated complex and the reactants.

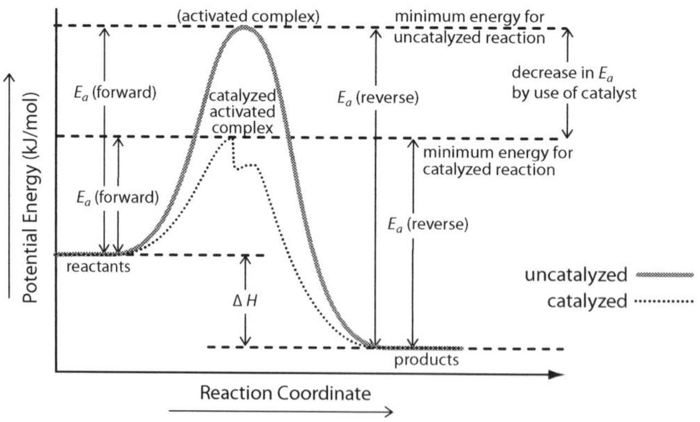

Figure 3.3.5 *The presence of a catalyst actually changes the energy profile to a lower activation energy pathway.*

Quick Check

Study the following potential energy diagrams for two independent reactions.

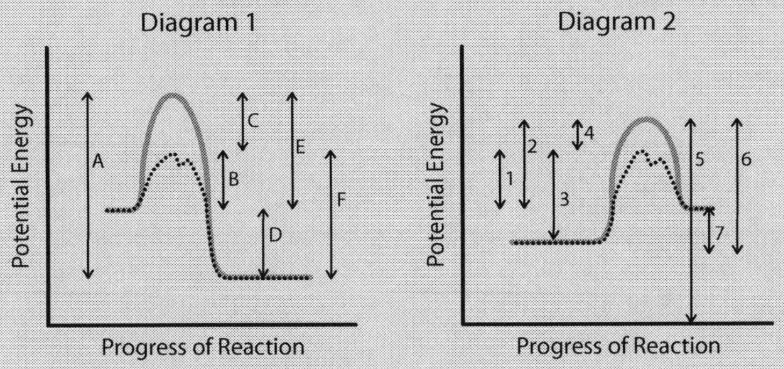

1. For diagram 1, indicate what each of the measurements shown by the lettered arrows represents. A is completed for you as an example.
2. From diagram 2, indicate the number that *represents* the same measurement in diagram 1. A is completed for you as an example.

A. Reverse uncatalyzed activation energy. $E_{a(\text{reverse uncatalyzed})}$ is #2 in diagram 2.

B.

C.

D.

E.

F.

3.3 Activity: Comparing and Contrasting Concepts in Kinetics

Question

How can you compare and contrast endothermic and exothermic processes?

Procedure

1. Use the outline provided below to organize what you've learned about endothermic and exothermic reactions.
2. The first row has been completed as an example of what is expected. Note that there may be many other comparisons and contrasts (or similarities and differences) that you can add to your table. Don't feel limited to only those lines where clues have been provided.

Characteristic	Endothermic	Exothermic
Sensation	Feels cold	Feels hot
Sign of ΔH		
Change in enthalpy		
PE ← → KE transformation		
Sample thermochemical equation		
Sample equation using ΔH		
Bond energy comparisons		
Energy involved in breaking vs. forming bonds		
Sample PE diagram		

Results and Discussion

You will find it very helpful to produce similar charts to help you summarize material for study in the remaining sections of this course. Add these to the dedicated section of your notebook for summary notes and refer to them from time to time to help you in preparing for your unit and final examinations.

3.3 Review Questions

1. Given the following ΔH values, write a balanced thermochemical equation and an equation using ΔH notation with the smallest possible whole number coefficients for each of the chemical changes given below.
   (a) The replacement of iron in thermite, $Fe_2O_3(s)$, by aluminum $\Delta H = -852$ kJ/molFe_2O_3

   (b) The formation of $Ca(OH)_2(s)$ from its elements $\Delta H = -986$ kJ/mol$Ca(OH)_2$

   (c) The decomposition of $H_2O(l)$ into its elements $\Delta H = +286$ kJ/molH_2O

2. Study the graphs shown below.
   (a) Draw a vertical line on the first graph to represent E_a. Place the line so that about 10% of the particles in the reacting sample have enough energy to react.
   (b) Rotate the first graph in such a way that the energy axes of the two graphs are both oriented up and down. Redraw the graph(s) in this orientation.
   (c) Explain what these graphs indicate about the reacting particles.

   (d) Repeat part (b) on the right side of the second graph.
   (e) What does this say about an endothermic reaction compared to an exothermic one?

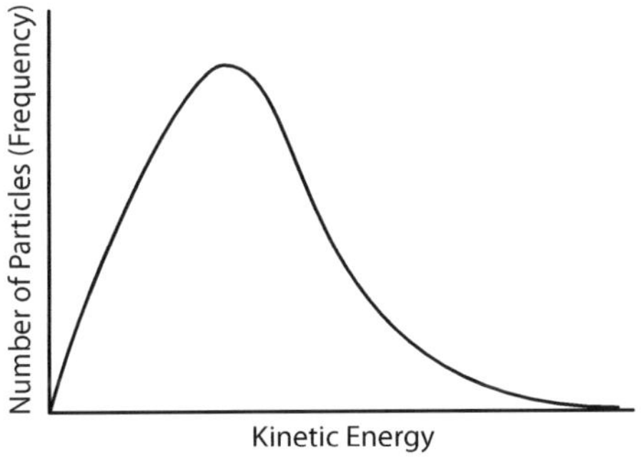

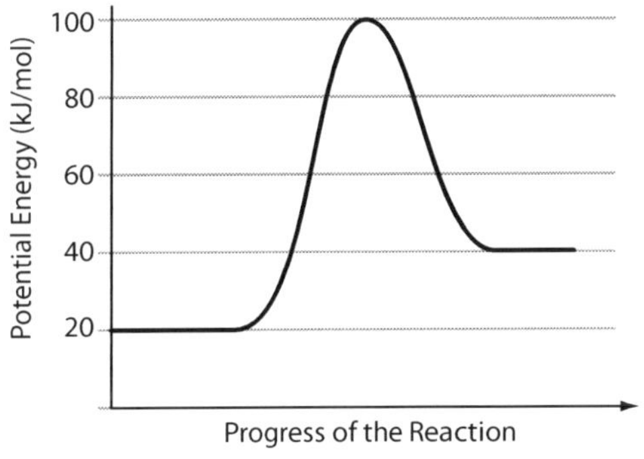

3. For a hypothetical reaction, $XY(g) \rightleftharpoons X(g) + Y(g)$ $\Delta H = 35$ kJ/mol. For the reverse reaction, $E_a = 25$ kJ/mol.
   (a) Sketch a potential energy diagram for this reaction (label general values as given).

   (b) What is the activation energy for the forward reaction?

   (c) What is ΔH for the reverse reaction?

4. Study the potential energy diagram shown below.

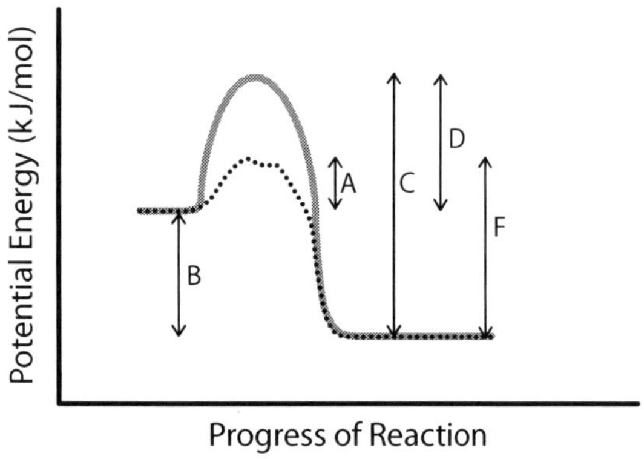

   (a) Indicate what each of the letters (A through E) represents.

   A.

   B.

   C.

   D.

   E.

   (b) Is this reaction endothermic or exothermic?

(c) How would the diagram be affected if the reacting system were heated?

5. Examine the following potential energy diagram for this reaction:
Q + S → T

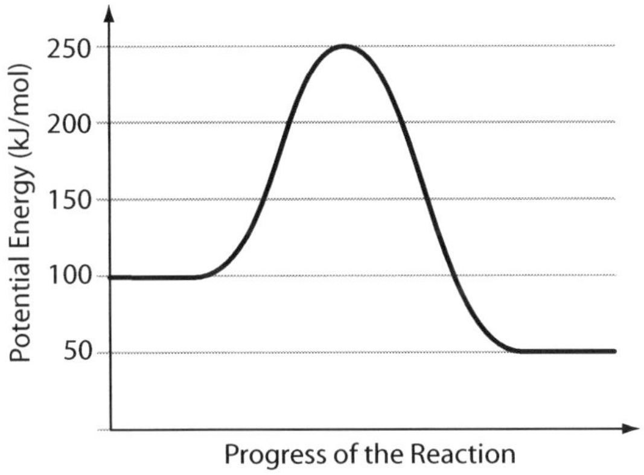

(a) Determine ΔH for the reaction.

(b) Write the thermochemical equation for the reaction.

(c) Rewrite the equation in ΔH notation.

(d) Classify the reaction as exothermic or endothermic.

(e) Determine the E_a of the reaction.

6. Why are exothermic reactions usually self-sustaining. In other words, why do they continue once supplied with activation energy? Use the burning of a pile of driftwood as an example.

7. Fill in the blanks for an EXOthermic reaction: The energy released during bond forming is ____________ than the energy required for bond ______________. As a result, there is a net ______________ of energy. The bonds formed have ____________ potential energy than the ________________ bonds did.

8. How would a PE diagram for a *fast* reaction compare to a PE diagram for a *slow* reaction? Explain.

9. (a) As two reactant particles approach one another for a collision, what happens to their kinetic energy? Why?

(b) What happens to their potential energy? Why?

(c) What happens to their total energy (sum of potential and kinetic)?

(e) Complete the following graph:

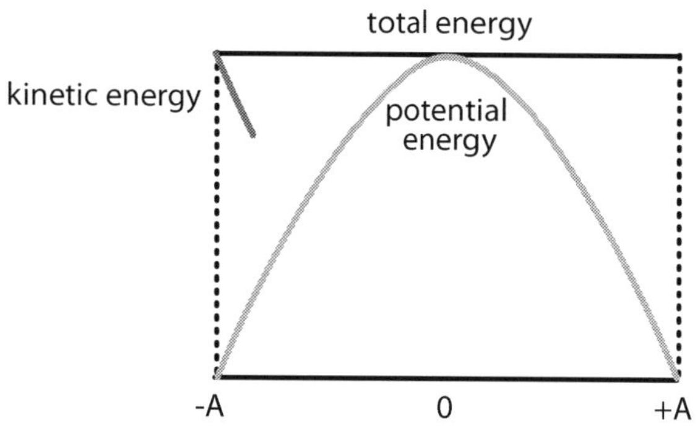

10. Study the following potential energy diagram.

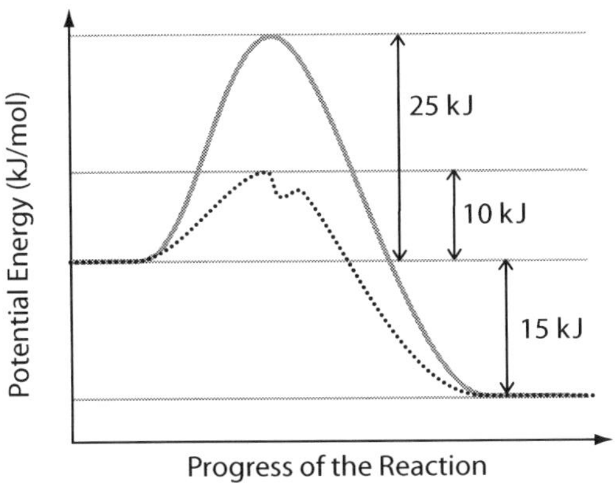

(a) Is this reaction endothermic or exothermic?

(b) What is E_a for the catalyzed pathway?

(c) What is E_a for the uncatalyzed pathway?

(d) What is ΔH for this reaction? How does this value change with a catalyst?

(e) How much lower is the potential energy of the activated complex with a catalyst?

(f) How does this affect the reaction rate?

3.4 Entropy Change versus Enthalpy Change

Warm Up

Everything around you can be perceived as being in a relative state of organization or disorganization. For each picture below, check the box that applies.

☐ organized
☐ disorganized

☐ organized
☐ disorganized

☐ organized
☐ disorganized

☐ organized
☐ disorganized

☐ organized
☐ disorganized

☐ organized
☐ disorganized

☐ organized
☐ disorganized

☐ organized
☐ disorganized

What Is Entropy?

Entropy is the amount of thermal energy in a closed system that is not available to do work. An analogy used to explain entropy in simple terms is that the entropy of a substance or a system correlates with its state of disorganization or energy dispersal.. The analogy of randomness or energy dispersal refers to the number of ways in which the energy of a system can be arranged. The possible ways in which energy can be distributed in a system are called microstates. . Every form of matter and every particle, except a fundamental particle, has a degree of energy dispersal which can be measured. Scientists use the letter S as the symbol for entropy. Standard molar entropies are expressed in joules per mole per kelvin (J/K • mol). Scientists view a more organized — lower entropy — system as one with fewer available variations or fewer microstates. In other words, a more organized state is a more "fixed" state with few possible ways in which energy can be distributed. Simpler things have lower entropies because they have fewer possible configurations or microstates.. What follows is a somewhat non-scientific example to help understand the concept of entropy. There are few microstates, or arrangements in which your bedroom is "neat", a neat bedroom is a system with a low entropy. However, there are a vast number of arrangements in which your bedroom can be "messy", a messy bedroom can be used as a simple analogy of a system with a high entropy. This example falls short for many reasons, not the least of which is that your bedroom is one system so both the neat and the messy microstates are actually part of the same system.

In a chemical system with a low entropy there are few species and few way of arranging the species that are present. A solid has a lower entropy than a liquid which, in turn, has a lower entropy than a gas. Entropy increases in a chemical system where one reactant species decomposes into two product species and decreases where two reactant species are synthesized into one product species.

Chemical Systems and Entropy

Atoms are organizations of subatomic particles; molecules are organizations of atoms; and molecular substances are organizations of molecules. A molecular substance's entropy is a function of its intramolecular (within molecules) relationships and its intermolecular (between molecules) relationships. The third law of thermodynamics states that a perfect crystal at 0 kelvin has 0 entropy.

For elements of the same state within a family, the higher the element's atomic number is, the greater its entropy. More electrons provide more variability in positions. For example, the entropies of the noble gases increase as you move down the periodic table (Table 3.4.1).

Table 3.4.1 *Standard Entropies (S°) of the Noble Gases*

Noble Gas	He	Ne	Ar	Kr	Xe
S° (J/mol·K)	126	147	155	164	170

Likewise, the heavier and more complex a molecule is, the greater its compound's entropy. As well as having more atoms (each with its own variability), more complex molecules have more possible rotational and vibrational orientations. This is exemplified by the entropies of nitrogen oxides (Table 3.4.2).

Table 3.4.2 *Standard Entropies (S°) of Some Nitrogen Oxides*

Substance	$NO(g)$	$N_2O(g)$	$N_2O_4(g)$	$N_2O_5(g)$
S° (J/mol·K)	211	220	304	356

The entropy of a substance is strongly dependent on its temperature. As particles gain kinetic energy, their motion becomes increasingly chaotic. The physical state or phase of a substance affects its entropy as illustrated by the standard entropies of different phases of molecular iodine shown in Table 3.4.3. Entropy increases from solid to liquid to gas. Particle motion (whether individual atoms or molecules) in the gas state is almost completely random. Particle motion in the liquid state is limited to within the body of the liquid but the particles can still slip past one another thereby allowing many different permutations (orders) of the same particles. The order of the particles is fixed in the solid state, thereby leaving only vibrational motion to provide for different possible inter-particle configurations.

Table 3.4.3 *Standard Entropies (S°) of Different Phases of Molecular Iodine*

Substance	$I_2(s)$	$I_2(aq)$	$I_2(g)$
S° (J/mol·K)	116	137	261

Quick Check

1. Define "entropy"?

____

2. Which of these two elements has greater entropy: Ag(*s*) or Cu(*s*)? Explain.

____

3. Which of these two compounds has greater entropy: water, $H_2O(l)$, or hydrogen peroxide, $H_2O_2(l)$? Explain.

____

Chemical Reactions and Entropy Change

A chemical equation alone does not contain enough information for you to reliably determine whether entropy increases or decreases during the reaction. This can only be determined with certainty by comparing the standard entropies of the reactants and products. The standard entropies are included in the examples below to verify each example's claim regarding entropy change. Standard entropies for many elements and compounds are found in the Thermodynamic Data in Appendix 8 of this text. Thermodynamic data for compounds not in this text can be found in a CRC Handbook or other reliable Chemical Handbook.

1. Entropy Changes in Reactions Involving Gases

Combining particles reduces their number but increases their complexity. The reduced number of particles usually decreases entropy more than the increased complexity increases it.

> Entropy usually decreases when gas particles combine into fewer particles.

The entropy of gases is considerably greater than the entropy of solids or liquids. For this reason, the entropy change in reactions involving gases is usually dominated by the increasing or decreasing moles of gas.

In the synthesis of water from its elements, entropy decreases as three gas molecules are organized into two.

$$2\,H_2(g) + O_2(g) \rightarrow 2\,H_2O(g)$$
$$2(131) + 205 \;>\; 2(189) \quad \text{J/K·mol}$$

Solids typically decompose by releasing a gas. Entropy increases in the following example as zero gas molecules are converted into one. The standard entropies show that entropy increases mainly because a gas is produced.

$$CaCO_3(s) \rightarrow CaO(s) + CO_2(g)$$
$$93 \;<\; 40 + 214 \quad \text{J/K·mol}$$

Despite the following reaction being a synthesis reaction, entropy increases because one gas molecule becomes two.

$$2\,C(s) + O_2(g) \rightarrow 2\,CO(g)$$
$$2(5.7) + 205 \;<\; 2(197.6) \quad \text{J/K·mol}$$

If the number of gas molecules doesn't change during the reaction then count the number of atoms that are part of gas molecules. Entropy decreases in the following example as there are 9 atoms (3 CO_2) in reactant gas molecules and only 6 atoms (3 CO) in product gas molecules.

$$2\,Fe(s) + 3\,CO_2(g) \rightarrow Fe_2O_3(s) + 3\,CO(g)$$
$$2(27.3) + 3(213.6) > 87.4 + 3(197.6) \quad J/K{\cdot}mol$$

Recall the caution given in the opening paragraph of this subsection. The standard entropies show that entropy increases in the following synthesis reaction despite six gas molecules combining into four. The phosphorus atoms changing from the solid state to the gas state in a compound with hydrogen has a greater influence on the entropy than the reduced number of gas particles.

$$P_4(s) + 6\,H_2(g) \rightarrow 4\,PH_3(g)$$
$$44 + 6(131) < 4(210) \quad J/K{\cdot}mol$$

2. The Reorganization of Atoms of the Same Element

What if a reaction the number of gas molecules does not change during a reaction and neither does the number of atoms that are part of gas molecules? If reactant molecules change from a solid phase to a liquid phase, entropy is usually increasing. If atoms of the same type, such as those found in a diatomic element, are rearranged into heterogeneous combinations of atoms, entropy is usually increasing.

(a) Phase Changes

Entropy decreases in the reaction below as three of the oxygen atoms go from being part of a gaseous compound (CO_2) to being part of a solid compound (Fe_2O_3). All the other atoms go from reactants to products of the same phase.

$$2\,Fe(s) + 3CO_2(g) \rightarrow Fe_2O_3(s) + 3\,CO(g)$$
$$2(27.3) + 3(213.6) > 87.4 + 3(197.6) \quad J/K{\cdot}mol$$

(b) Chemical Changes

A group of items has less entropy when the common items are grouped together. In the example below, nitrogen and oxygen atoms have less entropy when the "like" atoms are combined together than when the "unlike" atoms are combined.

$$N_2(g) + O_2(g) \rightarrow 2\,NO(g)$$
$$191.5 + 205 < 2(210.7) \quad J/K{\cdot}mol$$

Recall that a state's entropy increases with the number of ways it can be achieved or expressed. There is only one way to combine two nitrogen atoms ($^aN^bN$) where the superscripts "a" and "b" tag or distinguish the two atoms. Likewise, there is also only one way to combine two oxygen atoms ($^aO^bO$). On the other hand, there are two ways of combining the two nitrogen atoms with the two oxygen atoms to form NO ($^aN^aO$ & $^bN^bO$ or $^aN^bO$ & $^bN^aO$). Since the product condition has more variations (more microstates), it represents the less ordered system and therefore the one with greater entropy.

Entropy increases when common items split up to form or be part of more groups. In the example below, entropy increases as the oxygen atoms go from being in the same molecule (CO_2) to being in two molecules (CO and H_2O).

$$CO_2(g) + H_2(g) \rightarrow CO(g) + H_2O(g)$$
$$213.6 + 130.6 < 197.6 + 188.7 \quad J/K{\cdot}mol$$

Sample Problems — Predicting by Inspection Whether Entropy Increases or Decreases

Predict whether entropy increases or decreases in each of the following and provide your reasoning:

(a) $PCl_3(g) + Cl_2(g) \rightarrow PCl_5(g)$

(b) $Fe_2O_3(s) + 3\ H_2(g) \rightarrow 2\ Fe(s) + 3\ H_2O(g)$

What to Think About	How to Do It
For both problems, consider (in usual order of importance) the following: 1. Changes in the number of gas particles	(a) Entropy decreases because two gas molecules combine into one.
2. Reorganization of atoms of the same element	(b) Entropy increases because there are only six atoms in the reactant gas molecules and there are nine atoms in the product gas molecules..

Practice Problems — Predicting by Inspection Whether Entropy Increases or Decreases

Predict whether entropy increases or decreases in each of the following and provide your reasoning

1. $2\ FeO(s) \rightarrow 2\ Fe(s) + O_2(g)$

2. $S_8(s) + 8\ O_2(g) \rightarrow 8\ SO_2(g)$

3. $H_2O(s) \rightarrow H_2O(l)$

Natural Thermodynamic Drives

Two thermodynamic "drives" influence an equilibrium's position:

1. the drive toward decreasing enthalpy
2. the drive toward increasing entropy or disorder

1. The Drive Toward Decreasing Enthalpy

Objects naturally adopt the lowest energy state available to them. This is illustrated by placing a book on its edge in the trunk of a car. Nobody would expect the book to remain in this position after the car had moved. A slight jostle causes the book to adopt a more stable orientation as it falls onto its face. The book lowers its gravitational potential energy as its center of mass moves closer to Earth. The jostle plays the role of the activation energy in this analogy. This principle applies to all objects including molecules, atoms, and subatomic particles. It is responsible for atoms forming stronger bonding associations with lower potential energy. In other words, chemical reactions tend to proceed in the exothermic direction.

For example, consider this reaction: $N_2(g) + 2\ O_2(g) + 68\ kJ/mol \rightarrow 2\ NO_2(g)$

The tendency toward decreasing enthalpy (energy) pushes this reaction in the exothermic direction toward reactants (Figure 3.4.3).

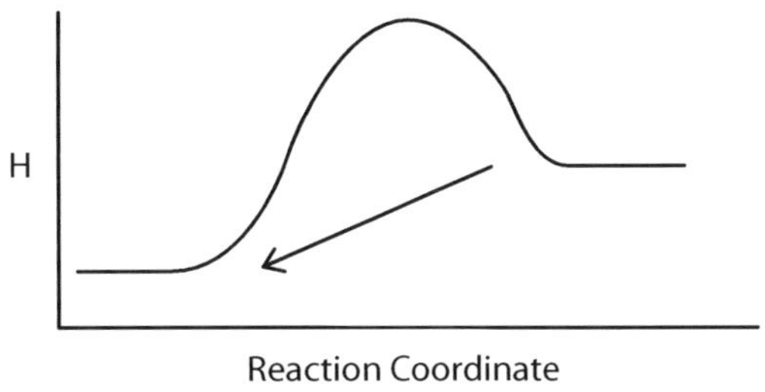

Figure 3.4.3 *Chemical reactions tend to proceed in the exothermic direction.*

2. The Drive Toward Increasing Entropy

Randomly moving objects such as liquid and gas molecules become disorganized when left on their own. It takes work to collect such objects and to keep them organized. Diffusion is an example of the tendency of objects toward disorder. Diffusion is the self-movement of chemicals from an area of greater concentration to an area of lesser concentration. If you open a bottle of perfume, its molecules will rapidly diffuse throughout the room. This tendency toward increasing entropy applies to chemical changes as well as to physical processes.

Enthalpy, Entropy, and Equilibrium

Chemical reactions are driven toward minimum or decreasing enthalpy and maximum or increasing entropy. If both drives are toward products then the reaction, having no opposition, will achieve an equilibrium position far to the right. If both drives are toward reactants, the forward reaction barely gets going before establishing equilibrium with a position far to the left. From a thermodynamic perspective, equilibria with a "reasonable" proportion of both reactants and products develop as a compromise between the two drives when they oppose each other.

> If the drive toward increasing entropy opposes the drive toward decreasing enthalpy, an equilibrium will develop with a "reasonable" proportion of both reactants and products.

Consider the following two examples:

$2\ CO_2(g) + 566\ \text{kJ/mol} \rightarrow 2\ CO(g) + O_2(g)$	$2\ H_2(g) + O_2(g) \rightarrow 2\ H_2O(g) + 483.6\ \text{kJ/mol}$
Decreasing enthalpy favors reactants. ←	Decreasing enthalpy favors products. →
→ Increasing entropy favors products.	← Increasing entropy favors reactants.

Figure 3.4.4 *The low enthalpy–low entropy option for water's movement*

The movement of rainwater is a good thermodynamic model of equilibrium. Water flows downhill and also seeps outward. Consider how rain distributes itself on a street. Some water covers the street but some also collects in the gutters and into puddles (Figure 3.4.4). The puddles and gutters are the low enthalpy–low entropy option while the street surface is the high enthalpy–high entropy option.

Figure 3.4.5 shows the four possible enthalpy-entropy combinations that could occur in a chemical reaction. Both the enthalpy and entropy could increase, they could both decrease, or one could increase and one could decrease. Although Figure 3.4.5 nicely lays out every possible thermodynamic scenario for reactions, there is absolutely no benefit to memorizing it. The thermodynamic drives themselves can easily be applied to any reaction rather than applying a table derived from them.

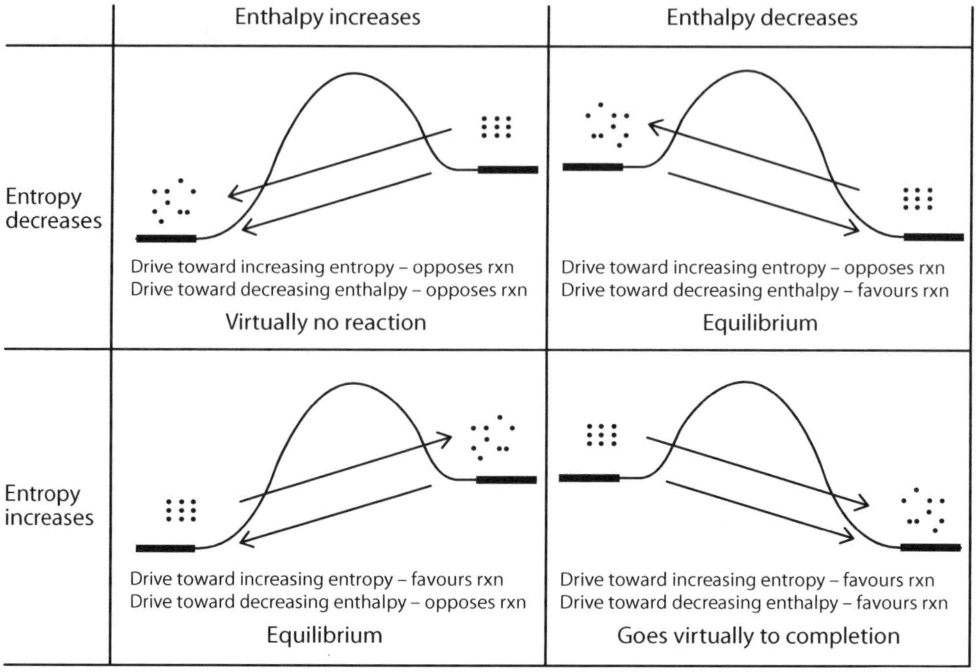

Figure 3.4.5 *The four thermodynamic categories of chemical reactions*

Why does a reaction not go entirely to completion when both drives are toward products? Maximum entropy is achieved just short of the completed reaction because even if the entropy of the products is much greater than the entropy of the reactants, a mixture containing a very small proportion of reactants will have a greater entropy than products alone. Chemists may say that such a reaction "goes to completion" because the equilibrium mixture consists of very nearly pure products.

Likewise, even if both drives are toward reactants, a mixture containing a very small proportion of products will still have greater entropy than the reactants alone. Chemists may say that such a reaction "does not occur" because the equilibrium mixture consists of very nearly pure reactants.

The relationship between enthalpy, entropy, and equilibrium facilitates a popular series of questions where students are directly or indirectly provided with two of these features of a reaction and asked for the third.

Sample Problem — Predicting an Equilibrium's Position from Its Thermodynamics

State whether the following reaction will achieve *equilibrium* (with a reasonable proportion of reactants and products), go nearly to *completion*, or virtually *not occur*.

$$N_2(g) + 3\,H_2(g) \rightarrow 2\,NH_3(g) \qquad \Delta H = -92\text{ kJ/mol}$$

What to Think About

1. Consider the two thermodynamic drives:
   - The drive toward increasing entropy is toward reactants.
   - The drive toward decreasing enthalpy is toward products.

How to Do It

Since the two drives are opposing each other, the reaction will achieve equilibrium with a reasonable proportion of reactants and products.

Sample Problem — Predicting an Equilibrium's Thermodynamics from Its Position

The following equilibrium has a reasonable proportion of reactants and products. State whether the forward reaction is endothermic or exothermic.

$$C(s) + H_2O(g) \rightleftharpoons H_2(g) + CO(g)$$

What to Think About	How to Do It
1. Determine from the equilibrium position whether the drives are opposed, both toward reactants, or both toward products.	The two thermodynamic drives are opposed because the reaction establishes equilibrium with a reasonable proportion of reactants and products.
2. By inspection, determine whether entropy is increasing or decreasing.	Entropy is increasing as one gas molecule reacts to produce two gas molecules.
3. Decide whether the reaction is endothermic or exothermic from steps 1 and 2.	The drives are opposed and the drive toward increasing entropy is toward products. Therefore the drive toward decreasing enthalpy must be toward reactants: the reaction is endothermic.

Practice Problems — Predicting an Equilibrium's Position from Its Thermodynamics or Vice Versa

1. State whether the following reaction will achieve *equilibrium* (with a reasonable proportion of reactants and products), go nearly to *completion*, or almost *not occur*. $3\ O_2(g) \rightleftharpoons 2\ O_3(g)$ $\Delta H = +285$ kJ/mol

2. The following reaction establishes equilibrium with a reasonable proportion of reactants and products. State whether this reaction is endothermic or exothermic. $CO(g) + H_2O(g) \rightleftharpoons CO_2(g) + H_2(g)$

3. The following equilibrium has a reasonable proportion of reactants and products. State whether entropy increases or decreases during the forward reaction. $CH_2O(g) + O_2(g) \rightleftharpoons CO_2(g) + H_2O(g)$ $\Delta H = -518$ kJ/mol

Enthalpy, Entropy, and Spontaneity

The spontaneity of a reaction is frequently a concern for chemists. A **spontaneous process** is one that happens "on its own" with no outside intervention.

> Chemical systems move spontaneously toward equilibrium.

The system's entropy change and enthalpy change both play a role in determining whether or not a reaction is spontaneous. You will learn much more about this in later chemistry courses. Do not confuse whether it's going to happen (spontaneity) with when it's going to happen (how quickly the final condition will be achieved). A spontaneous reaction can occur at a tediously slow rate. Nails spontaneously rust, and diamond spontaneously turns into graphite. Spontaneity is a thermodynamic function and depends only on the conditions at the start and the end of the process. Rate is a kinetic function and depends on the path taken between the two. The situation is loosely analogous to children telling their parents that they will take out the kitchen garbage but when this will occur is an entirely different matter.

3.4 Activity: Imitating Disorder

Question

Can you place some black dots in a matrix so that they appear to your classmates to be randomly distributed?

Background

When people attempt to randomize objects in space or time, they tend to err toward an even distribution.
Let's see if you and your classmates can identify which of each other's two matrices contains the set of dots that are actually randomly distributed.

Procedure

1. Attempt to randomly distribute 12 dots within the squares of one of the two matrices below. You may place more than one dot within a square.
2. Randomly place a single dot *in the other matrix* by rolling a dice twice to determine the row and column to place the dot in (e.g., a 1-1 roll would place the dot in the upper left hand corner of the matrix). Repeat this technique 11 more times to produce a matrix that actually contains 12 randomly distributed dots.

	1	2	3	4	5	6
1						
2						
3						
4						
5						
6						

	1	2	3	4	5	6
1						
2						
3						
4						
5						
6						

3. Exchange books with 10 classmates. Each time, attempt to identify which of your classmate's two matrices contains the set of dots that are actually randomly distributed.

Continued on next page

3.4 Activity: *Continued*

Results and Discussion

1. Keep a record (𝍸) in the table below of how many of your classmates chose correctly and how many times you chose correctly.

Your Guesses	
Correct	**Incorrect**

Your Classmates' Guesses	
Correct	**Incorrect**

If a person can't tell the difference between the two matrices then there is still a 50% chance that the person will choose the correct matrix. There is only a 17% probability that 7 or more of the 10 people could pick the correct (random) matrix by chance. If this happens, we'll declare your fake "busted." Likewise, if you can correctly identify the random distribution 7 out of 10 times then we'll declare you "randomly gifted."

Each trial tests two things: a person's ability to fake a random distribution and another person's ability to spot the fake. Correctly spotting the random distribution could indicate a "poor" fake or a "good" spotter.

2. Look around the room at your classmates' results and comment on whether there is a relationship between people who are good at faking random patterns and people who are good at recognizing random patterns.

3.4 Review Questions

1. Which substance in each of the following pairs would likely have the greater entropy? Explain.
   (a) $Br_2(l)$ or $Br_2(g)$

   (b) $SO_3(g)$ or $SO_2(g)$

   (c) $Sn(s)$ or $Pb(s)$

2. For each of the following state whether entropy is increasing or decreasing and briefly state your reasoning.
   (a) $2\ NH_3(g) \rightarrow N_2(g) + 3\ H_2(g)$

   (b) $NOCl_2(g) + NO(g) \rightarrow 2\ NOCl(g)$

   (c) $4\ Fe(s) + 3\ O_2(g) \rightarrow 2\ Fe_2O_3(s)$

   (d) $H_2(g) + Cl_2(g) \rightarrow 2\ HCl(g)$

   (e) $WO_3(s) + 3\ H_2(g) \rightarrow W(s) + 3\ H_2O(g)$

3. State whether each of the following reactions will achieve equilibrium with a reasonable amount of reactants and products, go almost to completion, or virtually not occur.

(a) $4\ NH_3(g) + 5\ O_2(g) \rightarrow 4\ NO(g) + 6\ H_2O(g)$ $\Delta H = -907.2$ kJ/mol

(b) $N_2(g) + 2\ O_2(g) \rightarrow 2\ NO_2(g)$ $\Delta H = +68$ kJ/mol

(c) $PCl_3(g) + Cl_2(g) \rightarrow PCl_5(g)$ $\Delta H = -92.5$ kJ/mol

(d) $S(s) + O_2(g) \rightarrow SO_2(g)$ $\Delta H = -297$ kJ/mol

4. For the following reaction, state whether the forward reaction is endothermic or exothermic, given that the two thermodynamic drives are opposed to each other. Explain your reasoning.
$CaCO_3(s) \rightleftharpoons CaO(s) + CO_2(g)$

5. Describe the thermodynamics of a reaction that establishes equilibrium so far toward reactants that it is said to virtually not occur.

6. The following equilibrium has a reasonable proportion of reactants and products. State whether entropy is increasing or decreasing during the forward reaction. Explain your reasoning.
$CO_2(g) + NO(g) \rightleftharpoons NO_2(g) + CO(g)$ $\Delta H = +82$ kJ/mol

7. Given that equilibrium is established with a reasonable proportion of reactants and products, in what direction will the system shift when the temperature is decreased? Explain your reasoning.
$2\ SO_2(g) + O_2(g) \rightleftharpoons 2\ SO_3(g)$

8. Why does a reaction that has both thermodynamic drives toward products (the drive toward increasing entropy and the drive toward decreasing enthalpy) not go entirely to completion?

3.5 Entropy — A Quantitative Treatment

Warm Up

In Grade 11, you learned that heat flows from a region of high energy to a region of low energy. This might lead to the conclusion that
spontaneous change must be exothermic.

1. Consider the following change occurring at room temperature:

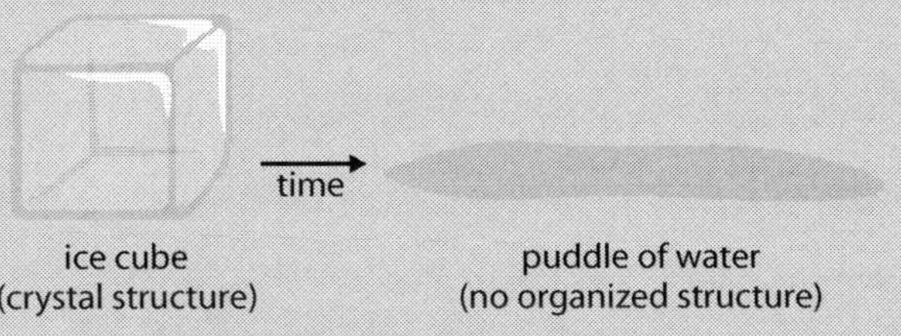

   (a) Is this change spontaneous (did it occur without outside intervention)? _______
   (b) Is this process endothermic or exothermic? _______________
   (c) What is the sign of ΔH? _______

2. Consider the change at a molecular level:

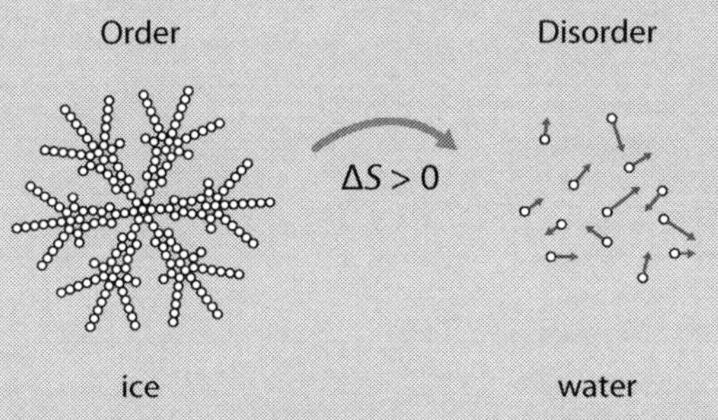

   (a) What is the sign for ΔS? _______
   (b) Is this process enthalpy driven or entropy driven? _____________

   Explain. ____

   ____

The First Law of Thermodynamics

Energy is conserved — never created or destroyed. When energy is released by an exothermic change, the potential energy stored in chemical bonds is converted to kinetic energy, which is the energy of motion of atoms and molecules. As the kinetic energy of the atoms and molecules in the system and the surroundings increases, the temperature rises. A system releases heat during an exothermic change. Heat is the energy transferred between a system and its surroundings. By convention, we indicate that the system is releasing heat by placing a negative sign in front of the enthalpy value.

Spontaneous Change

When thermodynamicists say that a reaction is spontaneous, they mean that the reaction will occur without any outside intervention. They do not mean the reaction occurs rapidly.

In contrast, a non-spontaneous event can continue only as long as it receives some sort of outside assistance. All non-spontaneous events occur at the expense of spontaneous ones. They can occur only when some spontaneous change occurs first.

Enthalpy and Spontaneity

When a change lowers the potential energy of a system, it tends to occur spontaneously. Fuels evolve heat as they combust to form H_2O and CO_2 and convert the potential energy in the bonds of the reactants to heat. Since a change that lowers the potential energy of a system is exothermic, we can say that exothermic changes have a tendency to occur spontaneously.

While many spontaneous changes are indeed exothermic, there are common examples of spontaneous endothermic changes including the melting of ice, the vaporization of water, and the dissolving of most salts in water to form aqueous solutions. Since each of these events is both endothermic AND spontaneous, they must have some other factor in common that allows them to overcome the unfavorable energy change. Careful examination shows that in each of these events, there is an increase in the randomness or disorder of the system. These observations led to the development of the **Second Law of Thermodynamics**.

Figure 3.5.1 *Every spontaneous process increases the entropy of the universe.*

Second Law of Thermodynamics: The entropy of the universe increases with every spontaneous process.

Quick Check

1. Use qualitative reasoning to decide which of the two options in each of these examples will occur spontaneously:

   (a) A mole of ice at 0°C *or* a mole of liquid water at the same temperature

   ____

   (b) Solid sodium chloride in the bottom of a bucket of water *or* a solution of the salt in water

   ____

   (c) A collection of jigsaw pieces *or* the completed puzzle

   ____

   (d) One kilogram of raw rubber *or* 1 kg of vulcanized rubber (Vulcanized rubber is rubber that is polymerized into long chains; vulcanized rubber is used to make tires.)

   ____

   (e) A pack of cards arranged in suits *or* a pack of cards that is randomly shuffled

   ____

The Boltzmann Equation

Ludwig Boltzmann, a famous physicist, studied fluid mechanics in the late 1800s. During this time, Boltzmann determined the probability that a group of particles might occupy a particular set of positions in space at any particular time. These sets of positions are referred to as **microstates**. It has been suggested that this term, microstates (states), may have led to the symbol ***S*** being selected to represent entropy. Boltzmann noted that entropy is directly proportional to the natural log of the number of microstates available. In 1872, Boltzmann derived his famous equation to represent entropy:

$$\boldsymbol{S = k_B \ln W}$$

where S = entropy

k_B = Boltzmann's constant = $R/N_A = \dfrac{8.314\ \text{L·kPa/mol·K}}{6.02 \times 10^{23}\ \text{mol}^{-1}} = 1.38 \times 10^{-23}$ J/K

W = number of microstates

In a pure crystal at absolute zero (0 K), the particles orient themselves in only one possible microstate. At absolute zero, the entropy is $S = 1.38 \times 10^{-23}$ J/K (ln 1). Since the natural log of 1 = 0, the *entropy of a pure crystal at 0 K equals zero*. This is the **Third Law of Thermodynamics**.

Third Law of Thermodynamics: The entropy of a *pure crystal* at absolute zero is zero ($S = 1.38 \times 10^{-23}$ J/K × ln (1) = 0).

Increasing the number of electrons in an element or increasing the number of atoms in a molecule leads to an increase in entropy. More electrons or atoms mean more possible microstates and therefore a higher entropy according to the Boltzmann equation.

Dependence of Entropy on Temperature

The Second Law of Thermodynamics states "the entropy of the universe increases with every spontaneous change." The "universe" is the *system* plus the *surroundings* and the entropy of a system is a quantitative measure of the disorder or randomness within a system. There are two kinds of disorder in a system: **positional disorder**, depending on the arrangement of particles (molecules and atoms) in space, and **thermal disorder**, depending on how the total energy is distributed among all the particles. The more random the distribution of particles in space, the higher the entropy. The more randomly energy is distributed among the particles, the greater the entropy.

Table 3.5.1 shows all possible arrangements for two identical particles among three relative energy levels. The most likely total energy is 2 kJ. Maximizing positional disorder does not necessarily lead to maximum overall energy.

Table 3.5.1 *All possible two-particle arrangements among three relative energy levels*

Energy Level	Particle Arrangements					
2 kJ			X		X	XX
1 kJ		X		XX	X	
0 kJ	XX	X	X			
Total energy	0 kJ	1 kJ	2 kJ	2 kJ	3 kJ	4 kJ

Adding heat to a system results in greater disorder and, therefore, greater entropy. The entropy increase is directly proportional to the amount of heat added. However, the increase in entropy is more significant when we add heat to a system at a lower temperature where little disorder exists, rather than at high temperature where there is already substantial disorder. For a given quantity of heat, the entropy change is inversely proportional to the temperature at which we add the heat. Thus entropy can be determined as:

$$S_{surroundings} = \frac{q}{T} = \frac{-\Delta H}{T}$$

The equation above shows that entropy has units of energy divided by temperature (J/K). If an entropy change is being calculated for a particular quantity of material undergoing a physical or chemical change, the units may be J/K·mol.

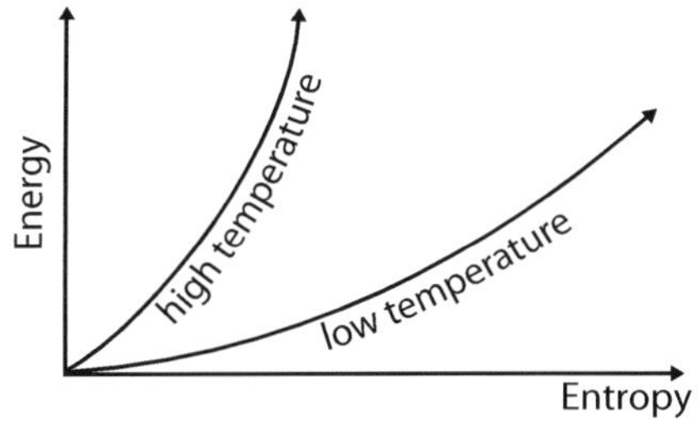

Figure 3.5.2 *The change in entropy (ΔS) is most noticeable at a low temperature.*

Quick Check

1. When 1.0 mole of steam condenses to form 1.0 mole of liquid water at 100.0° C, 40.7 kJ of heat is released. What is ΔS for the surroundings?

2. Select the example with greater entropy in each case.

   (a) $F_2(g)$ or $Cl_2(g)$

   (b) $CO_2(g)$ or $CO(g)$

   (c)

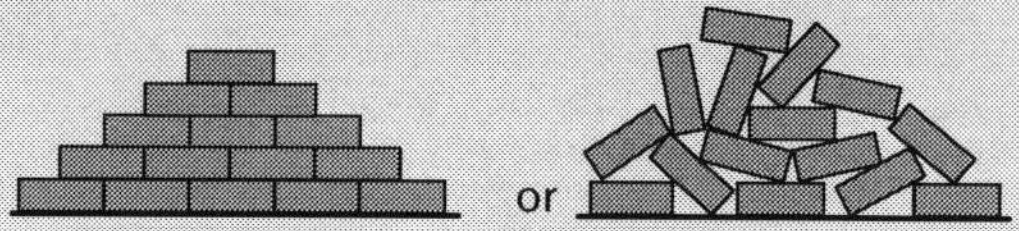

Entropy Is a State Function

We know the Third Law of Thermodynamics states that at absolute zero, the entropy of a pure crystal is equal to zero joules. Mathematically, we can state:

$$S = 0 \text{ J when } W = 1 \text{ at } T = 0 \text{ K}$$

Entropy has a value of 0 J at absolute zero and it is therefore possible to determine the amount of entropy that a substance possesses at temperatures above 0 K. If we determine the entropy of 1 mole of a substance at a temperature of 298 K (25°C) and a pressure of 1 atm, we call it the standard entropy or $S°$. Standard entropy values at STP for several species are listed in Table A8 in the appendix at the back of this book. (Notice that the standard entropy values of pure elements in their standard states are *not* equal to zero because standard entropy values are not recorded at 0 K.) Once we know the entropies of a variety of substances we can calculate the standard entropy change, or $\Delta S°$, for chemical reactions in the same way as we calculated $\Delta H°$ earlier.

Entropy is a state function — it is not pathway dependent. Therefore, we can use the same logic as that of a Hess's Law type of calculation to determine the entropy change for a given chemical reaction. It is important to note that like enthalpy, entropy is an extensive property — it depends on the amount of substance present. This means that the number of moles of all species in the reaction must be taken into account. Hence:

$$\Delta S°_{\text{reaction}} = \sum nS°_{\text{products}} - \sum nS°_{\text{reactants}}$$

For a process to be spontaneous, there must be an overall increase in the entropy of the universe. If the entropy change of the universe is negative, the process is non-spontaneous. For an individual reaction, which would be the system, the change may be spontaneous, even if the entropy change for the reaction is negative. However the overall change in entropy of the universe (system + surroundings) as a result of the reaction would be positive .

Sample Problem — Quantifying Entropy Change

Urea (from urine) hydrolyzes slowly in the presence of water to produce ammonia and carbon dioxide.

$$CO(NH_2)_2(aq) + H_2O(l) \rightarrow CO_2(g) + 2\,NH_3(g)$$

What is the standard entropy change, for this reaction when 1 mol of urea reacts with water? Is the process spontaneous? The standard entropies for reactants and products are:

Substance	$S°$ (J mol^{-1} K^{-1})	Substance	$S°$ (J mol^{-1} K^{-1})
$CO(NH_2)_2(aq)$	173.7	$CO_2(g)$	213.8
$H_2O(l)$	70.0	$NH_3(g)$	192.8

What to Think About

1. Calculate the change in entropy using the equation:

   $\Delta S°_{rxn} = \sum nS°_{products} - \sum nS°_{reactants}$

2. After determining the stoichiometrically correct entropy values, substitute and solve.

3. Does the answer make sense?
   One mole of aqueous substance and 1 mole of liquid form *3 moles of gas*.

4. What does the answer mean?

How to Do It

Determine $S°$ values for all reactants and products. These are listed in the table given above in this example.

$$\left[\frac{1 \text{ mol } CO_2}{\text{mol rxn}} \times \frac{213.8 \text{ J}}{\text{mol K}} + \frac{2 \text{ mol } NH_3}{\text{mol rxn}} \times \frac{192.8 \text{ J}}{\text{mol K}}\right] - \left[\frac{1 \text{ mol } CO(NH_2)_2}{\text{mol rxn}} \times \frac{173.7 \text{ J}}{\text{mol K}} + \frac{1 \text{ mol } H_2O}{\text{mol rxn}} \times \frac{70.0 \text{ J}}{\text{mol K}}\right]$$

$= 599.4 - 243.7 = 355.7 \text{ J/mol}_{rxn}\cdot\text{K}$

The number of microstates (W) has increased. So we expect a positive ΔS value. ✓

A positive ΔS value is indicative of a spontaneous change

Practice Problems — Quantifying Entropy Change

1. Use qualitative reasoning (no calculations are necessary) to predict whether the entropy change in each of the following processes is positive or negative. Does the entropy change of the system favor spontaneous change or not?
   (a) The evaporation of 1 mole of rubbing alcohol

   (b) $2\,Ca(s) + O_2(g) \rightarrow 2\,CaO(s)$

   (c) $XeF_4(g) \rightarrow Xe(g) + 2\,F_2(g)$

   (d) The dilution of an aqueous solution of lime Kool-Aid

2. Use the standard entropy table in Table A8 in the appendix at the back of this book to calculate the standard entropy change for each of the following reactions. Is the reaction thermodynamically favorable (spontaneous) based on the $\Delta S°$ value?
   (a) $CaO(s) + 2\,HCl(g) \rightarrow CaCl_2(s) + H_2O(l)$

   (b) $C_2H_4(g) + H_2(g) \rightarrow C_2H_6(g)$

3.5 Review Questions

1. Predict the sign you would expect for $\Delta S°$ in each of the following processes. Give a short explanation of why you think it is (+) or (–). Do NOT do any calculations.
   (a) Blowing up a building

   (b) Organizing a stack of files in alphabetical order

   (c) $AgCl(s) \rightarrow Ag^+(aq) + Cl^-(aq)$

   (d) $2\ H_2(g) + O_2\ (g) \rightarrow 2\ H_2O(l)$

   (e) $Na(s) + ½\ Cl_2(g) \rightarrow NaCl(s)$

   (f) Removing medication from bottles and organizing the pills by the day in "blister packs"

2. Predict the sign of $\Delta S°$ you would expect for each of the following changes. Give a short explanation of why you think it is (+) or (–). Do NOT do any calculations.

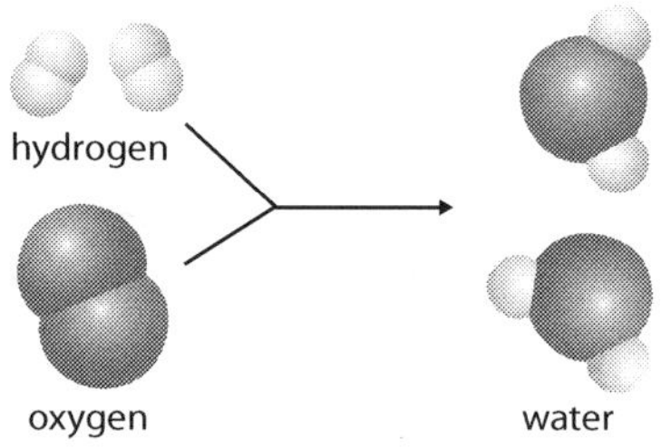

(a)

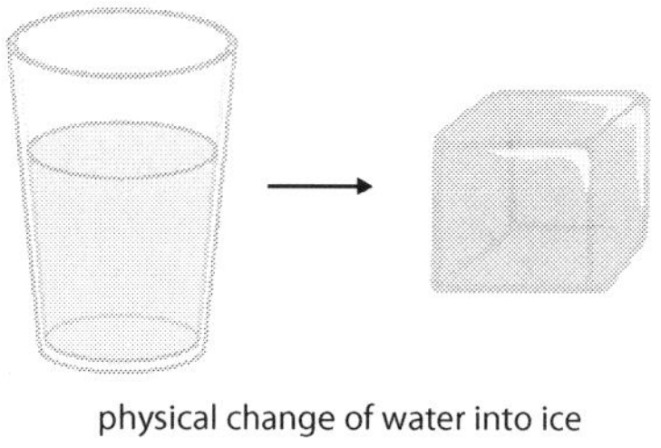

(b)

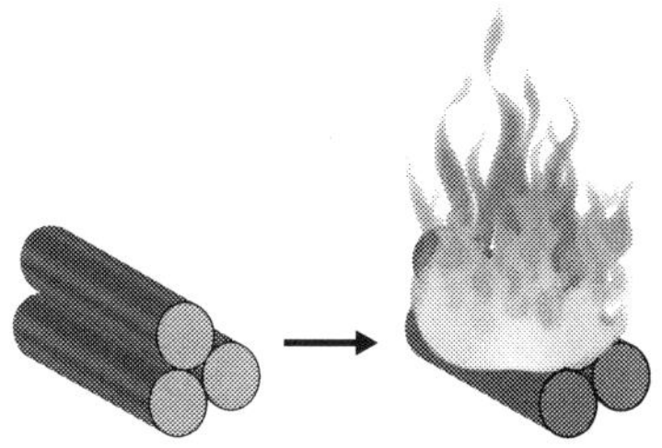
(c)

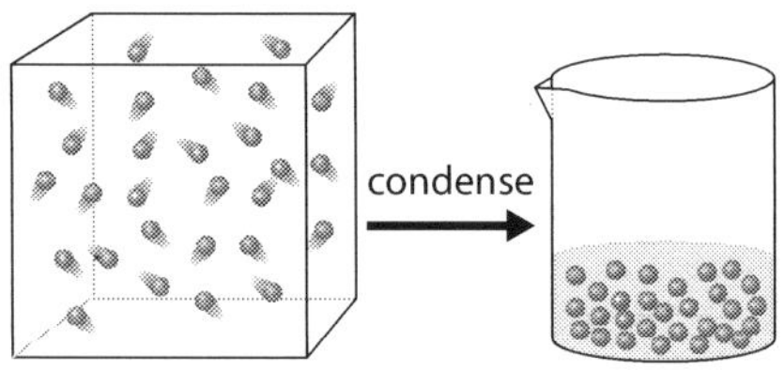

(d)

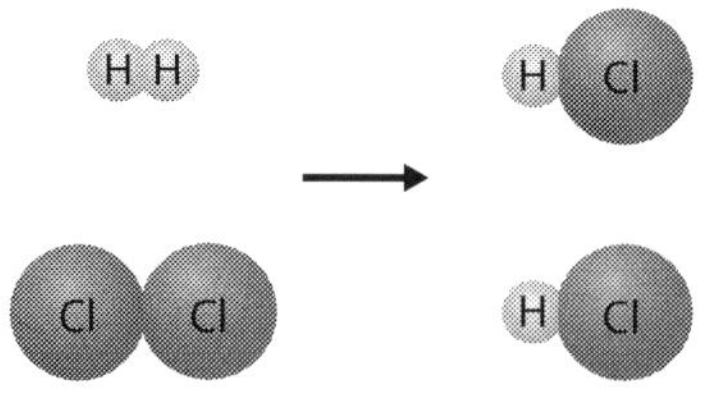

(e)

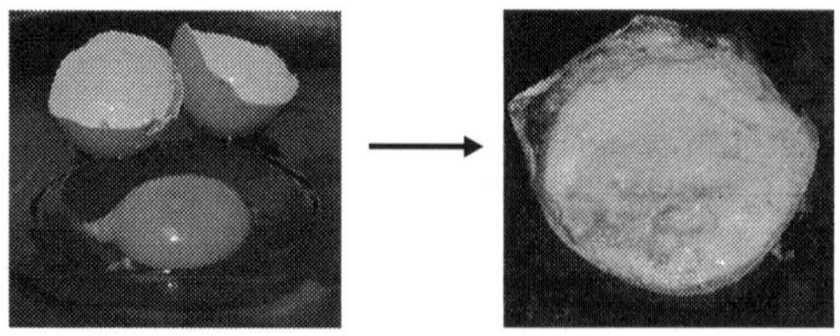
(f)

3. The boiling point of chloroform ($CHCl_3$) is 61.7°C. The enthalpy of vaporization is 31.4 kJ/mol. Calculate the entropy of vaporization. Does the sign for entropy of vaporization make sense? Explain.

4. (a) What is the normal boiling point for formic acid, HCOOH?
Given: $\Delta H_f^\circ = -424.72$ kJ/mol for liquid HCOOH and −379.1 kJ/mol for gaseous HCOOH
$S^\circ = 128.95$ J/mol K for liquid HCOOH and 251.0 J/mol K for gaseous HCOOH

(b) Based on the calculated boiling point, in what state does formic acid exist at room temperature? Explain.

5. The normal boiling point of water is 100.0°C, and its molar enthalpy of vaporization is 40.7 kJ/mol. What is the change in entropy in the system in J/K when 39.3 g of steam at 1 atm condenses to a liquid at the normal boiling point? Does the sign for the value you calculate make sense? Explain.

6. Iodine is an unusual element that sublimes under standard conditions. If the ΔS°_{subl} of iodine is 145 J/mol K and the ΔH°_{subl} of iodine is 62 kJ/mol, what is the standard sublimation temperature for iodine?

7. Consider the following addition reaction: $C_2H_2(g) + 2\,H_2(g) \rightarrow C_2H_6(g)$
The following data is known for this reaction:

Substance	S° (J/mol K)	ΔH_f (kJ/mol)
$C_2H_2(g)$	200.9	226.7
$H_2(g)$	130.7	0
$C_2H_6(g)$	????	−84.7

(a) If the value of ΔS° for the reaction is −232.7 J/mol K, calculate the value of S° for C_2H_6 gas.

(b) Calculate the enthalpy change ΔH° for the reaction.

(c) Assume that Boltzmann's equation applies when the system is in equilibrium. What is the temperature at this point (use the non-SI unit of °C)?

8. Consider the following reaction: $2\ H_2S(g) + SO_2(g) \rightarrow 3\ S(s) + 2\ H_2O(g)$
(a) Predict the sign of $\Delta S°$ for the reaction at 298 K. Explain the basis of your prediction.

(b) Calculate the actual value of $\Delta S°$ for the reaction. Assume the sulfur produced is the *rhombic* form. Does your calculation justify your prediction? Explain.

(c) Assume that Boltzmann's equation applies when the system is in equilibrium. What is the temperature at this point (use the non-SI unit of °C)?

9. The combustion of methanol is described by the following equation:

$$2\ CH_3OH(l) + 3\ O_2(g) \rightarrow 4\ H_2O(l) + 2\ CO_2(g)$$

The value of $\Delta S°$ for this reaction is −38.6 cal/mol K at 25°C. One calorie is the energy required to warm 1 g of water by 1°C. One calorie is equivalent to 4.18 J.
Data collected for this reaction:

Reaction Species	**$\Delta H°_f$ (kcal/mol) at SATP**	**$S°$ (cal/mol K) at SATP**
$CH_3OH(l)$	−57.0	30.3
$H_2O(l)$	−68.3	16.7
$CO_2(g)$	−94.0	51.1

Calculate the standard absolute entropy $S°$ per mole of $O_2(g)$. Convert this value to units of J/mol K.

10. Use the values in Table A8 in the appendix to calculate $\Delta S°$ for each of the following equations. (It is important to use the values in the appendix because entropy values may differ slightly from one source to another. It is important to refer to the recommended source for reference values to ensure consistency in answers.)

(a) $H_2(g) + ½\,O_2(g) \rightarrow H_2O(g)$

(b) $3\,O_2(g) \rightarrow 2\,O_3(g)$

(c) $CH_4(g) + 2\,O_2(g) \rightarrow CO_2(g) + 2\,H_2O(g)$

(d) $P_4O_{10}(s) + 6\,H_2O(l) \rightarrow 4\,H_3PO_4(s)$
(Given $S°$ for solid phosphoric acid = 110.54 J/mol K.)

(e) The complete combustion of octane in gasoline

3.6 Gibbs Free Energy

Warm Up

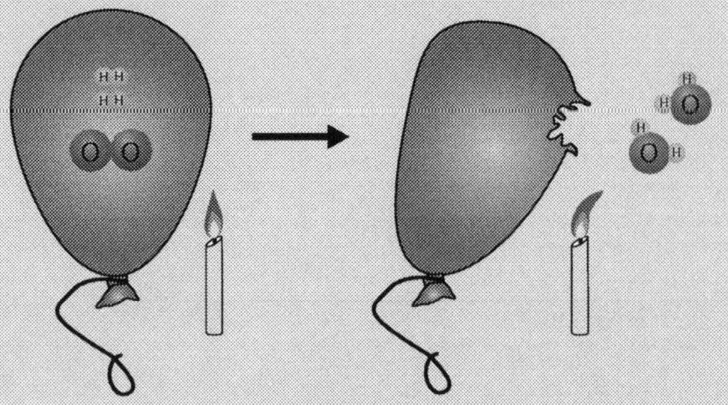

1. Write a balanced chemical equation (including phase subscripts) for the reaction shown in the diagram.

2. Use the values in Table A8 in the appendix at the back of this book to calculate ΔH_{rxn} and ΔS_{rxn} for the reaction.

3. What is the function of the candle in this process?

4. Is this spontaneous process *enthalpy driven* or *entropy driven*? Explain.

Free Energy — Enthalpy and Entropy Combine

We have now seen that two factors — enthalpy and entropy — determine whether or not a physical or chemical event is spontaneous or thermodynamically favorable. Sometimes these two factors work together. For example, when a stone wall crumbles, its enthalpy decreases and its entropy increases. Since a decrease in enthalpy and an increase in entropy both favor a spontaneous change, the two factors complement one another. In other situations, the effects of enthalpy and entropy are in opposition. Such is the case in the melting of ice, the vaporization of water and even the formation of water from its elements as in the Warm Up.

When enthalpy and entropy effects oppose one another, the overall reaction spontaneity is less obvious. We can determine the net effect of the two factors through another thermodynamic quantity called **Gibbs free energy, *G***, named after Josiah Willard Gibbs (1839–1903), a U.S. scientist (Figure 3.6.1). Gibbs free energy is defined as: $G = H - TS$. For a chemical or physical *change* at constant temperature and pressure, the equation becomes:

$$\Delta G = \Delta H - T\Delta S$$

A change is spontaneous only if it is accompanied by a decrease in free energy. In other words, ΔG must be negative for a spontaneous change. A spontaneous change is also termed a **thermodynamically favorable** change.

Figure 3.6.1 *American scientist Josiah Willard Gibbs*

Spontaneous change must be accompanied by a decrease in free energy. That is, ΔG must be *NEGATIVE* for a spontaneous change.

Table 3.6.1 shows the effects of positive and negative values of ΔH and ΔS on ΔG. The table shows the importance of the absolute temperature in determining whether a change will occur spontaneously. Temperature is important in cases where ΔH and ΔS have the same signs.

Table 3.6.1 *Impact of ΔH and ΔS at various temperatures on the thermodynamic favorability (spontaneity) of chemical reactions*

ΔH	ΔS	ΔG	Reaction Characteristics	Examples
–	+	Always negative	Reaction is spontaneous at all temperatures; reverse reaction is always non-spontaneous.	$2\,O_3(g) \rightarrow 3O_2(g)$
+	–	Always positive	Reaction is non-spontaneous at all temperatures; reverse reaction occurs spontaneously.	$3\,O_2(g) \rightarrow 2\,O_3(g)$
–	–	Negative at low temps; positive at high temps	Reaction is spontaneous at low temperatures and becomes non-spontaneous as temperature is raised.	$CaO(s) + CO_2(g) \rightarrow CaCO_3(s)$
+	+	Positive at low temps; negative at high temps	Reaction is non-spontaneous at low temperatures but becomes spontaneous as temperature is raised.	$CaCO_3(s) \rightarrow CaO(s) + CO_2(g)$

Reactions that occur with a free energy decrease in the system are **exergonic**. Those that occur with a free energy increase are **endergonic**.

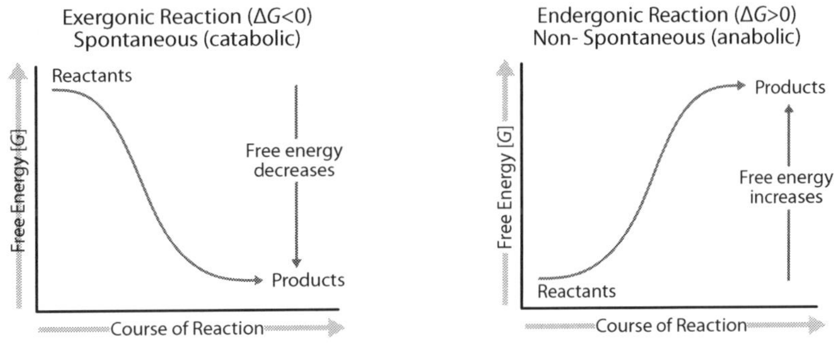

Figure 3.6.2 *Exergonic (left) and endergonic reactions*

The terms *exergonic* and *endergonic* are most commonly applied in biological contexts (Figure 3.6.2). Catabolic processes break down large proteins and lipids into amino and fatty acids producing many small molecules, each resulting in a large number of bond formations. These catabolic processes are exergonic. Anabolic processes form biological macromolecules following a multitude of bond breakages. Anabolic processes are endergonic. Essentially, *anabolic processes* are "powered" by *catabolic processes* during the metabolic processes that occur in our bodies. When one reaction is "powered" by another, the reactions are said to be **coupled**.

Free Energy and Maximum Work

Spontaneous chemical reactions perform useful work. The burning of fuels in heat engines, chemical reactions in batteries, and the catabolic portion of metabolism within our bodies are all spontaneous processes that produce useful work. We cannot harness all of the energy released when spontaneous chemical reactions occur. Some energy is lost as heat. Engineers seek to maximize the efficiency of converting chemical energy to work and to minimize the amount of energy transferred unproductively to the environment as heat.

Is there a limit to the amount of energy in a reaction that can be harnessed as useful work? The maximum amount of energy we can harness from a reaction, as work is equal to ΔG. This is the energy that is not lost as heat and is *therefore free* (or available) to be used for work. By determining the value of ΔG, we can find out whether or not a given reaction will be an effective source of energy. By comparing the actual work derived from a given system with the ΔG value for the reactions involved, we can measure the efficiency of the system.

Free Energy and Equilibrium

Reactions with a negative free energy change are spontaneous (thermodynamically favorable), while those with a positive free energy change are non-spontaneous. The negative sign in front of the Free Energy value indicates that the energy is released in the process. A positive sign in front of the Free Energy value indicates that Free Energy from the surrounding is required to drive the process All reactions proceed spontaneously until they reach equilibrium. When the value of ΔG is equal to zero, the reaction is at equilibrium. We will learn later that at equilibrium the forward and reverse reactions occur at equal rates.

For the state change, $H_2O(l) \rightleftharpoons H_2O(s)$, equilibrium exists at 0°C and atmospheric pressure. Above 0°C, only liquid water can exist, and below 0°C, all the liquid will freeze to form ice. This gives us an interesting relationship between ΔH and ΔS.

$$\Delta G = 0 = \Delta H - T\Delta S$$

Therefore at equilibrium, $\Delta H = T\Delta S$; and

$$\boldsymbol{\Delta S_{system} = \frac{\Delta H}{T}}$$

Thus, if we know ΔH and ΔS, we can calculate the temperature at which equilibrium will occur. This is the temperature at which a state change occurs.

Quick Check

1. For the process $Br_2(l) \rightleftharpoons Br_2(g)$, $\Delta H = +31.0$ kJ/mol and $\Delta S = 92.9$ J/mol K.
   (a) Explain why a (+) value for the enthalpy change is reasonable for this process.

   ____

   ____

   (b) Why would we expect the entropy change to be (+) for this process?

   ____

   (c) Assuming that ΔH and ΔS are temperature independent, calculate the temperature at which $Br_2(l)$ will be in equilibrium with $Br_2(g)$. Give the answer in °C.

   (d) What property does this temperature represent for bromine?

   ____

Standard Free Energies

About the same time the American Josiah Gibbs derived the free energy equation, German physicist Hermann von Helmholtz deduced the same thing. For this reason, the Gibbs-Helmholtz equation is a common name for $\Delta G = \Delta H - T\Delta S$. The equation is valid under all temperature, pressure, and concentration conditions. We will begin by restricting all of our calculations to standard conditions of pressure (1 atm) and concentration (1 *M*, where it applies). In other words, we will use the equation in the form:

$$\Delta G° = \Delta H° - T\Delta S$$

Where $\Delta G°$ is the standard free energy change (determined at 1 atm, 1 *M*), $\Delta H°$ is the standard enthalpy change calculated from reference values, $\Delta S°$ is the standard entropy change calculated from reference values, and *T* is the Kelvin temperature.

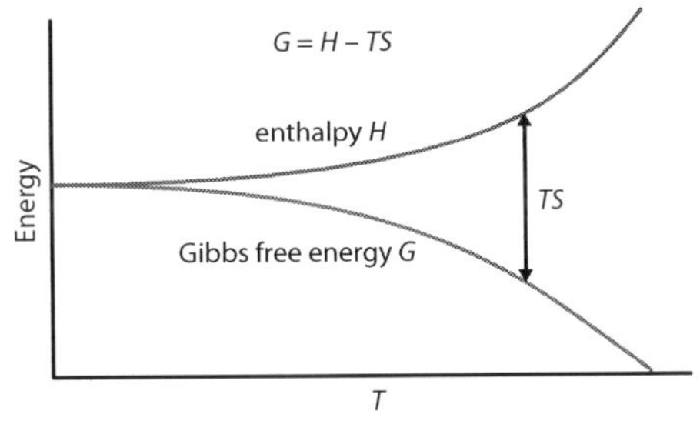

Figure 3.6.3 *This graph of energy vs. temperature shows that the difference between enthalpy (H) and free energy (G) is equal to TS. The graph shows that as the temperature increases, the difference between these two forms of energy becomes larger.*

Since enthalpy and entropy are state functions, it follows that Gibbs free energy is also a state function. We can use Hess's law and we can calculate standard free energies of formation as follows:

$$\Delta G° = \sum n\Delta G°_{prod} - \sum n\Delta G°_{react}$$

Note: $\Delta G°_f = 0$ for an element in its normal state at 25°C and 1 atm.

Sample Problem — Using the Gibbs-Helmholtz Equation to Calculate a Free Energy Change at Standard Temperature

For the process $NaCl(s) \rightarrow Na^+(aq) + Cl^-(aq)$, use the tables in Table A8 in the appendix at the back of this book to calculate:

(a) $\Delta H°$

(b) $\Delta S°$

(c) Use the values from (a) and (b) to calculate $\Delta G°$.

(d) According to your results, is this a spontaneous process?

What to Think About

1. As $\Delta H°$ is a state function, calculate it. The $\Delta H_f°$ values are listed in Table A8 in the appendix.

   Notice that while *elements in their standard states have $\Delta H_f°$ values of 0 kJ/mol,* this is *not* the case for ions in solution.

2. We use a similar process to determine $\Delta S°$, also a state function.

   Absolute entropy values of formation $S_f°$ are in Table A8 in the appendix.

3. Instructions indicate that you should calculate $\Delta G°$ using the answers to (a) and (b). Use the Gibbs- Helmholtz equation.

   It is important to ensure that the ***units are consistent*** *throughout the equation.* In other words, you must convert $\Delta S°$ to kJ/K mol before substituting the values into the Gibbs equation.

   In general, if a question requiring the Gibbs Equation does *not provide* a specific *temperature*, assume ***SATP conditions (or T = 25°C = 298 K) apply***. The presence of the ° symbol, however, does **not** restrict all calculations to a temperature of 25°C.

4. A (–) ΔG value indicates spontaneity (also called ***thermodynamic favorability***) though the magnitude is not very large.

How to Do It

a) $\Delta H°_{(overall)} = \Sigma n\Delta H°_{f(prod)} - \Sigma n\Delta H°_{f(react)}$

$\Delta H_f°$ for $Na^+(aq) = -240.12$ kJ/mol

$\Delta H_f°$ for $Cl^-(aq) = -167.16$ kJ/mol

$\Delta H_f°$ for $NaCl(s) = -411.15$ kJ/mol

$$\Delta H° = \left[\frac{1\ \text{mol Na}^+}{\text{mol rxn}}\left(\frac{-240.12\ \text{kJ}}{\text{mol Na}^+}\right) + \frac{1\ \text{mol Cl}^-}{\text{mol rxn}}\left(\frac{-167.16\ \text{kJ}}{\text{mol Cl}^-}\right)\right]$$

$$\left[-\frac{1\ \text{mol NaCl}}{\text{mol rxn}}\left(\frac{-411.15\ \text{kJ}}{\text{mol NaCl}}\right)\right] = 3.87\ \text{kJ/mol rxn}$$

(b) $\Delta S° = \Sigma nS°_{prod} - \Sigma nS°_{react}$

$S_f°$ for $Na^+(aq) = 59.0$ J/K mol

$S_f°$ for $Cl^-(aq) = 56.5$ J/K mol

$S_f°$ for $NaCl(s) = 72.13$ J/K mol

$$\Delta S° = \left[\frac{1\ \text{mol Na}^+}{\text{mol rxn}}\left(\frac{0.0590\ \text{kJ}}{\text{K mol Na}^+}\right) + \frac{1\ \text{mol Cl}^-}{\text{mol rxn}}\left(\frac{0.0565\ \text{kJ}}{\text{K mol Cl}^-}\right)\right]$$

$$-\left[\frac{1\ \text{mol NaCl}}{\text{mol rxn}}\left(\frac{0.07213\ \text{kJ}}{\text{K mol NaCl}}\right)\right] = 0.04337\ \text{kJ/K mol rxn}$$

(c) $\Delta G° = \Delta H° - T\Delta S°$

$$\Delta G° = 3.87\ \frac{\text{kJ}}{\text{mol}_{rxn}} - 298\ \text{K}\left(\frac{0.04337\ \text{kJ}}{\text{K mol}_{rxn}}\right)$$

$$= -9.05\ \text{kJ/mol}_{rxn}$$

(d) The dissolving of the salt has a (–) ΔG value meaning it is spontaneous as would be expected for dissolving a salt at room temperature.

In fact, endothermicity and an increased number of microstates also make sense for the dissolving process. This process is entropy driven.

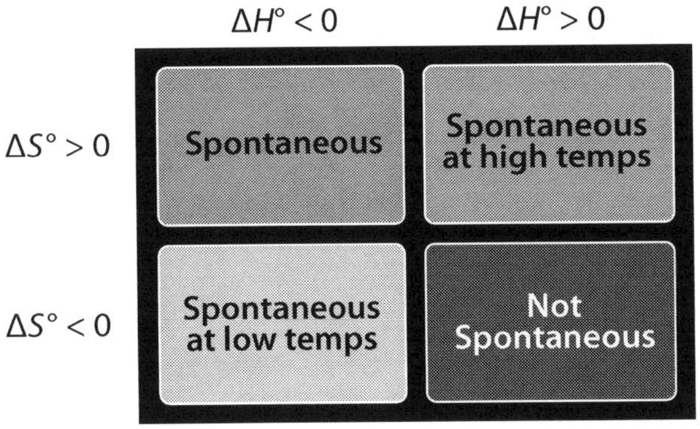

Figure 3.6.4 *Examination of the equation, $\Delta G° = \Delta H° - T\Delta S°$, shows that if $\Delta H°$ and $\Delta S°$ share the same sign, temperature will determine spontaneity. The temperature at which $\Delta H°$ and the term $T\Delta S°$ are equal is the temperature at which equilibrium will occur. "High" and "low" temperatures are relative and refer to temperatures above or below the equilibrium T value.*

It is significant that $\Delta S°$ values are usually very small compared to $\Delta H°$. Only multiplication by T causes subtraction of the $T\Delta S°$ term from $\Delta H°$ to have a significant impact on the value of $\Delta G°$. In an example such as the dissolving of table salt, both $\Delta H°$ and $\Delta S°$ are positive. This dissolution process is spontaneous only when the temperature is large enough to allow subtraction of the $T\Delta S°$ term from $\Delta H°$ to result in a negative $\Delta G°$.

The values of standard free energies of formation of pure compounds and elements and aqueous ions are listed in Table A8 in the appendix. As is the case for the $S°$ and $\Delta H_f°$ values in the appendix, standard conditions for $\Delta G_f°$ are 25°C and 1 atm.

Sample Problem — Using Free Energies of Formation to Calculate a Free Energy Change at Standard Temperature

For the process $NaCl(s) \rightarrow Na^+(aq) + Cl^-(aq)$, use the tables in Table A8 in the appendix to calculate:

(a) $\Delta G°$

(b) According to your results in (a), is this a spontaneous process?

What to Think About

1. As $\Delta G°$ is a state function, calculate the value using the equation introduced earlier in this section. The $\Delta G_f°$ values are listed in Table A8 in the appendix.

   As with $\Delta H°_f$ values, ***elements in their standard states have $\Delta G_f°$ values of 0 kJ/mol***. This is *not* the case for ions in solution.

   The value calculated for $\Delta G°$ using reference values and the state function equation is very close to the value calculated using the Gibbs-Helmholtz equation. Using the state function algorithm to calculate $\Delta H°$ and $\Delta S°$ values introduces further approximations due to rounding to appropriate significant figures. This leads to differences between the two calculated values.

2. A (–) ΔG value indicates spontaneity even though the magnitude is not very large.

How to Do It

(a) $\Delta G° = \Sigma n\Delta G°_{(prod)} - \Sigma n\Delta G°_{(react)}$

$\Delta G_f°$ for $Na^+(aq)$ = –261.91 kJ/mol

$\Delta G_f°$ for $Cl^-(aq)$ = –131.23 kJ/mol

$\Delta G_f°$ for $NaCl(s)$ = –384.12 kJ/mol

$$\Delta G° = \left[\frac{1\ \text{mol}\ Na^+}{\text{mol rxn}}\left(\frac{-261.91\ \text{kJ}}{\text{mol}\ Na^+}\right) + \frac{1\ \text{mol}\ Cl^-}{\text{mol rxn}}\left(\frac{-131.23\ \text{kJ}}{\text{mol}\ Cl^-}\right)\right] - \left[\frac{1\ \text{mol NaCl}}{\text{mol rxn}}\left(\frac{-384.12\ \text{kJ}}{\text{mol NaCl}}\right)\right] = -9.02\ \text{kJ/mol rxn}$$

b) This is a spontaneous process. This makes sense for the dissolving of a salt at room temperature. We know that virtually all salts dissolve spontaneously at room temperature. This is generally entropy driven. It is interesting that the dissolving of NaCl is very nearly at equilibrium under SATP conditions.

Practice Problems — Using the Gibbs-Helmholtz Equation and Free Energies of Formation to Calculate a Free Energy Change at Standard Temperature

1. Use the ΔG_f° values in Table A8 in the appendix to calculate ΔG_{comb}° for the combustion of ethanol under SATP conditions.

2. Calculate the maximum work available from the oxidation of 1 mole of octane at 25°C and 1 atm. Use the ΔH_f° and the S_f° values from Table A8 in the appendix along with the Gibbs-Helmholtz equation.

3. Calculate ΔG_{rxn}° for the reaction of $N_2(g) + O_2(g) \rightarrow 2\ NO(g)$. Do the calculation *two* ways. First by determining ΔH_f°, then ΔS_f° followed by the Gibbs-Helmholtz equation. Then use the ΔG_f° values and see how the values compare.

Calculation of Free Energy at Non-Standard Temperatures

ΔG° *is the most temperature dependent* of the thermodynamic functions. We can use the Gibbs-Helmholtz equation to calculate ΔG° at temperatures other than 25°C. To do this, we neglect the variations of ΔH° and ΔS° with temperature because they are relatively temperature independent quantities compared to ΔG°.

ΔH° is essentially independent of temperature and the variations of ΔS° with temperature are ordinarily very small — entropy is most dependent on temperature near absolute zero. Near room temperature, variations in ΔS° are negligible.

In other words, we take the values of ΔH° and ΔS° from the tables and simply insert them into the Gibbs-Helmholtz equation using the appropriate value of T (in Kelvin degrees) to calculate ΔG°.

Sample Problem — Using the the Gibbs-Helmholtz Equation to Calculate a Free Energy Change at Non-Standard Temperatures

Calculate $\Delta G°$ for the reaction $Cu(s) + H_2O(g) \rightarrow CuO(s) + H_2(g)$ at a temperature of 227.0°C.

What to Think About

1. As the temperature is non-standard, you must use the Gibbs-Helmholtz equation to solve the problem.

2. Use reference tables to determine the $\Delta H°$ and $\Delta S°$ values of each compound or element in the reaction first.

3. Calculate the overall enthalpy change for the reaction.

4. Evaluate the sign of the enthalpy value and its significance.

5. Calculate the overall entropy change for the reaction

6. Consider the sign of the overall entropy change of the reaction and its significance.

7. Finally, use the Gibbs-Helmholtz equation to calculate $\Delta G°$ at a temperature of 227.0 °C, but first convert the temperature to Kelvin degrees.

How to Do It

$\Delta H°_{(overall)} = \Sigma n\Delta H°_{f(prod)} - \Sigma n\Delta H°_{f(react)}$

$\Delta H°_f$ for CuO (s) = −157.3 kJ/mol

$\Delta H°_f$ for H_2 (g) = 0 kJ/mol

$\Delta H°_f$ for Cu (s) = 0 kJ/mol

$\Delta H°_f$ for H_2O (g) = −241.82 kJ/mol

$$\Delta H° = \left[\frac{1\ \cancel{\text{mol CuO}}}{\text{mol rxn}}\left(\frac{-157.3\ \text{kJ}}{\cancel{\text{mol CuO}}}\right) + \frac{1\ \cancel{\text{mol H}_2}}{\text{mol rxn}}\left(\frac{0\ \text{kJ}}{\cancel{\text{mol H}_2}}\right)\right]$$

$$- \left[\frac{1\ \cancel{\text{mol Cu}}}{\text{mol rxn}}\left(\frac{0\ \text{kJ}}{\cancel{\text{mol Cu}}}\right) + \frac{1\ \cancel{\text{mol H}_2\text{O}}}{\text{mol rxn}}\left(\frac{-241.82\ \text{kJ}}{1\ \cancel{\text{mol rxn}}}\right)\right]$$

$= 84.5\ \text{kJ/mol}_{rxn}$

A slightly endothermic process

$\Delta S° = \Sigma nS°_{(prod)} - \Sigma nS°_{(react)}$

$S°_f$ for CuO(s) = 42.63 J/K mol

$S°_f$ for H_2(g) = 130.68 J/K mol

$S°_f$ for Cu(s) = 33.15 J/K mol

$S°_f$ for H_2O(g) = 188.83 J/K mol

$$\Delta S° = \left[\frac{1\ \cancel{\text{mol CuO}}}{\text{mol rxn}}\left(\frac{42.63\ \text{kJ}}{\text{K}\ \cancel{\text{mol CuO}}}\right) + \frac{1\ \cancel{\text{mol H}_2}}{\text{mol rxn}}\left(\frac{130.68\ \text{kJ}}{\text{K}\ \cancel{\text{mol H}_2}}\right)\right]$$

$$- \left[\frac{1\ \cancel{\text{mol Cu}}}{\text{mol rxn}}\left(\frac{33.15\ \text{kJ}}{\text{K}\ \cancel{\text{mol Cu}}}\right) + \frac{1\ \cancel{\text{mol H}_2\text{O}}}{\text{mol rxn}}\left(\frac{188.83\ \text{kJ}}{\text{K}\ \cancel{\text{mol rxn}}}\right)\right]$$

$= -48.67\ \text{kJ/mol}_{rxn}\ \text{K}$

A (−) value for ΔS makes sense as the O atoms have moved from a gaseous compound to a solid compound. Additionally the H has moved from gaseous water where it was combined with oxygen to pure gaseous hydrogen.

$$227\ \cancel{°\text{C}}\left(\frac{1\text{K}}{1\cancel{°\text{C}}}\right) + 273\ \text{K} = 500.\text{K}$$

$\Delta G° = \Delta H° - T\Delta S°$

$$\Delta G° = 84.5\frac{\text{kJ}}{\text{mol}_{rxn}} - 500.\ \cancel{\text{K}}\left(\frac{-0.04867\ \text{kJ}}{\cancel{\text{K}}\ \text{mol}_{rxn}}\right)$$

$= 108.8\ \text{kJ/mol}_{rxn}$

Note that the (+) $\Delta G°$ value indicates a non-spontaneous reaction. The (+) $\Delta H°$ and the (−) $\Delta S°$ both favor a non-spontaneous reaction. Hence this reaction would be non-spontaneous under any temperature conditions.

Practice Problems — Using the Gibbs-Helmholtz Equation to Calculate a Free Energy Change at Non-Standard Temperatures

1. The mineral calcite decomposes according to the following reaction:
   $CaCO_3(s) \rightarrow CaO(s) + CO_2(g)$ in which $\Delta H° = 178.3$ kJ/mol$_{rxn}$ and $\Delta S° = 160.6$ J/mol$_{rxn}$ K.
   (a) Calculate $\Delta G°$ at 750.0°C.

   (b) Calculate $\Delta G°$ at 950.0°C.

   (c) Does the reaction become more or less spontaneous (thermodynamically favorable) as temperature increases?

Experimental Manipulation of the Gibbs-Helmholtz Free Energy Equation

We can arrange the equation, $G = H - TS$ to the form $G = -ST + H$. A plot of G vs. T will be a straight line with a slope of $-S$ and a y-intercept of H. Various experiments may be set up to study the variables in the Gibbs-Helmholtz equation. These experiments produce graphs such as those shown in Figure 3.6.5.

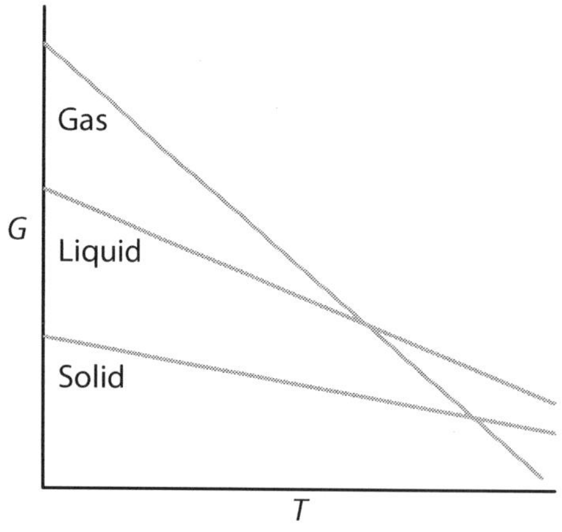

Figure 3.6.5 *The graph above shows that free energy (G) varies with temperature (T).*

Since all chemical species have a positive value for entropy, G decreases with an increase in temperature (at constant pressure and state). Gases have far greater entropy than liquids, which have greater entropy than solids. Figure 3.6.5 shows the free energies of gases are more temperature dependent than liquids, which are more temperature sensitive than solids.

The direct measurement of free energy is not easily accomplished. In the next section, we will apply our understanding of equilibrium to a more detailed investigation of free energy and how it varies with temperature.

3.6 Review Questions

1. (a) What two factors, other than temperature, influence the spontaneity of a process?

   (b) Describe each factor.

   (c) What sign is associated with spontaneity for each factor?

2. Complete the following table for the equation: $\Delta G^\circ = \Delta H^\circ - T\Delta S^\circ$.

Sign of ΔH°	Sign of ΔS°	Temperature	Sign of ΔG°	Spontaneous /Non-Spontaneous
–	+	low		
–	+	high		
+	–	low		
+	–	high		
–	–		–	
+	+			spontaneous
–	–	high		
+	+		+	

3. Examine the representation of ice melting and water condensing on a glass of ice water. Consider circled areas A and B.
   Circle A:
   (i) What are the signs of ΔH° and ΔS° for this process? Explain your answers.

   (ii) Is this process spontaneous at all temperatures, only low temperatures, only high temperatures or never? Explain.

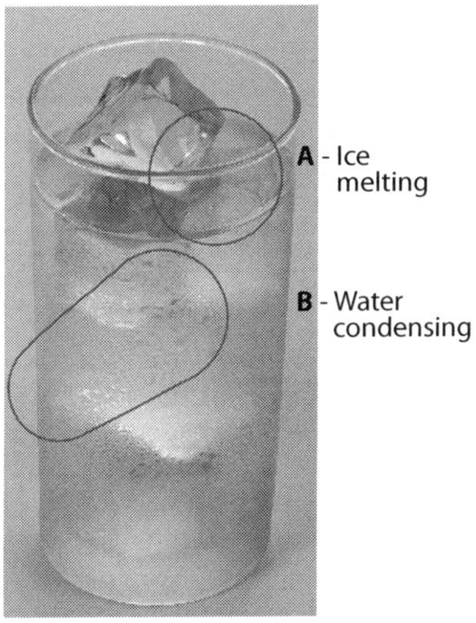

   Circle B:
   (i) What are the signs of ΔH° and ΔS° for this process? Explain your answers.

   (ii) Is this process spontaneous at all temperatures, only low temperatures, only high temperatures or never? Explain.

4. $\Delta H°$ is –196.1 kJ/mol$_{rxn}$ for the following representation of a reaction of $H_2O_2(l)$.

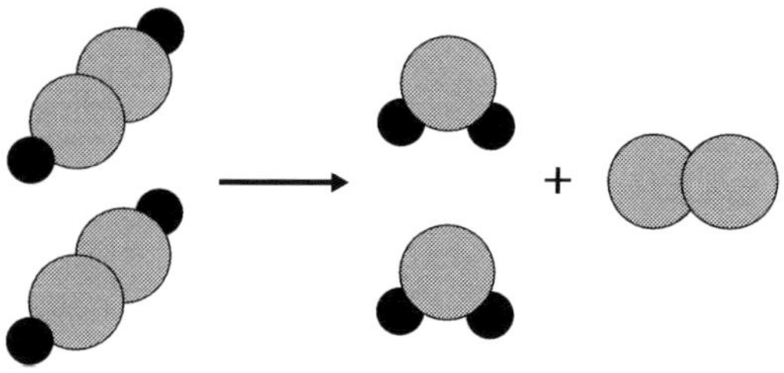

(a) What are the signs of $\Delta S°$ and $\Delta G°$ for the reaction? Explain.

(b) Is the process spontaneous at all temperatures, only low temperatures, only high temperatures or never? Explain.

5. (a) Use the representation below to produce a balanced chemical equation. Use the lowest possible whole number coefficients in your equation.

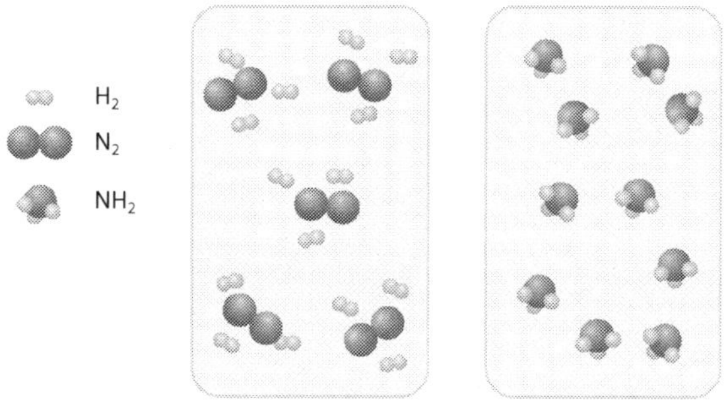

Before the reaction After the reaction

(b) Use Table A8 in the appendix to calculate $\Delta H°_{rxn}$ for the reaction. Show your work.

(c) Predict the *sign* of $\Delta S°_{rxn}$ for the reaction (do not calculate).

(d) Is this process spontaneous at all temperatures, only low temperatures, only high temperatures or never? Explain.

(e) Determine the temperature (in °C) at which the spontaneity of this reaction changes.

6. Shiny silver iodine crystals are deposited on the surface of ice placed into a test tube filled with purple iodine vapor.

(a) Write a balanced chemical equation to describe the process pictured here.

(b) Use Table A8 in the appendix to calculate the sublimation temperature (same as the deposition temperature) for iodine.

7. Consider the following reaction: $2\ O_3(g) \rightarrow 3\ O_2(g)$. $\Delta H° = -285.4$ kJ/mol$_{rxn}$.
(a) Predict the signs for $\Delta S°_{rxn}$ and $\Delta G°_{rxn}$ and the spontaneity of the reaction (no calculations required).

(b) Use values from Table A8 in the appendix to calculate $\Delta S°_{rxn}$ and $\Delta G°_{rxn}$ and to determine the accuracy of your prediction.

8. Calculate $\Delta G°_{rxn}$ for each of the following reactions using Table A8 in the appendix.
(a) $NH_3(g) + HCl(g) \rightarrow NH_4Cl(s)$

(b) $AgNO_3(aq) + NaI(aq) \rightarrow AgI(s) + NaNO_3(aq)$ (Hint: Use the net ionic equation.)

(c) $P_4O_{10}(s) + H_2O(l) \rightarrow H_3PO_4(l)$ (Hint: The reaction is unbalanced.)

9. Government requirements in the United States and Canada state that fuels should contain a "renewable" component. Fermentation of glucose isolated from a variety of garden products such as sugar cane, beets, and corn produces ethanol. Producers can add ethanol to gasoline to fulfill the renewable fuel requirement. Here is the fermentation reaction for glucose:
$C_6H_{12}O_6(s) \rightarrow 2\ C_2H_5OH(l) + 2\ CO_2(g)$

Calculate:

(a) $\Delta H°$

(b) $\Delta S°$

(c) $\Delta G°$

(d) Under what temperature conditions does this reaction occur spontaneously? Justify.

(e) How might this impact the economic feasibility of producing renewable fuels in this way?

10. In low concentrations, phosgene is a colorless to pale yellow cloud with the pleasant odor of freshly cut hay. In higher concentrations, phosgene becomes a choking agent toxic to the pulmonary system. Armies used phosgene to kill hundreds of people during the World War 1. Carbon monoxide and chlorine combine to form phosgene, $COCl_2(g)$.

(a) Calculate $\Delta S°_{rxn}$ given that $\Delta H° = -220.\ \text{kJ/mol}_{rxn}$ and $\Delta G° = -206\ \text{kJ/mol}_{rxn}$ at 25 °C.

(b) The (–)$\Delta G°$ value means the production of the war gas is spontaneous under SATP conditions. Considering the signs of $\Delta S°$ and $\Delta H°$, what temperature conditions should further favor the spontaneous production of phosgene?

(c) Assuming the temperature effects on $\Delta S°$ and $\Delta H°$ are negligible, calculate $\Delta G°$ at 435°C. Is the reaction spontaneous at this higher temperature?

4 Reaction Kinetics

By the end of this chapter, you should be able to do the following:

- Demonstrate awareness that reactions occur at differing rates
- Experimentally determine rate of a reaction
- Demonstrate knowledge of collision theory
- Describe the energies associated with reactants becoming products
- Apply collision theory to explain how reaction rates can be changed
- Analyze the reaction mechanism for a reacting system
- Represent graphically the energy changes associated with catalyzed and uncatalyzed reactions
- Describe the uses of specific catalysts in a variety of situations

By the end of this chapter, you should know the meaning of these **key terms**:

- activated complex
- activation energy
- bimolecular
- catalyst
- catalytic converter
- collision theory
- ΔH notation
- elementary processes
- endothermic
- enthalpy
- enzymes
- exothermic
- heterogeneous catalysts
- homogeneous catalysts
- initial rate
- integrated rate law
- KE distribution curve
- kinetic energy (KE),
- metalloenzymes
- molecularity
- overall order
- potential energy (PE)
- product
- rate-determining step
- reactant
- reaction intermediate
- reaction mechanism
- reaction rate
- successful collision
- termolecular
- thermochemical equation

External tanks of liquid oxygen and hydrogen fuel react to create the energy needed to launch a rocket carrying the space shuttle.

4.1 Measuring the Rate of Chemical Reactions

Warm Up

In previous years, you were introduced to the concept of rate of change in the position of an object as it moves. You learned that this is the object's velocity. If we don't consider the object's direction, we might use the more general terms, "speed" or "rate." Velocity is a vector quantity while speed is a scalar quantity. When dealing with chemical reactions, we need not concern ourselves with vectors.

Assume a vehicle moves the following distances over the stated periods of time as it travels from the eastern Fraser Valley into Vancouver:

Distance Travelled (km)	Time (min)
0	0
22	20.0
62	50.0
117	90.0
125	100.0

What is the average velocity (rate) of the car (over the entire time period)?

(a) in km/min ______________

(b) in km/h ______________

(c) Why do we refer to this as an *average* rate?

____

____

(d) A unit of __________ is always placed in the denominator when calculating rate.

Measuring Reaction Rate

Chemical reactions involve the conversion of reactants with a particular set of properties into products with a whole new set of properties.

Chemical kinetics is the investigation of the rate at which these reactions occur and the factors that affect them.

If you consider familiar reactions like the explosion of a firecracker, the metabolism of the lunch you ate today and the rusting of your bicycle, it is evident that chemical reactions occur at a wide variety of rates (Figure 4.1.1).

Time for reaction: < 1 s several hours weeks to many months

Figure 4.1.1 *An explosion, food digestion, and rusting metal all involve chemical reactions but at very different rates.*

Reaction rates may be determined by observing either the disappearance of a reactant or the appearance of a product. Deciding exactly what to measure can be a tricky business. There are several things the chemist needs to consider:

- Is there a measurable property associated with the change in quantity of a reactant or product you might use to determine the rate?

- Exactly how might you measure the quantity of reactant or product in the laboratory?
- Finally, what units would be associated with the quantity you measure and consequently, what units will represent the reaction rate?

Once these questions have been answered, it is simply a matter of determining the rate using the following equation:

$$\text{average reaction rate} = \frac{\text{change in a measurable quantity of a chemical species}}{\text{change in time}}$$

Experimentally, it turns out that, for most reactions, the rate is greatest at the beginning of the reaction and decreases as the reaction continues. Because the rate changes as a reaction proceeds, reaction rates are generally expressed as averages over a particular time period. As reactants are being consumed during a reaction, the forward rate might be thought of as having a negative value. However, we generally report the rate as an absolute or positive value.

Quick Check

Thionyl chloride is a reactive compound used in a variety of organic synthesis reactions. Due to its potential to release dangerous gases explosively on contact with water, it is controlled under the Chemical Weapons Convention in the United States. It can be decomposed in solution with an organic solvent according to the reaction:

$SO_2Cl_2(soln) \rightarrow SO_2(g) + Cl_2(g)$

Removal of small samples called aliquots and titration of these samples as the reaction proceeds produces the data given in the table on the next page.

Note: Ideally, a reaction should be *monitored* as it proceeds without interference. In a technique such as this, it is critical to remove as small an aliquot as possible so that the sampling's interference with the subject reaction is minimal. It is also important to complete the titration as quickly as possible because the reaction, of course, continues to occur within the sample. Nonetheless, removal and sampling of small aliquots is one technique for monitoring the rate of a chemical reaction.

Use the grid provided on the next page to produce a graph of concentration of thionyl chloride versus time.

$[SO_2Cl_2]$ (mol/L)	Time (seconds)
0.200	0
0.160	100.
0.127	200.
0.100	300.
0.080	400.
0.067	500.
0.060	600.

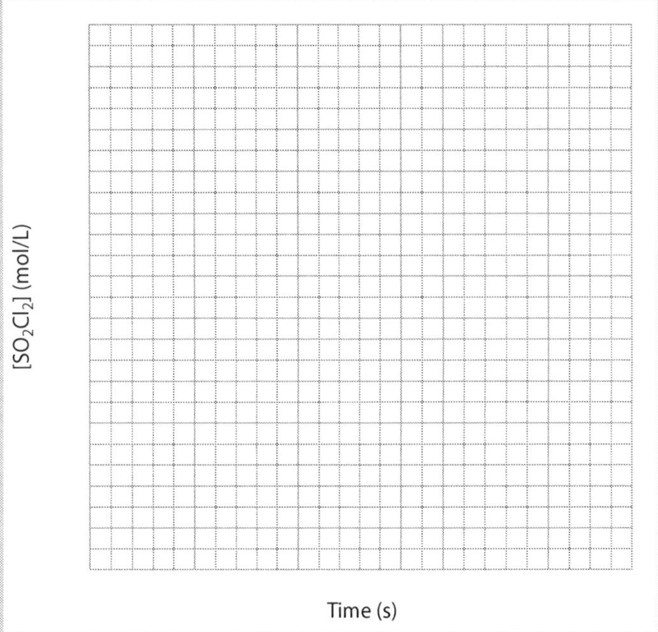

(Quick Check continued on next page)

Quick Check *(continued)*

1. What would the slope of this graph ($\Delta[SO_2Cl_2]/\Delta time$) represent?

2. How does the slope of the graph change as time passes?

3. What does this indicate about the reaction rate?

4. What is the average rate of decomposition of thionyl choride?

5. How does the rate at 500 s compare to the rate at 300 s?

6. Suggest a way to determine the rate at the particular times mentioned in question 5. The rates at those particular instants are called **instantaneous rates.**

7. Calculate the instantaneous rates of reaction at 500 s and 300 s (if you're unsure of how to do this, ask a classmate or your teacher).

Reaction Measuring Techniques

The technique used to measure the change in the quantity of reactant or product varies greatly depending on the reaction involved and the available apparatus. In many cases, the reactant or product involved in a reaction may be measured directly. As in the Quick Check above, the concentration of a reactant in solution may be determined from time to time as the reaction proceeds by the titration of an aliquot of the reacting species. If a gas is being formed or consumed in a closed system, a manometer may be used to measure the change in pressure (Figure 4.1.2(a)). Gas production might also be measured using a pneumatic trough and a gas volume measuring tube called a eudiometer (Figure 4.1.2(b)). Of course, if a gas is leaving an open system, there will be a change in mass that could easily be measured using a balance.

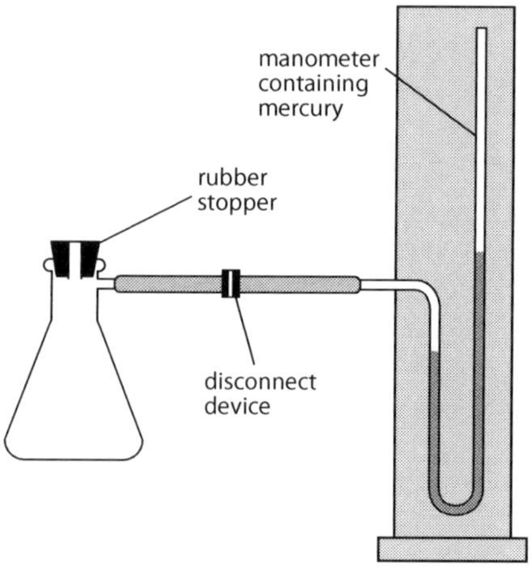

(a) A manometer measures the partial pressure of a gas formed in a reaction

Figure 4.1.2 *A manometer (a) and a eudiometer (b) are two different devices that can be used to measure the production of a gas from a reaction in a closed system.*

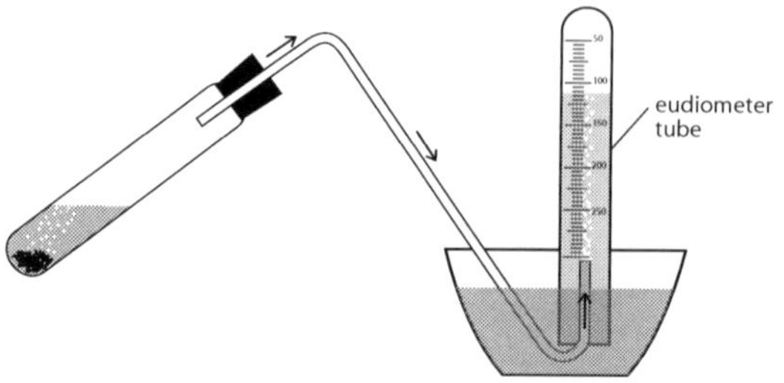

(b) A eudiometer measures the volume of gas produced during a reaction.

If the amount of a reactant or a product can't be monitored directly, a chemist can monitor some property of the reacting mixture that correlates in a known manner with the quantity of a reactant or a product. If a reaction is occurring in aqueous solution, the solution's color and pH (acidity) are properties that might indicate the quantity of reactant or product present.

A pH electrode is one type of ion selective electrode (ISE) that can be used to measure acidity. The concentrations of many types of ions can be measured with different ISEs. The ion's concentration correlates with the charge that builds up as the ion diffuses across the ISE's membrane. It is simplest if only one chemical involved in the reaction affects the monitored property. If the property is influenced by more than one chemical, then their relative influences must be known. Reactions involving color changes may be colorimetrically analyzed using a spectrophotometer.

Sample Problem — Determining the Rate of a Reaction in the Laboratory State five different methods for measuring the rate of the reaction of an iron nail in concentrated hydrochloric acid.

What to Think About	How to Do It
1. Begin by writing a balanced chemical equation. It is very important to consider the states (and any colors) of all species.	$Fe(s) + 2\,HCl(aq) \rightarrow FeCl_2(aq) + H_2(g)$ colorless — yellow-orange color (like rust)
2. Decide if there is a property associated with the quantity of reactant consumed or product produced that you might measure to monitor the reaction rate.	The first species, Fe(s) is a solid that will be consumed during the reaction.
3. Decide exactly how you might measure this property and what unit would be associated with it.	A balance could be used to determine the mass of the iron before and after the reaction was completed. The time would also need to be recorded. The resulting rate of reaction would be recorded in units of g Fe used/unit of time.

4. A repeat of the same steps would reveal more than five different ways to determine the rate of this particular reaction. Other answers might include:

$\frac{\Delta[HCl]}{\text{time}}$	$\frac{\Delta pH}{\text{time}}$	$\frac{\Delta Vol\ H_2}{\text{time}}$	$\frac{\Delta P_{(H_2)}}{\text{time}}$	$\frac{\Delta mass_{H_2}}{\text{time}}$
titrate	pH meter	eudiometer	manometer	balance (open system)
M/s	pH units/s	mL/s	kPa/s	g/s

Practice Problems — Determining the Rate of a Reaction in the Laboratory

1. Indicate two methods for determining the rate of each of the following reactions:

   (a) $Cu(s) + 2\ AgNO_3(aq) \rightarrow Cu(NO_3)_2(aq) + 2\ Ag(s)$ (Cu^{2+} ions are blue.)

   (b) $PCl_5(g) \rightarrow PCl_3(g) + Cl_2(g)$

   (c) $CaCO_3(s) \rightarrow CaO(s) + CO_2(g)$

   (d) $H_2SO_4(aq) + Ba(OH)_2(aq) \rightarrow BaSO_4(s) + 2\ H_2O(l)$

2. Why would volume of water **not** be an acceptable answer for question 1(d) above?

3. Why would concentration of copper metal, [Cu(*s*)], **not** be an acceptable answer for question 1(a) above?

Calculating Reaction Rate

Once the chemist has decided what quantity of a particular chemical species to measure, he or she may begin to gather data. These data may be used to calculate the rate of the chemical reaction. Data may be presented graphically to monitor the rate throughout the entire reaction, or initial and final data may be used to determine the reaction's average rate as indicated earlier.

$$\text{average reaction rate} = \frac{\Delta\ \text{measurable quantity of a chemical species}}{\Delta\ \text{time}}$$

As chemistry often involves the application of a balanced chemical equation, it is possible to convert from the rate of one reacting species to another by the simple application of a **mole ratio**.

Sample Problem — Calculating Average Rate from Laboratory Data

A paraffin candle ($C_{28}H_{58}$) is placed in a petri dish on an electronic balance and combusted for a period of 15.0 min. The accompanying data is collected.

(a) Calculate the average rate of combustion of the paraffin over the entire 15 min period.

(b) Calculate the average rate of formation of water vapor for the same period.

(c) Note the mass loss in each 3.0 min time increment. Comment on the rate of combustion of the candle during the entire trial. Suggest a reason why the rate of this reaction isn't greatest at the beginning, with a steady decrease as time passes.

(d) Why don't the mass values drop in a completely constant fashion?

Time (min)	Mass (g)
0	180.00
3.0	178.00
6.0	175.98
9.0	173.99
12.0	172.00
15.0	170.01

Continued opposite

Sample Problem (*Continued*)

What to Think About	How to Do It
1. Write a balanced chemical equation. Hydrocarbon combustion always involves reaction with oxygen to form water vapor and carbon dioxide.	$2\ C_{28}H_{58}(s) + 85\ O_2(g) \rightarrow 56\ CO_2(g) + 58\ H_2O(g)$
2. Think about the system carefully. Consider the balanced equation. What is causing the loss of mass?	In this case, all mass loss is due to the combusted paraffin. This paraffin is converted into two different gases: carbon dioxide and water vapor.
Question (a) 3. Apply the equation with appropriate significant figures to calculate the rate. Note that the rate is a negative value as paraffin is lost. To simplify things, reactant and product rates are often expressed as absolute values. Consequently they appear positive.	$\frac{170.01\ g - 180.00\ g}{15.0\ min - 0\ min} = -0.666\ g/min$
Question (b) 4. Now apply appropriate molar masses along with the mole ratio to convert the rate of consumption of paraffin to the rate of formation of water vapor as follows: mass paraffin (per minute) → moles paraffin → moles water vapor → mass water vapor (per min)	$\frac{0.666\ g\ C_{28}H_{58}}{min} \times \frac{1\ mol\ C_{28}H_{58}}{394.0\ g\ C_{28}H_{58}} \times \frac{58\ mol\ H_2O}{2\ mol\ C_{28}H_{58}} \times \frac{18.0\ g\ H_2O}{1\ mol\ H_2O} = 0.882\ g\ H_2O/min$
Question (c) 5. Notice the mass loss in each 3.0 min time increment recorded in the table.	The rate of consumption of paraffin seems to be nearly constant. This may be due to the [O_2] being very plentiful and so essentially constant. As well, the quantity of molten paraffin at the reacting surface stays constant through the entire reaction. As this reaction proceeds, there is no decrease in [reactants] to lead to a decrease in reaction rate.
Question (d) 6. Explain why the mass values do not drop in a completely constant fashion.	There is some variation in rate. This is due to the expected uncertainty associated with all measuring devices (in this case, the balance).

Practice Problems — Calculating Average Rate

1. A piece of zinc metal is placed into a beaker containing an aqueous solution of hydrochloric acid. The volume of hydrogen gas formed is measured by water displacement in a eudiometer every 30.0 s. The volume is converted to STP conditions and recorded.

   (a) Determine the average rate of consumption of zinc metal over the entire 150.0 s in units of g/min.

Volume H_2 (STP) (mL)	0	15.0	21.0	24.0	25.0	25.0
Time (seconds)	0	30.0	60.0	90.0	120.0	150.0

   (b) When is the reaction rate the greatest?

   (c) What is the rate from 120.0 to 150.0 s?

   (d) Assuming there is still a small bit of zinc left in the beaker, how would you explain the rate at this point?

2. A 3.45 g piece of marble ($CaCO_3$) is weighed and dropped into a beaker containing 1.00 L of hydrochloric acid. The marble is completely gone 4.50 min later. Calculate the average rate of reaction of HCl in mol/L/s. Note that the volume of the system remains at 1.00 L through the entire reaction.

Using Rate as a Conversion Factor

In Grade 11, you may have learned about **derived units**. A derived unit is a unit that consists of two or more other units. A quantity expressed with a derived unit may be used to convert a unit that measures one thing into a unit that measures something else completely. One of the most common examples is the use of a rate to convert between distance and time.

The keys to this type of problem are:

- determining which form of the conversion factor to use, and
- deciding where to start.

Sample Problem — Using Rate as a Conversion Factor

A popular organic chemistry demonstration is the dehydration of sucrose, $C_{12}H_{22}O_{11}$, using sulfuric acid to catalyze the dehydration. The acid is required for the reaction, but it is still present once the reaction is complete, primarily in its intact form and partially as dissolved sulfur oxides in the water formed. Because of this, it does not appear at all in the reaction. The product is a large carbon cylinder standing in a small puddle of water as follows: $C_{12}H_{22}O_{11}(s) \rightarrow 11\ H_2O(g) + 12\ C(s)$. Due to the exothermicity of the reaction, much of the water is released as steam, some of which contains dissolved oxides of sulfur. Ask your teacher to perform the demonstration for you, ideally in a fume hood.

Given a rate of decomposition of sucrose of 0.825 mol/min, how many grams of C(*s*) could be formed in 30.0 s?

Continued opposite

Sample Problem (*Continued*)

What to Think About

1. In this problem, you want to determine the mass of carbon in grams. Essentially, the question is: Do you use the rate as is or do you take the reciprocal? As time needs to be cancelled, use the rate as is. Once you have determined the need to convert time into mass, consider which form of the conversion factor to use.

2. Now design a "plan" for the "conversion route," using the rate, the mole ratio, and the molar mass.

How to Do It

As your answer contains one unit, begin with a number having one unit, in this case the time.

time → moles sucrose → moles carbon → mass of carbon

$$30.0\ s \times \frac{1\ min}{60\ s} \times \frac{0.825\ mol\ C_{12}H_{22}O_{11}}{1\ min} \times \frac{12\ mol\ C}{1\ mol\ C_{12}H_{22}O_{11}} \times \frac{12.0\ g\ C}{1\ mol\ C}$$

$= 59.4\ g\ C$

Practice Problems — Using Rate as a Conversion Factor

1. Ozone is an important component of the atmosphere that protects us from the ultraviolet rays of the Sun. Certain pollutants encourage the following decomposition of ozone: $2\ O_3(g) \rightarrow 3\ O_2(g)$, at a rate of 6.5×10^{-4} M O_3/s. How many molecules of O_2 gas are formed in each liter of atmosphere every day by this process? (As this problem provides a rate in units of mol/L/s and requires molecules/L as an answer, we can simply leave the unit "L" in the denominator the entire time.)

2. Propane gas combusts in camp stoves to produce energy to heat your dinner. How long would it take to produce 6.75 L of CO_2 gas measured at STP? Assume the gas is combusted at a rate of 1.10 g C_3H_8/min. Begin by writing a balanced equation for the combustion of C_3H_8.

3. A 2.65 g sample of calcium metal is placed into water. The metal is completely consumed in 25.0 s. Assuming the density of water is 1.00 g/mL at the reaction temperature, how long would it take to consume 5.00 mL of water as it converts into calcium hydroxide and hydrogen gas?

4.1 Review Questions

1. Give three reasons why the distance-time data in the Warm Up at the beginning of this section is so different from the property-time data collected for a typical chemical reaction.

2. Consider the following reaction, which could be done in either flask, using any of the equipment shown:

   $6\ Cu(s) + 8\ HNO_3(aq) + O_2(g) \rightarrow 6\ CuNO_3(aq) + 4\ H_2O(l) + 2\ NO_2(g)$

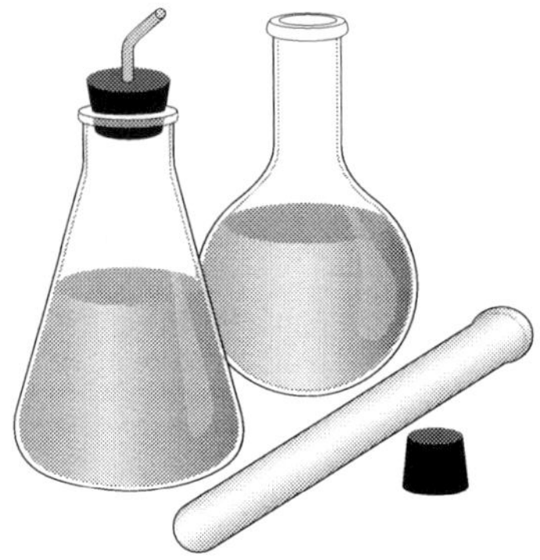

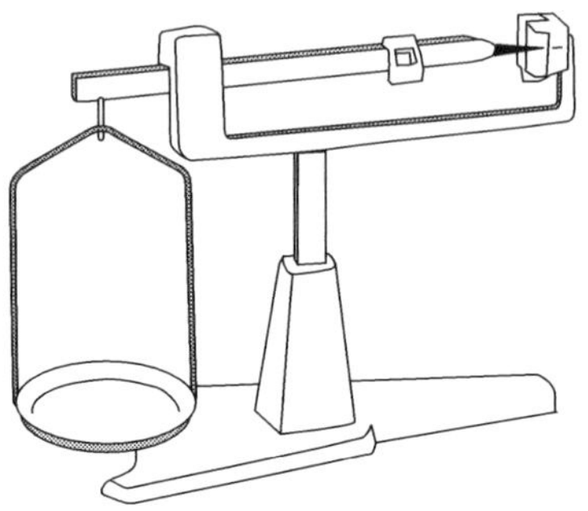

   (a) If 5.00 g of copper solid is completely reacted in 250.0 mL of excess nitric acid in 7.00 min at STP, calculate the rate of the reaction in:

   (i) g Cu/min   (ii) g NO_2/min   (iii) mol HNO_3/min

   (b) Assume the reaction continues at this average rate for 10.0 min total time. Determine the final:

   (i) mL NO_2 formed at STP   (ii) molarity of $CuNO_3$

   (c) Describe SIX ways you might measure the reaction rate. Include the equipment required, measurements made and units for the rate. You may use a labeled diagram.

3. Consider the graph for the following reaction:
$CaCO_3(s) + 2\ HCl(aq) \rightarrow CaCl_2(aq) + CO_2(g) + H_2O(l)$

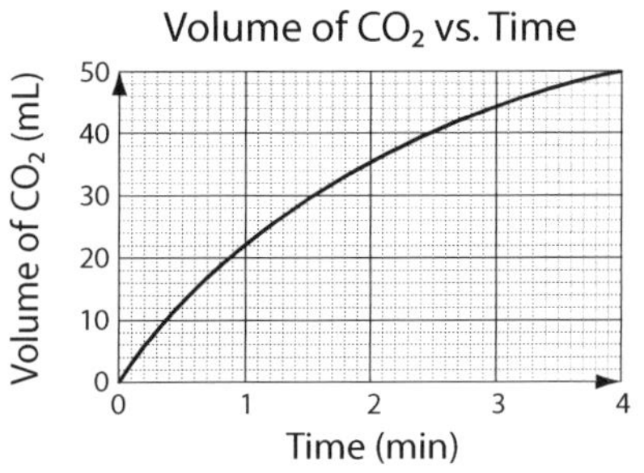

Recall the discussion of the *instantaneous rate* earlier in this section.

(a) Determine the instantaneous rate at the following times:
(i) an instant after 0 min (This is the *initial rate*.)

(ii) 1 min

(iv) 4 min

(b) How do these rates compare? What do you suppose causes this pattern?

4. Here is a table indicating the volume of gas collected as a disk of strontium metal reacts in a solution of hydrochloric acid for 1 min.
$Sr(s) + 2\ HCl(aq) \rightarrow SrCl_2(aq) + H_2(g)$

Time (seconds)	Volume of Hydrogen at STP (mL)
0	0
10.0	22.0
20.0	40.0
30.0	55.0
40.0	65.0
50.0	72.0
60.0	72.0

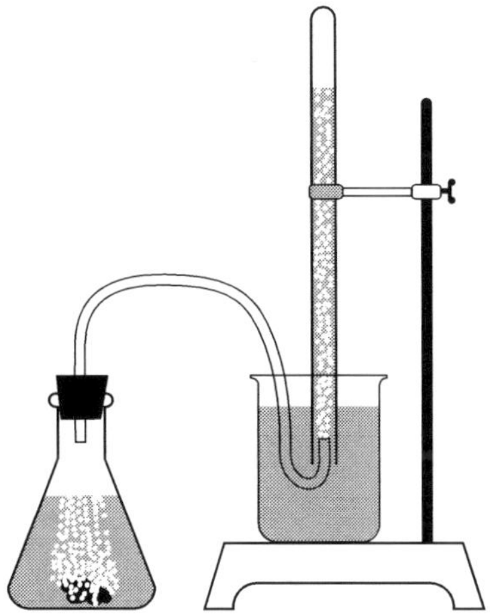

(a) Calculate the average rate of reaction in moles of HCl consumed/second over the first 50.0 s.

(b) Calculate the mass of strontium consumed in this 50.0 s period.

(c) Why did the volume of gas collected decrease in each increment until 50.0 s?

(d) Why did the volume of gas remain unchanged from 50.0 s to 60.0 s?

5. The spectrophotometer works by shining a single wavelength of light through a sample of a colored solution. A photocell detects the amount of light that passes through the solution as **% transmittance** and the amount of light that does not pass through as the **absorbance**. The more concentrated the solution, the darker the color. Dark color leads to a lower percentage of light transmitted and thus a higher absorbance. There is a direct relationship between absorbance and the concentration of a colored solution. The "calibration curve" (actually a straight line) below was created using solutions of *known* $Cu(NO_3)_2$ concentration.

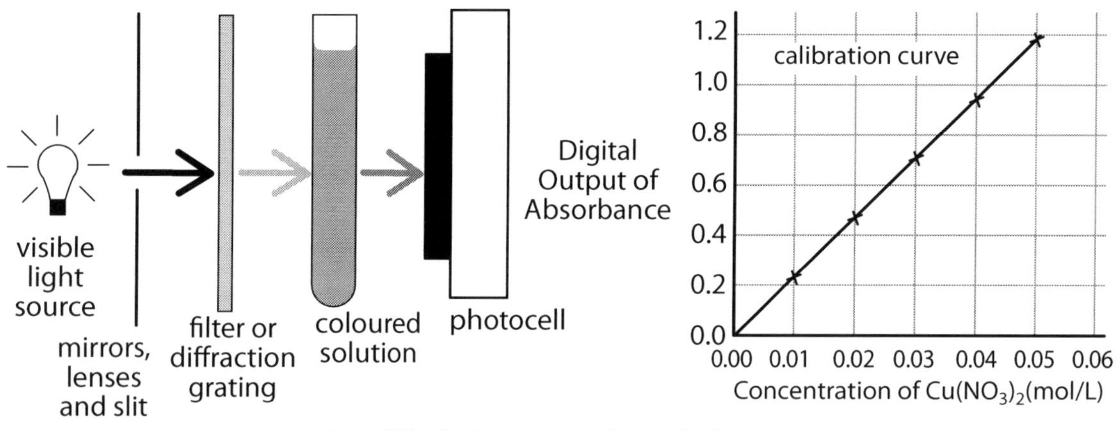

A simplified diagram of a colorimeter

A copper sample was reacted with 250 mL of nitric acid by the following reaction:

$3\ Cu(s) + 8\ HNO_3(aq) \rightarrow 3\ Cu(NO_3)_2(aq) + 2\ NO(g) + 4\ H_2O(l)$

As the reaction proceeded, small aliquots were removed and placed in a cuvette (the special test tube used to hold a sample in the spectrophotometer). The cuvettes were then placed in the instrument and the absorbances were recorded as follows:

Time (seconds)	**Absorbances (no unit)**	**Concentration of Copper(II) Ion (mol/L)**
0	0	0 mol/L
20.	0.40	
40.	0.70	
60.	0.90	
80.	1.00	

Find the absorbances on the standard graph and record the corresponding concentrations of the copper(II) ions (equal to the concentration of $Cu(NO_3)_2$) in the table.

(a) Calculate the average rate of the reaction from time 0 s to 80. s in units of $ML^{-1}s^{-1}$ of $HNO_3(aq)$.

(b) What mass of Cu(*s*) will be consumed during the 80. s trial?

(c) What will you observe in the main reaction flask as the reaction proceeds?

4.2 Factors Affecting Rates of Reaction

Factors Affecting Reaction Rate

In section 4.1, we discovered that reactions tend to slow down as they proceed. What might cause this phenomenon? What is true about a reacting system when it contains lots of reactants? Consideration of this question leads us to recognize there are more particles available to react when a reaction first starts. Intuition tells us in order for a reaction to occur, the reacting particles must contact each other. If this is so, anything that results in an increased frequency of particle contact must make a reaction occur faster.

The three factors of surface area, concentration, and temperature may all be manipulated to increase the frequency with which particles come together. Different chemicals inherently react at different rates so the nature of the reactants affects reaction rate. Finally, you may recall from previous years that a chemical species called a *catalyst* may be used to increase the rate of a reaction. We will consider each of these five factors in turn.

Surface Area

Most reactions in the lab are carried out in solution or in the gas phase. In these states, the reactants are able to intermingle on the molecular or atomic level and contact each other easily. When reactants are present in different states in a reacting system, we say the reaction is **heterogeneous.** Most heterogeneous systems involve the reaction of a *solid* with a solution or a gas. In a heterogeneous reaction, the reactants are able to come into contact with each other only where they meet at the interface between the two phases. The size of the area of contact determines the rate of the reaction. Decreasing the size of the pieces of solid reactant will increase the area of contact (Figure 4.2.1).

Increasing the surface area of a solid will increase the rate of a heterogeneous reaction.

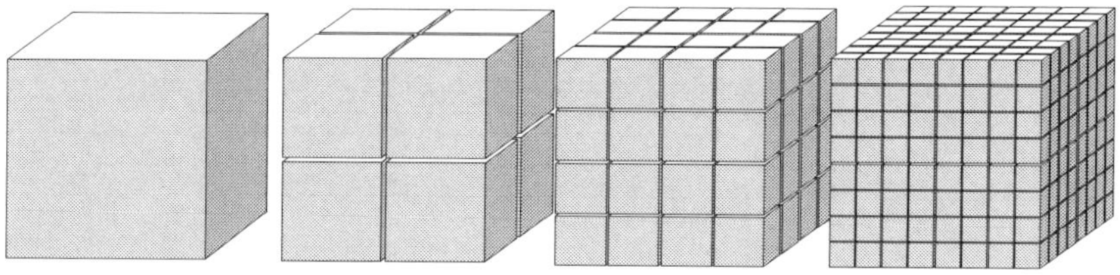

Figure 4.2.1 *Increasing the number of pieces leads to a significant increase in the surface area.*

Concentration (Pressure)

The rates of all reactions are affected by the concentrations of the dissolved or gaseous reactants. When more solute is placed in the same volume of solvent, the solution's concentration is increased (Figure 4.2.2).

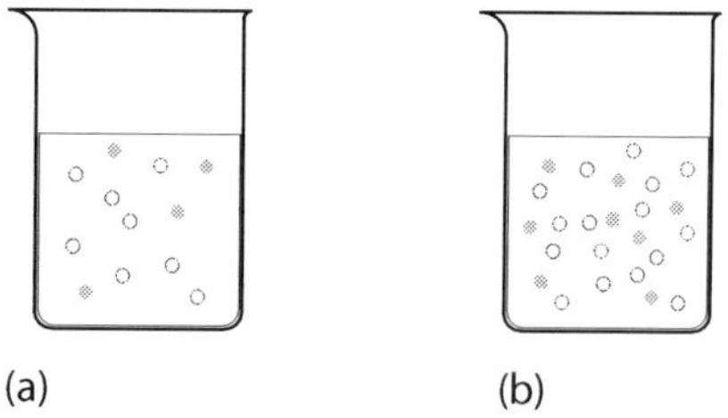

Figure 4.2.2 *Solution (b) contains twice the number of solute particles in the same volume as solution (a). The opportunity for particle contact is doubled in solution (b).*

When more gas particles are placed in the same volume of a container, the **partial pressure** of the gas has increased. In Figure 4.2.3, container (b) has twice as many gas particles in the same volume as container (a). This, of course, means the concentration has been doubled. We might also say the *partial pressure* of the gas has doubled. In container (c), the piston has been lowered to half the volume. The result is another doubling of concentration (and pressure).

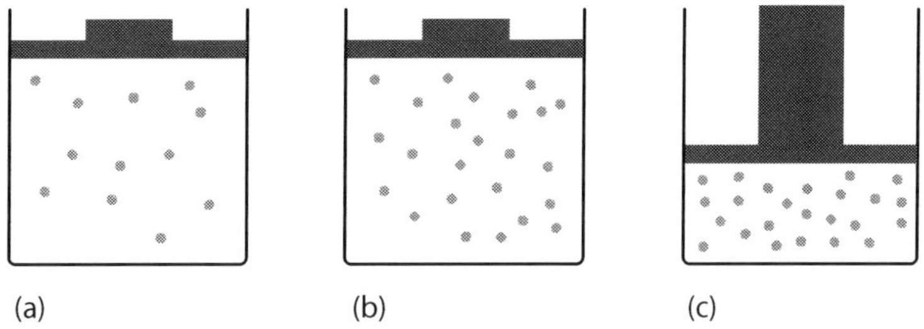

Figure 4.2.3 *The partial pressure in (b) is greater than in (a) because of the increased concentration of particles. In (c), decreasing the volume increases the concentration and the pressure.*

Increasing the concentration (or partial pressure of a gas) will increase the rate of a chemical reaction.

Always remember the concentration of pure solids and liquids cannot be increased because adding more substance increases both the moles and the liters, so the molarity or moles per liter remains constant. Also remember that crushing or breaking a solid will increase its surface area. However it is impossible to cut a piece of liquid or gas into smaller bits. The surface area of liquids can be increased by spreading them over a larger area.

Temperature

There is a qualitative relationship between temperature and kinetic energy. Mathematically speaking, KE = $3/2RT$ where R is a constant having the value 8.31 J/mol K, and T is the Kelvin temperature. From this relationship, we see that temperature and kinetic energy are directly related to one another. If the temperature is doubled, the kinetic energy is doubled (as long as the temperature is expressed in units of Kelvin degrees).

An increase in temperature will lead to particles striking one another more frequently. However, we now see that it will also result in the particles striking one another with more energy. In other words, an increase in temperature means that the same particles are travelling faster. As a consequence, they hit each other more frequently and more forcefully. As a result, *temperature is the most significant factor* that affects reaction rate.

Another thing you may have learned in previous years is within any substance there is a "normal" distribution of kinetic energies among the particles that make up the system due to their random collisions. Such a distribution might be graphed as shown in Figure 4.2.4.

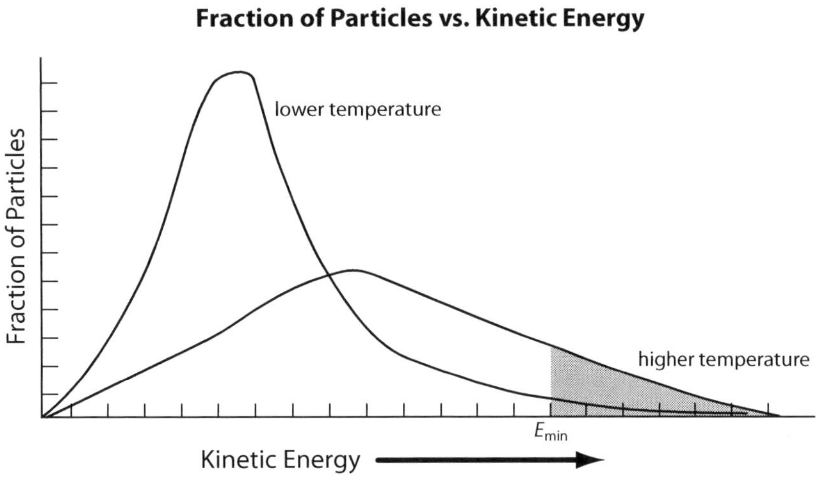

Figure 4.2.4 *Kinetic energy shows a "normal" distribution at both lower and higher temperatures.*

Note that some of the particles have very little energy and others have a lot. The *x*-axis value associated with the peak of the curve indicates the kinetic energy of most of the particles. The second curve indicates how the distribution would change if the temperature were increased. The area under the curves represents the total number of particles and therefore should be the same for both curves. The gray area represents the particles that have sufficient energy to *collide successfully* and produce a product. Notice that this has increased with an increase in temperature. A common generalization is that an increase of 10°C will double reaction rate. This is true for some reactions around room temperature.

Increasing temperature will increase the rate of a reaction for *two* reasons: *more frequent* and *more forceful* collisions.

The Nature of Reactants

Fundamental differences in chemical reactivity are a major factor in determining the rate of a chemical reaction. For instance, zinc metal oxidizes quickly when exposed to air and moisture, while iron reacts much more slowly under the same conditions. For this reason, zinc is used to protect the integrity of the iron beneath it in galvanized nails.

Generally reactions between simple monoatomic ions such as Ag^+ and Cl^- are almost instantaneous. This is due to ions being extremely mobile, in close proximity to one another, having opposite charges, and requiring no bond rearrangement to react. However, more complicated ionic species such as CH_3COO^- react more slowly than those that are monoatomic.

In general, differences in chemical reactivity can be attributed to factors that affect the breaking and forming of chemical bonds. Ionization energy, electronegativity, ionic and molecular polarity, size, and complexity of structure are some of these factors. The state of the reacting species may also play a role.

In general, at room temperature the rate of (*aq*) reactants > (*g*) > (*l*) > (*s*).

Precipitation occurs quickly between ions in solution. In Figure 4.2.5(a), the AgCl forms as a heavy, white precipitate the instant the silver ions contact the chloride in solution. In (b), the $AgCH_3COO$ precipitate is less heavy and forms over a period of 10 s to 20 s. The complex structure of the acetate ion makes it more difficult to achieve the correct orientation to bond successfully.

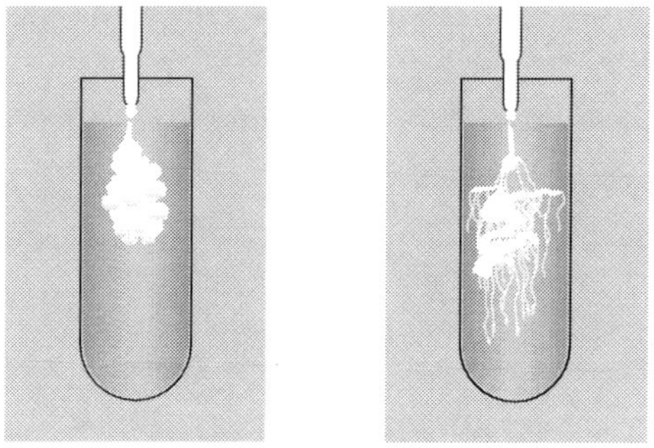

(a) (b)

Figure 4.2.5 *(a) AgCl quickly forms a precipitate. (b) $AgCH_3COO$ forms a precipitate more slowly.*

Presence of a Catalyst

Catalysts are substances that increase the rates of chemical reactions without being used up. Because they remain in the same quantity and form when a reaction is completed, the formulas of catalysts are not included in the chemical reaction. Sometimes the formula is shown above the arrow between the reactants and products like this:

$$2\,H_2O_2(l) \xrightarrow{MnO_2} 2\,H_2O(l) + O_2(g)$$

What actually happens is that catalysts are consumed during an intermediate step in a reaction and regenerated in a later step. The catalysts most familiar to you are probably the enzymes produced by living organisms as they catalyze digestive and other biochemical processes in our bodies. We will discuss catalysts in more detail later in this chapter.

The reaction depicted in graduated cylinders in Figure 4.2.6 is the catalyzed decomposition of hydrogen peroxide as shown in the equation above. In addition to the H_2O_2, there is a bit of dish soap and some dye in the cylinders so the oxygen gas bubbles through the soap solution and produces foam. This demonstration is often called "elephant toothpaste." Note that the cylinder in (b) contained 30% hydrogen peroxide while the cylinder in (a) was only 6%, so the effect of concentration was demonstrated in addition to the catalytic effect.

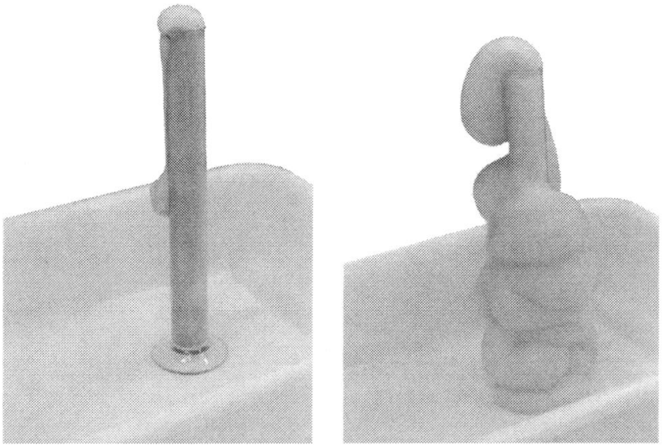

(a) (b)

Figure 4.2.6 *"Elephant toothpaste" is produced through a catalytic reaction. The concentration of H_2O_2 is greater in (b) than in (a).*

> A catalyst increases reaction rate without itself being consumed or altered.

An **inhibitor** is a species that reduces the rate of a chemical reaction by combining with a reactant to stop it from reacting in its usual way. A number of pharmaceuticals are inhibitors. Drugs that act through inhibition are called *antagonists*.

Sample Problem — Factors Affecting Reaction Rate

Which of the following reactions is faster at room temperature?

(a) $H_2(g) + I_2(s) \rightarrow 2\,HI(g)$ (b) $Ba^{2+}(aq) + SO_4^{2-}(aq) \rightarrow BaSO_4(s)$

List two ways to increase the rate of each reaction.

What to Think About	How to Do It
1. First consider the nature of the reactants.	The reactant states lead us to believe that reaction (b) involving aqueous species would be the fastest.
2. To increase the rate of reaction (a), start by recognizing this is a heterogeneous reaction. This means that, in addition to the usual factors, surface area can be considered.	• Increase surface area of iodine solid. • Increase temperature. • Increase concentration of hydrogen gas. • Increase partial pressure of hydrogen gas (decrease container volume). • Add an appropriate catalyst.
3. To increase the rate of reaction of the homogeneous reaction in (b), apply all the usual factors except surface area. *Note that you must be specific when mentioning the factors.* For example, what species' concentration will be increased?	• Increase temperature. • Increase concentration of either or both reactant ions (Ba^{2+} and/or SO_4^{2-}). • Add an appropriate catalyst.

4.2 Activity: Graphic Depiction of Factors Affecting Reaction Rates

Question

How do concentration, surface area, and temperature affect reaction rate?

Background

Four trials were carried out in which a chunk of zinc was reacted with hydrochloric acid under four different sets of conditions. In all four trials, the chunk of zinc was of equal mass. The data collected indicate that varying factors have a significant impact on reaction rate. These data can be represented in tabular and graphical form.

The reaction was allowed to proceed for the same time period in each trial. In all four trials, the gas was collected in a eudiometer using the apparatus shown below.

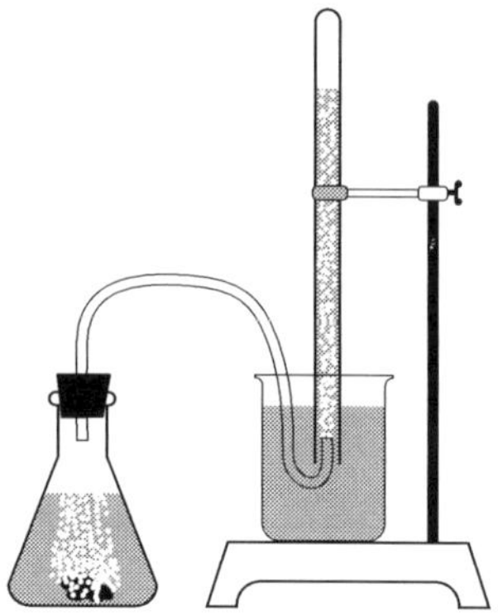

Time (s)	Trial 1 25°C, 1 M HCl (mL)	Trial 2 50°C, 1 M HCl (mL)	Trial 3 25°C, 2 M HCl (mL)	Trial 4 25°C, 1 M HCl, zinc powder (mL)
0	0	0	0	0
30.	12	34	20	26
60.	19	56	34	44
90.	24	65	44	57
120.	27	65	51	65
150.	29	65	54	65

Procedure

1. Use the following grid to graph all four sets of data. Vary colors for each trial line.

Results and Discussion

1. Write a balanced equation for the reaction that was studied.

2. Rank the conditions from those producing the fastest to slowest reaction rates. What factor influences reaction rate the most? Which factor is second most effective? Which factor has the least influence on the rate?

3. Calculate the average reaction rate in mL H_2/min for each trial. Use the time required to collect the maximum amount of hydrogen gas formed (e.g., the time for trial 2 will be 90. s). Place the rates on the graphed lines.

4. How many milligrams of zinc were used in 1.50 min for each trial? Assume a molar volume for $H_2(g)$ of 24.5 L/mol. (This is for SATP conditions or 25°C and 101.3 kPa or the pressure at sea level.) For the 50°C trial, use 26.5 L/mol.

5. What error is introduced by the assumption in question 4? Would the actual mass of Zn be larger or smaller than that calculated? Explain.

4.2 Review Questions

1. Identify the four factors that affect the rate of any reaction. Give a brief explanation as to how each one applies. Which of these factors can be altered to change the rate of a particular chemical reaction?

2. Identify the one factor that affects only the rate of heterogeneous reactions. Explain why it does not affect homogeneous reaction rates.

3. Use the Internet to find examples of catalysts that do the following:
   (a) Convert oxides of nitrogen into harmless nitrogen gas in the catalytic converter of an automobile.

   (b) Increase the rate of the Haber process to make ammonia.

   (c) Found on disinfectant discs to clean contact lenses.

   (d) Found in green plants to assist in photosynthesis.

4. How would each of the following changes affect the rate of decomposition of a marble statue due to acid rain? Begin by writing the equation for the reaction between marble (calcium carbonate) and nitric acid below.

   (a) The concentration of the acid is increased.

   (b) Erosion due to wind and weathering increases the surface area on the surface of the statue.

   (c) The statue is cooled in cold winter weather.

   (d) The partial pressure of carbon dioxide gas in the atmosphere is increased due to greenhouse gases.

5. (a) At room temperature, catalyzed decomposition of methanoic acid, HCOOH, produced 80.0 mL of carbon monoxide gas in 1.00 min once the volume was adjusted to STP conditions. The other product was water. Calculate the average rate of decomposition of methanoic acid in moles per minute.

(b) Give general (approximate) answers for the following:

(i) How long would you expect the production of 40.0 mL of gas to take?

(ii) How long would you expect the production of 80.0 mL to take without a catalyst?

(iii) How long would you expect the production of 80.0 mL of gas to take at 10°C above the experimental conditions?

6. Answer the questions below for each of the following reactions:

(i) $C(s) + O_2(g) \rightarrow CO_2(g)$

(ii) $Pb^{2+}(aq) + 2\,I^-(aq) \rightarrow PbI_2(s)$

(iii) $Mg(s) + CuCl_2(aq) \rightarrow MgCl_2(aq) + Cu(s)$

(a) Indicate whether you think it would be fast or slow if performed at room temperature. Then rank the three reactions from fastest to slowest.

(b) List which of the five factors could be used to increase the rate of each reaction.

7. Rank the diagrams below in order of expected reaction rate for this reaction:

$G(g) + B(g) \rightarrow GB(g)$

where G = gray, B = black and GB is the product. Explain your ranking. Assume the same temperature in all three reacting systems.

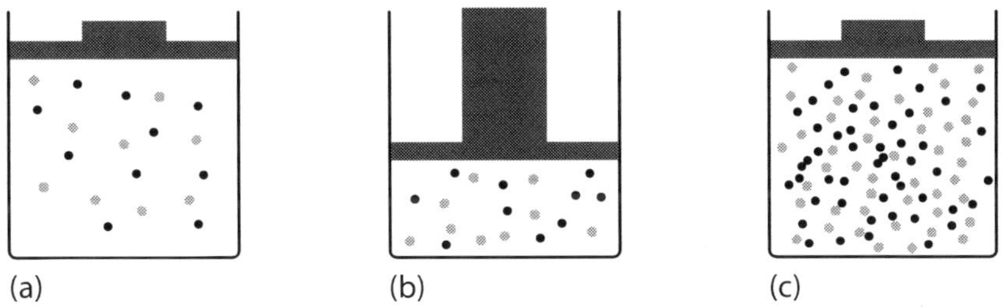

4.3 Collision Theory

Warm Up

Consider a hypothetical reaction between two gas particles, A and B, to form AB according to the reaction, $A(g) + B(g) \rightarrow AB(g)$. Determine the total number of possible distinct collisions that could occur between the A particles and the B particles in each situation shown in the diagram below. Let □ represent A and ● represent B. Draw arrows from each A particle to each B particle in turn to help you track each possible collision. The third case is done as an example for you.

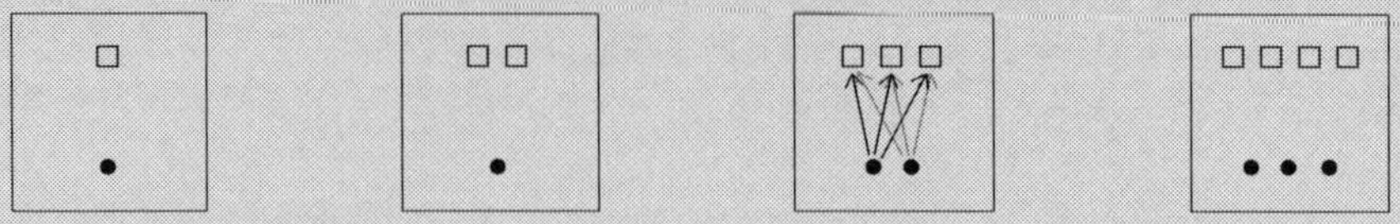

Total possible collisions: ________ ________ ___6___ ________

What is the relationship between the number of A and B particles and the total number of distinct collisions possible?

____

What might this relationship indicate regarding the rate of a reaction between A and B?

____

Collisions and Concentrations

From our study of the factors affecting reaction rates, it seems obvious that a successful reaction requires the reacting particles to collide with one another. The series of diagrams in the Warm Up above show that the more particles of reactant species present in a reacting system, the more collisions can occur between them in a particular period of time. Careful examination of the situations described in the Warm Up reveals that the number of possible collisions between the reactant molecules, A and B, is simply equal to the product of the number of molecules of each type present. That is:

number of A × number of B = total possible collisions between A and B

The number of particles per unit volume may be expressed as a concentration. In the example, all of the particles are in the same volume so we can think of the number of particles of each type as representing their concentrations. From this, we can infer that the concentration of the particles colliding must be related to the rate. These two statements allow us to represent the relationship discovered in the Warm Up as follows.

The rate of a reaction is directly proportional to the product of the concentrations of the reactants.

When two variables are directly proportional to one another there is a constant that relates the two. In other words, multiplying one variable by a constant value will always give you the other variable. We call this multiplier a *proportionality constant*. In science, proportionality constants are commonly represented by the letter k.

The slope of any straight-line graph is a proportionality constant. A quick review of this concept can be found in your M4 Chemistry textbook. Applying this concept to the relationship discovered in the Warm Up results in the following.

$$\text{reaction rate} = k[A]^x[B]^y$$

The relationship above is called a **rate law**. The proportionality constant in this case is called a **rate constant**. Every reaction has its own unique rate law and its own unique rate constant. For many reactions, the exponents, x and y, are each equal to 1. The values of x and y are called **reactant orders**. In this section, we will focus on reactions that are first order with respect to all reactants. In other words, both $x = 1$ and $y = 1$. Be aware, however, that there are reactions involving second and even third order reactants. Clearly, the higher the order of a particular reactant, the more a change in the concentration of that reactant affects the reaction rate.

Quick Check

1. Write the general form for a rate law in which two reactants, C and D, react together. Assume the reaction is first order for each reactant. Explain what the rate law means.

____

____

____

2. Assume a reaction occurs by this rate law: rate = k[A]. How would the rate be affected by each of the following changes in concentration?
   (a) [A] is doubled.

   ____

   (b) [A] is halved.

   ____

3. Assume a gaseous reaction occurs by this rate law: rate = k[A][B]. How would the rate be affected if the volume of the container were halved?

____

4. How is the rate of a reaction affected by increasing the temperature? What part of the rate law must be affected by changing temperature?

____

____

A Distribution of Collisions

When reacting particles collide with one another, each collision is unique in its energy and direction. If you've ever played a game of billiards, snooker, or 8-ball, you're familiar with the transfer of energy from the shooter's arm to the pool stick to the cue ball to the ball being shot. Only when the shooter sends the cue ball directly into the ball being shot with a controlled amount of strength are the momentum and direction of the ball easily predictable.

This control is required in a "direct shot" or in a classic "bank shot" where, much like a beam of reflected light, the angle of incidence equals the angle of reflection (Figure 4.3.1(a)). Bank shots may be necessary when an opponent's balls are blocking a clear shot. In most cases, however, collisions between the cue ball, the ball being shot, and other balls on the table are different in direction and amount of energy transferred (Figure 4.3.1(b)). Skillful players may intentionally play "shape" or put "English" on the ball to manipulate the direction and the amount of energy transfer involved in collisions.

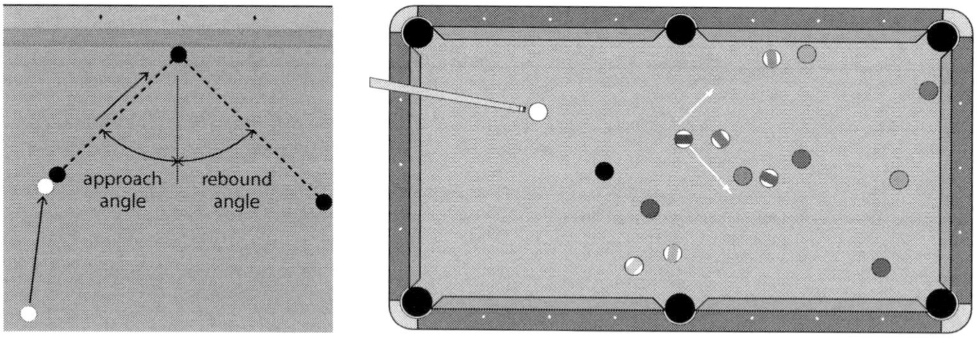

(a) (b)

Figure 4.3.1 *(a) A bank shot involves predictable collisions. (b) Skilled players determine exactly what type of collision is required for the shot they need to make.*

The break at the start of the game is probably the best model of the distribution of collision energies involved between the reacting particles in a chemical reaction (Figure 1.3.2). Some of the particles move quickly and collide directly with others to transfer a great deal of energy. Others barely move at all or collide with a glancing angle that transfers very little energy. In addition, we must remember that real reactant collisions occur in three dimensions, while our pool table model is good for two dimensions only (Figure 4.3.3).

Figure 4.3.2 *The break at the start of a game provides a large distribution of collision energies.*

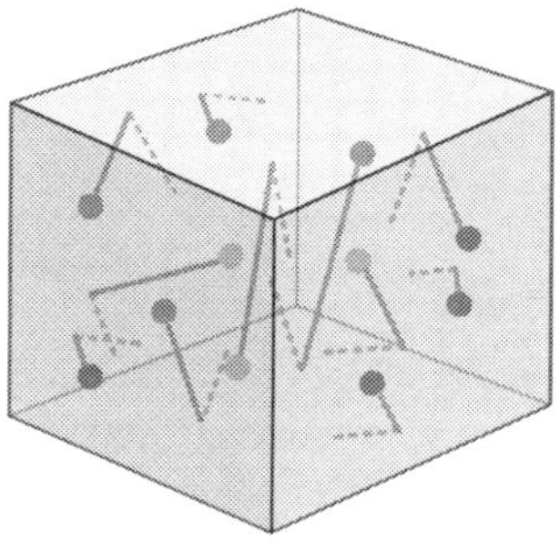

Figure 4.3.3 *The collisions occurring between species in a chemical reaction occur in three dimensions.*

Collision Theory

Regardless of the fact that the energy of particle collisions is distributed in a regular way, the rate of a reaction actually depends on *two* considerations.

Collision theory states that reaction rates depend upon:
- the number of collisions per unit time, and
- the fraction of these collisions that succeed in producing products.

Requirements for Effective Collisions

A mixture of hydrogen and oxygen gas may sit indefinitely inside a balloon at room temperature without undergoing any apparent reaction regardless of concentrations. Addition of a small amount of energy such as a spark to the system, however, causes the gases to react violently and exothermically. How can this phenomenon be explained?

In 1 mol of gas under standard conditions, there are more than 10^{32} collisions occurring each second. If the rate of collisions per second were equal to the rate of reaction, every reaction would be extremely rapid. Since most gaseous reactions are slow, it is evident that only a small fraction of the total collisions effectively result in the conversion of reactants to products.

As discussed earlier, the tremendous number of collisions in a reacting sample results in a wide

Quick Check

Consider the factors affecting reaction rate that you studied in section 4.2.

1. Which of these factors do you think increase reaction rate by increasing the number of collisions per unit time?

   ____

2. Which of the factors do you think increase reaction rate by increasing the fraction of collisions that succeed in producing products?

   ____

3. Do you think any of the factors increase *both* the number of collisions per unit time and the fraction of successful collisions? If so, which one(s)?

   ____

range of velocities and kinetic energies. Only a small percentage of the molecules in a given sample have sufficient kinetic energy to react.

The minimum kinetic energy that the reacting species must have in order to react is called the **activation energy** or E_a of the reaction.

Only collisions between particles having the threshold energy of E_a are energetic enough to overcome the repulsive forces between the electron clouds of the reacting molecules and to weaken or break bonds, resulting in a reaction. Most gaseous reactions have relatively high E_a values; hence reactions like the one between hydrogen and oxygen gas do not occur at room temperature.

The activation energy of a reaction depends on a comparison of the energy released during the formation of new chemical bonds and the energy required to break existing bonds. As bond energies are a characteristic of a particular chemical species, the only thing that can change the activation energy of a reaction is to change the pathway between reactant and product species. This is precisely what occurs when a reaction is catalyzed.

In section 4.2, a kinetic energy distribution diagram was shown for a sample of matter at two different temperatures. Figure 4.3.4 shows a similar pair of energy distributions at two different temperatures. It also shows two different activation energies. E_{a2} represents the activation energy without a catalyst present. E_{a1} represents a lowered activation energy that results in the presence of a catalyst. Note that in both cases, with and without a catalyst, the number of particles capable of colliding effectively (as represented by the shaded area under the curve) increases at the higher temperature.

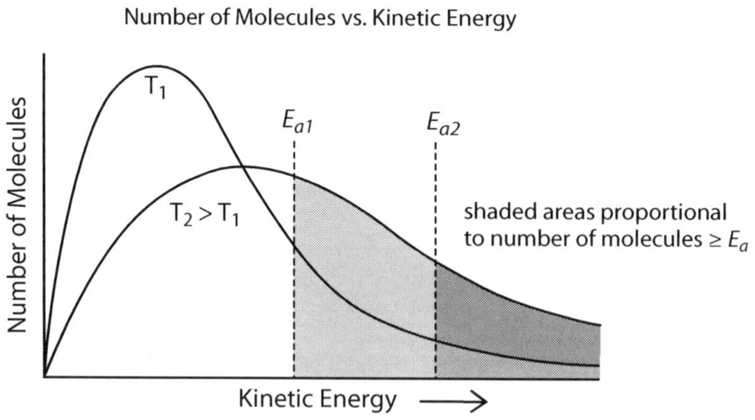

Figure 4.3.4 *With higher temperatures, the number of particles capable of colliding effectively increases.*

It turns out there is one further factor that complicates collision theory even more. Particles having the activation energy associated with a given reaction don't always react when they undergo a collision. Even very high-energy collisions may not be effective unless the molecules are properly oriented toward one another.

In addition to attaining E_a, the *geometric shape* and the *molecular orientation* of reacting particles must also be favorable for a successful collision to occur.

Consider the reaction $CO(g) + NO_2(g) \rightarrow CO_2(g) + NO(g)$

Figure 4.3.5 shows two different ways the reactants CO and NO_2 could collide. Here we see a successful collision followed by an unsuccessful collision between carbon monoxide and nitrogen dioxide in an attempt to form carbon dioxide and nitrogen monoxide. No matter how energetic the collision, it will succeed only when the carbon and oxygen atoms in the respective molecules are oriented properly. For the CO molecule to become CO_2, the oxygen from the NO_2 molecule must collide with the carbon atom in the CO molecule so that a bond can form.

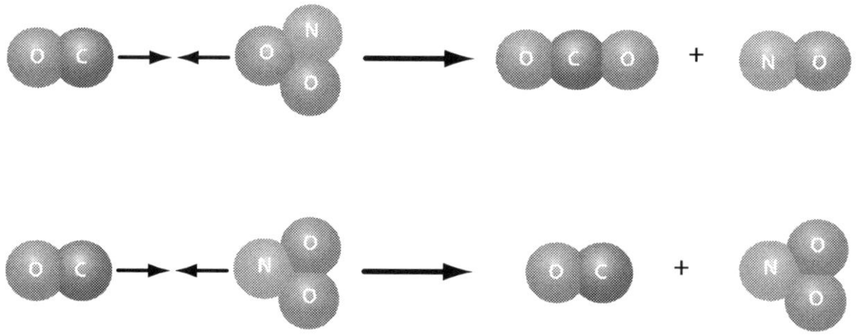

Figure 4.3.5 *The top collision is successful because the molecules are oriented so that the carbon and oxygen atoms can bond to form CO_2.*

Collision Theory and Factors Affecting Reaction Rate

Increased temperature, concentration, and surface area all increase the frequency of collisions leading to an increase in reaction rate. The presence of a catalyst and temperature both increase the fraction of collisions that are successful.

Sample Problem — Collision Theory

Study the following data for 1 mol of reactants at two different temperatures. $T_1 < T_2$.

	Temperature 1	Temperature 2
Frequency of collisions:	$1.5 \times 10^{32}\ s^{-1}$	$3.0 \times 10^{32}\ s^{-1}$
% of collisions > E_a:	10%	30%

(a) How many collisions exceed activation energy per second at each temperature?

(b) How many times greater is the reaction rate at temperature 2 than temperature 1? (Assume the percent of collisions with correct geometry is the same at both temperatures.)

(c) If the frequency of collisions was only doubled by increasing the temperature from T_1 to T_2, why is the rate increased by a factor of six?

What to Think About	How to Do It
1. Multiply the percentage by the frequency at each temperature.	$0.10(1.5 \times 10^{32}\ s^{-1}) = 1.5 \times 10^{31}\ s^{-1}$ at T_1 $0.30(3.0 \times 10^{32}\ s^{-1}) = 9.0 \times 10^{31}\ s^{-1}$ at T_2
2. Divide the result for T_2 by the result for T_1.	$\frac{9.0 \times 10^{31}\ s^{-1}}{1.5 \times 10^{31}\ s^{-1}} = 6.0 \times$ greater
3. Decide what, in addition to collision frequency, must be influenced by reaction temperature.	Increasing reaction temperature increases the energy of collisions as well as collision frequency.

Practice Problems — Collision Theory

1. For slow reactions, at temperatures near 25°C, an increase of 10°C will approximately double the number of particles that have enough energy to react. At temperatures much higher than that, increasing temperature leads to smaller and smaller increases in the number of successful collisions. In the graph below, the area under the kinetic energy distribution curve represents the total number of particles.
   (a) Assume the curve shown represents the kinetic energy distribution for a sample of reacting particles at room temperature. Add a curve to represent the kinetic energy distribution for a sample of reacting particles at 10°C above room temperature.
   (b) Add a second curve to represent the kinetic energy distribution for a sample of reacting particles at a temperature 100°C above curve (a).
   (c) Add a third curve for a temperature 10°C above curve (b).

Number of Particles vs. Energy

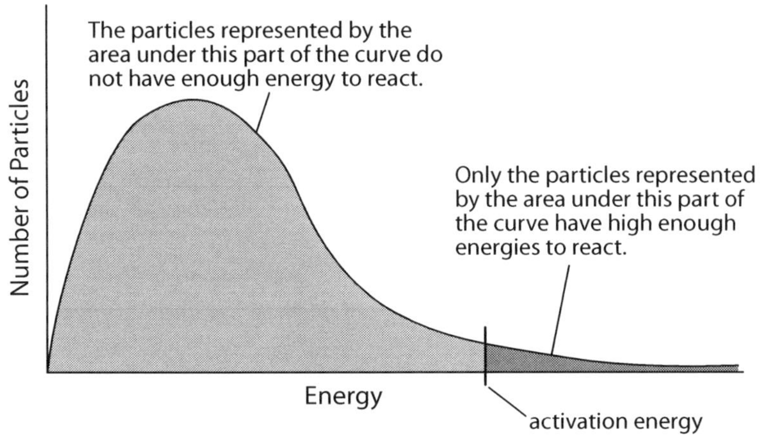

Continued on the next page

Practice Problems (*Continued*)

2. At higher temperature ranges, that is, for reactions already occurring at a high rate, most of the collisions already possess E_a. Hence, an increase in temperature increases the rate primarily because of the increased frequency of collisions. Although the particles hit each other harder and with more energy, this is not really relevant because they have already achieved E_a. Complete the following table for a reacting particle sample.

Temperature	**100°C**	**300°C**
Frequency of collisions	$2.00 \times 10^{15}\ s^{-1}$	$3.00 \times 10^{15}\ s^{-1}$
Force of collisions (% possessing E_a)	95.0%	97.0%
Frequency of collisions possessing activation energy		

(a) Calculate the fraction by which the percentage of particles possessing E_a increases with an increase of 200°C. Divide the percentage for 300°C by the percentage for 100°C.

(b) Calculate the fraction by which the frequency of collisions increases with an increase of 200°C.

(c) Calculate the fraction by which the frequency of collisions possessing E_a increases with an increase of 200°C.

(d) The data in the table shows that at higher temperatures the increase in rate is almost entirely due to what?

(e) Why might increasing the force of collisions eventually produce less successful reactions?

4.3 Review Questions

1. List the two things that affect the rates of all chemical reactions according to collision theory.

2. What are the two requirements for a collision to be successful?

3. One chunk of zinc is left whole and another is cut into pieces as shown. Both samples of zinc are reacted in an equal volume of 6.0 mol/L aqueous hydrochloric acid.

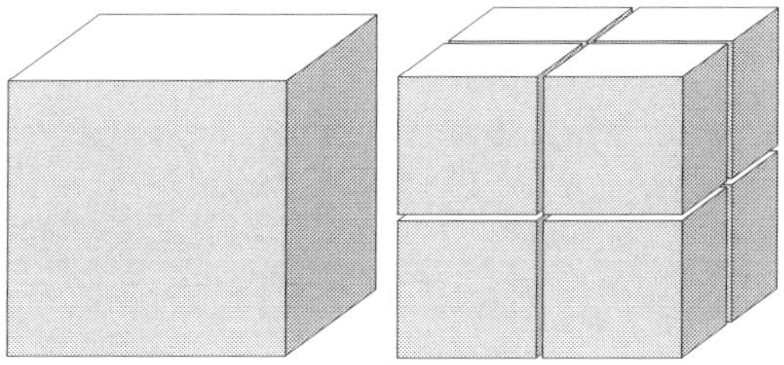

   (a) Assuming the surface area of the first zinc sample is 6.00 cm^2, what is the surface area of the second sample of zinc?

   (b) Compare the frequency of collisions between the hydrochloric acid and the single piece of zinc with those between the acid and the cut sample of zinc.

   (c) Assuming the average rate of reaction for the single piece of zinc with the acid is 1.20×10^{-3} mol Zn/min, calculate the rate of reaction for the cut sample of zinc.

   (d) Assuming this rate is maintained for a period of 4.50 min, how many milliliters of hydrogen gas would be collected at STP?

4. A reaction between ammonium ions and nitrite ions has the following rate law:

$$\text{rate} = k[NH_4^+][NO_2^-]$$

Assume the rate of formation of the salt is 3.10×10^{-3} mol $L^{-1}s^{-1}$. Note that the units may also be expressed as mol/(L s). The reaction is performed in aqueous solution at room temperature.

(a) What rate of reaction would result if the $[NH_4^+]$ was tripled and the $[NO_2^-]$ was halved?

(b) Determine the reaction rate if the $[NH_4^+]$ was unchanged and the $[NO_2^-]$ was increased by a factor of four?

(c) If the $[NH_4^+]$ and the $[NO_2^-]$ were unchanged, but the rate increased to 6.40×10^{-3} mol/(L s), what must have happened to the reacting system?

(d) What would the new reaction rate be if enough water were added to double the overall volume?

5. A student reacts ground marble chips, $CaCO_3(s)$, with hydrochloric acid, $HCl(aq)$, in an open beaker at constant temperature.

(a) In terms of collision theory, explain what will happen to the rate of the reaction as it proceeds from the beginning to completion.

(b) Sketch a graph of volume of $CO_2(g)$ vs. time to show the formation of product with time as the reaction proceeds.

6. Consider the following three experiments, each involving the same mass of zinc and the same volume of acid at the same temperature. Rank the three in order from fastest to slowest, and explain your ranking using collision theory.

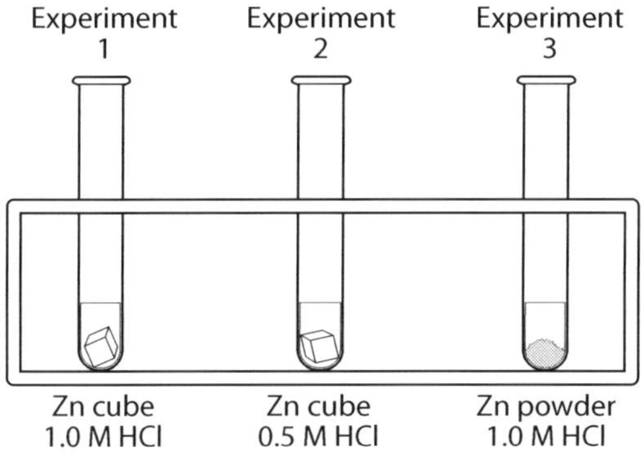

7. Is the following collision likely to produce Cl_2 and NO_2 assuming the collision occurs with sufficient energy? If not, redraw the particles in such a way that a successful collision would be likely.

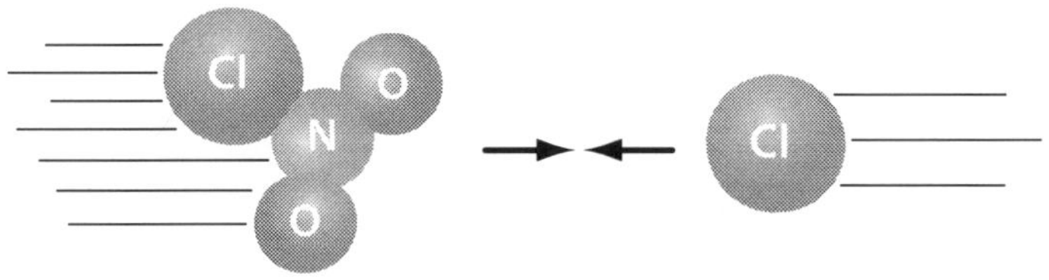

8. Use collision theory to explain each of the following.
   (a) Food found in camps half way up Mount Everest is still edible once thawed.
   (b) Campers react magnesium shavings with oxygen to start fires.
   (c) A thin layer of platinum in a vehicle's exhaust system converts oxides of nitrogen into non-toxic nitrogen gas.

4.4 Determining Rate Laws from Experimental Data

Warm Up

In section 4.3, we introduced the concept of a *rate law*. Rate laws express rates of reaction in the following form: reaction rate = $k[A]^x[B]^y$, where [A] and [B] represent the concentrations of the reactants, and *x* and *y* represent the orders with respect to reactants A and B.

The following diagrams represent systems of gaseous reactants A (symbolized by **O**) and B (symbolized by ■) at a fixed temperature and volume. The equation for the reaction is $A(g) + B(g) \rightarrow C(g)$.

The rate law equation uses only the reactant concentrations, so we did not depict the presence of the product C in these diagrammatic representations. Below the containers, we have provided the instantaneous rate of reaction for each system in units of mol/L of C produced per second.

System 1 System 2 System 3

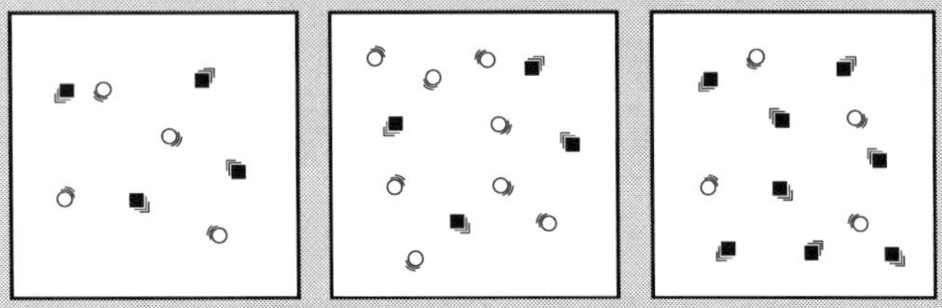

Rate = 0.010 mol $L^{-1}s^{-1}$ 0.020 mol $L^{-1}s^{-1}$ 0.040 mol $L^{-1}s^{-1}$

1. By what factor did the concentration of A (**O**) change from System 1 to 2?

____

2. How did this affect the reaction rate?

____

3. By what factor did the concentration of B (■) change from System 1 to 3?

____

4. How did this affect the reaction rate?

____

5. Complete the following expression:

rate = k[A]$^{\square}$[B]$^{\square}$

Determining an Initial Reaction Rate

In section 4.1, we discussed methods of determining rates of chemical reactions. In that same section, we determined both the average and instantaneous rates of reaction from a graph of data we collected for the decomposition of thionyl chloride. We call the instantaneous rate determined at the very beginning of a reaction the **initial rate** (Figure 4.4.1).

Concentration of Product vs. Time

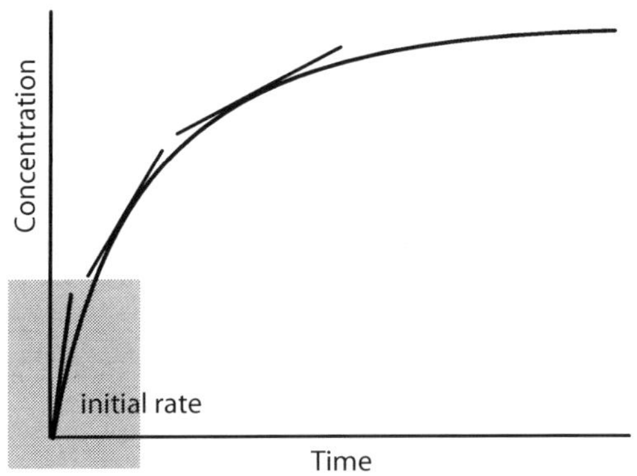

Figure 4.4.1 *The slope of a tangent line drawn to the curve at the beginning of a reaction is greater than that of any other tangent. This slope gives the initial rate of a reaction.*

As predicted by collision theory, the initial rate of a reaction depends on the concentration of the reactants present. Increasing the number of reactant particles in a particular volume leads to more frequent collisions between particles, which usually increases the reaction rate. Performing multiple trials with different concentrations of reactants shows how varying the reactant concentration affects the rate of a reaction (Figure 4.4.2).

Concentration of Reactants vs. Time

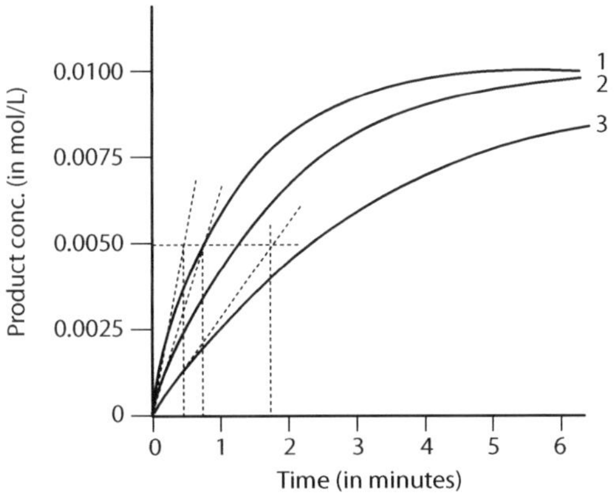

Figure 4.4.2 *The graph shows the relationship between concentration and time for three different initial reactant concentrations. Trial 1 has the greatest initial reactant concentration. The reaction rate increases from Trial 3 to 2 to 1. We determine the initial rate of each reaction from the slope of the tangent at the beginning of the reaction.*

Determining Reaction Orders

We can summarize data from a series of trials such as those shown in the Warm Up in a tabular form. If we assume that each **O** represents 1.00 mmol of A, and each ■ represents 1.00 mmol of B, all of which are contained in a 1.00 L container, the table would look like Table 4.4.1.

Table 4.4.1 *Data Table for Three Trials*

Trial Number	Initial Rate ($molL^{-1}s^{-1}$)	Initial [A] (mol/L)	Initial [B] (mol/L)
1	0.010	0.00400	0.00400
2	0.020	0.00800	0.00400
3	0.040	0.00400	0.00800

From Trial 1 to 2, we double [A] and hold [B] constant. The result is a doubling of the reaction rate. This implies that the rate is directly proportional to the [A], and the process is first order with respect to A. We can demonstrate the relationship mathematically by setting up a ratio of the rate laws for the two trials:

$$\frac{\text{rate 2}}{\text{rate 1}} = \frac{k[A]^x[B]^y}{k[A]^x[B]^y} \text{ thus } \frac{0.020 \text{ mol/L/s}}{0.010 \text{ mol/L/s}} = \frac{\cancel{k}(0.00800 \text{ mol/L})^x(\cancel{0.00400} \text{ mol/L})^y}{\cancel{k}(0.00400 \text{ mol/L})^x(\cancel{0.00400} \text{ mol/L})^y}$$

or $2 = 2^x$ so $x = 1$ (*first order with respect to A*)

From Trial 1 to 3, [A] is constant, while [B] doubles. The result is a quadrupling of the reaction rate. This implies an exponential relationship between the reaction rate and [B] in which the rate is proportional to the [B] squared, and the process is second order with respect to B. Setting up a ratio of the rate laws for these two trials gives:

$$\frac{\text{rate 3}}{\text{rate 1}} = \frac{k[A]^x[B]^y}{k[A]^x[B]^y} \text{ thus } \frac{0.040 \text{ mol/L/s}}{0.010 \text{ mol/L/s}} = \frac{\cancel{k}(\cancel{0.00400 \text{ mol/L}})^x(0.00800 \text{ mol/L})^y}{\cancel{k}(\cancel{0.00400 \text{ mol/L}})^x(0.00400 \text{ mol/L})^y}$$

or $4 = 2^y$ so $y = 2$ (*second order with respect to B*)

The data indicates the following rate law:

reaction rate = $k[A][B]^2$

The **overall order** for a reaction is the sum of the orders with respect to each reactant; hence, in this case, the overall reaction order is 1 + 2 = 3 or third order.

Determining the Rate Constant

Once we have determined the orders with respect to each of the individual reactants, we can determine the numerical rate constant by substituting the rate and concentration values from any of the trials. In the example from the Warm Up, the rate law is: reaction rate = $k[A][B]^2$.

Therefore, the rate constant, $k = \frac{\text{reaction rate}}{[A][B]^2}$

Substitution of the values from Trial 1 in the table gives

$$k = \frac{0.010 \cancel{\text{mol/L}}/\text{s}}{(0.00400 \cancel{\text{mol/L}})(0.00400 \text{ mol/L})^2} = 1.6 \times 10^5 \text{ L}^2\text{mol}^{-2}\text{s}^{-1}$$

We determine the units for the rate constant by canceling the units in the substituted equation. As the overall orders for reactions become larger, the units for rate constants become more complex. We observe a general pattern for the rate constant units as shown in Table 4.4.2.

Table 4.4.2 *Pattern of Rate Constants from Zero to nth Order*

Zero Order	First Order	Second Order	*n*th Order (n >1)
$M\,L^{-1}s^{-1}$	s^{-1}	$M^{-1}\,L\,s^{-1}$	$mol^{(1-n)}\,L^{(n-1)}s^{-1}$

The magnitude of rate constants varies from one reaction to another. However, for a particular reaction, the value of the rate constant changes only if the temperature changes. In an actual experiment, the process of substitution to determine the numerical value of the rate would be repeated for each trial and all values would be averaged.

Sample Problem — Determining a Rate Law from Experimental Data

Bromate and bromide ions react in acidic solution to form bromine:

$$BrO_3^-(aq) + 5\,Br^-(aq) + 6\,H^+(aq) \rightarrow 3\,Br_2(l) + 3\,H_2O(l)$$

Use the data from this table to determine the rate law expression and the rate constant for the reaction.

Run	$[BrO_3^-]_{initial}$ (mol/L)	$[Br^-]_{initial}$ (mol/L)	$[H^+]_{initial}$ (mol/L)	Initial Rate (mol/L^{-1}s^{-1})
1	0.10	0.10	0.10	0.00080
2	0.20	0.10	0.10	0.00160
3	0.20	0.20	0.10	0.00320
4	0.10	0.10	0.20	0.00320

What to Think About

1. Identify two trials for which the concentration of only one reactant changes.
2. Set up a ratio to compare these two trials to one another. The value of the exponent that makes the ratio of the concentration change equal the ratio of the rates is the order with respect to the reactant for which the concentration changes between the two trials.
3. Repeat, comparing trials for which the concentration of a different reactant changes while the concentration of all other reactants remains constant.
4. Repeat this process for all reactants.
   Note that once the order of a particular species is known, we can calculate the order with respect to another reactant even if the concentration of the reactant with the known order changes. We substitute the value of the known order into the equation and attribute the changes in reaction rate to two different concentration changes.
5. Substitute the values for Trial 1 into the rate law and solve for the rate constant, *k*.

How to Do It

$$\frac{\text{rate 2}}{\text{rate 1}} = \frac{\cancel{k}(0.20)^x\cancel{(0.10)^y}\cancel{(0.10)^z}}{\cancel{k}(0.10)^x\cancel{(0.10)^y}\cancel{(0.10)^z}} = \frac{0.00160\ \cancel{M/s}}{0.00080\ \cancel{M/s}}$$

hence $2^x = 2$; therefore $x = 1$

$$\frac{\text{rate 3}}{\text{rate 2}} = \frac{\cancel{k(0.20)^x}(0.20)^y\cancel{(0.10)^z}}{\cancel{k(0.20)^x}(0.10)^y\cancel{(0.10)^z}} = \frac{0.00320\ \cancel{M/s}}{0.00160\ \cancel{M/s}}$$

hence $2^y = 2$; therefore $y = 1$

$$\frac{\text{rate 4}}{\text{rate 1}} = \frac{\cancel{k(0.10)^x}\cancel{(0.10)^y}(0.20)^z}{\cancel{k(0.10)^x}\cancel{(0.10)^y}(0.10)^z} = \frac{0.00320\ \cancel{M/s}}{0.00080\ \cancel{M/s}}$$

hence $2^z = 4$; therefore $z = 2$

$$\text{rate} = k[BrO_3^-][Br^-][H^+]^2$$

$$k = \frac{\text{rate}}{[BrO_3^-][Br^-][H^+]^2}$$

$$k = \frac{0.00080\ \cancel{mol/L}\cdot s}{(0.10\ \cancel{mol/L})(0.10\ mol/L)(0.10\ mol/L)^2}$$

$$k = 8.0\ L^3mol^{-3}s^{-1}$$

Practice Problems — Determining Rate Laws from Experimental Data

1. Use the information in the table below to write the rate-law expression for the reaction, and explain how you obtained your answer. Determine the rate constant with units.

   $2\ NO(g) + O_2(g) \rightarrow 2\ NO_2(g)$

Experiment Number	Initial $[O_2]$ ($mol{\cdot}L^{-1}$)	Initial [NO] ($mol{\cdot}L^{-1}$)	Initial Rate of Formation of NO_2 ($mol{\cdot}L^{-1}{\cdot}s^{-1}$)
1	0.0010	0.0010	x
2	0.0010	0.0020	$2x$
3	0.0020	0.0010	$2x$
4	0.0020	0.0020	$4x$

2. Consider an imaginary reaction: $2\ X + Y \rightarrow Z$. Determine the rate law and the rate constant, with units, from the experimental data in the table below.

Initial Rate of Formation of Z ($mol{\cdot}L^{-1}{\cdot}s^{-1}$)	Initial $[X]_o$ ($mol{\cdot}L^{-1}$)	Initial $[Y]_o$ ($mol{\cdot}L^{-1}$)
7.0×10^{-4}	0.20	0.10
1.4×10^{-3}	0.40	0.20
2.8×10^{-3}	0.40	0.40
4.2×10^{-3}	0.60	0.60

3. The following systems represent gaseous reactants A (symbolized by ○ and B (symbolized by ■) at a fixed temperature and volume. The equation for the reaction is $A(g) + B(g) \rightarrow C(g)$.

   Assume the rate law for the reaction is: rate = $k[A][B]^3$

   System 1 represents a reaction with a rate of 0.010 $molL^{-1}s^{-1}$. Complete the diagrams for the other systems as follows:

   (a) Adding enough particles of A ○) to System 2 to represent a system that would react with an initial rate of 0.020 $molL^{-1}s^{-1}$.

   (b) Adding enough particles of B (■) to System 3 to represent a system that would react with an initial rate of 0.080 $molL^{-1}s^{-1}$.

System 1 System 2 System 3

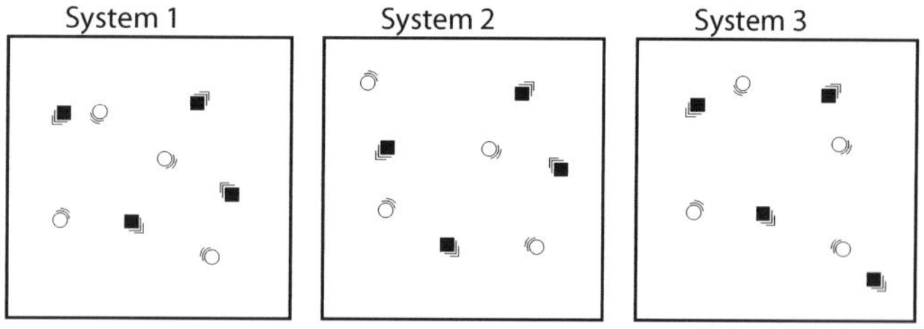

Rate = 0.010 mol $L^{-1}s^{-1}$ 0.020 mol $L^{-1}s^{-1}$ 0.080 mol $L^{-1}s^{-1}$

Determining a Rate Law from Laboratory Data

In summary, to determine a rate law for a reaction, we start by measuring the initial rate of reaction for at least two trials while varying the concentration of one of the reacting species and keeping the concentrations of the other reactants constant. We continue the experimental analysis by continuing to perform comparison trials varying the concentration of each reacting species while keeping the concentrations of the other reactants constant until we collect enough data to determine the rate law (Figure 4.4.3). Once we have determined the general rate law expression, we can calculate the rate constant by algebraic substitution.

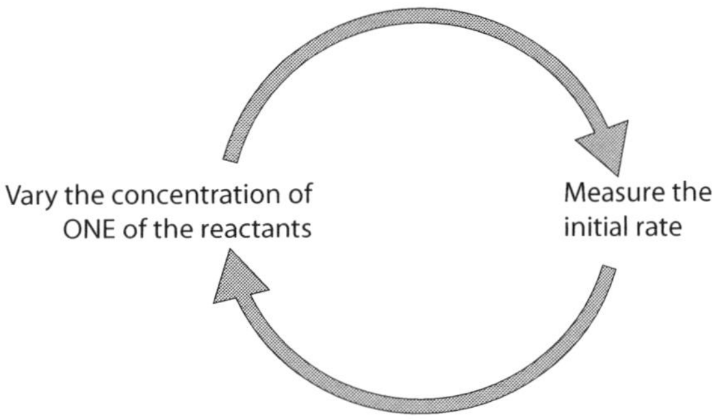

Figure 4.4.3 *A cycle to determine rate laws from experimental data. Continue this cycle until the orders with respect to all reactants have been determined.*

4.4 Review Questions

1. Consider the hypothetical reaction: X + Y → Z and the following data:

Initial Rate of Appearance of Z ($mol\ L^{-1}s^{-1}$)	$[X]_0$ (mol/L)	$[Y]_0$ (mol/L)
0.053	0.05	0.25
0.127	0.10	0.15
1.02	0.20	0.30
0.254	0.10	0.30
0.509	0.20	0.15

(a) Use the data in the table to determine the rate law for the reaction.

(b) Determine the value of the rate constant with units.

(c) Determine the initial rate of appearance of Z when the concentration of X is 0.15 mol/L and that of Y is 0.20 mol/L.

2. Nitrosyl fluoride, NO_2F, can be made by reacting NO_2 and F_2 gases as follows:

$$2\ NO_2(g) + F_2(g) \rightarrow 2\ NO_2F(g)$$

The following table represents data collected for the rate of formation of nitrosyl fluoride at room temperature. Recall that $mol\ L^{-1}$ is equivalent to mol/L.

$[NO_2]_0$ ($mol \cdot L^{-1}$)	$[F_2]_0$ ($mol \cdot L^{-1}$)	Rate ($mol \cdot L^{-1} \cdot s^{-1}$)
0.00100	0.00100	4.00×10^{-5}
0.00100	0.00300	1.20×10^{-4}
0.00500	0.00300	6.00×10^{-4}
0.00500	0.00500	1.00×10^{-3}

(a) Use the data in the table to determine the rate law for the reaction.

(b) Calculate the rate constant at room temperature. Include appropriate units.

3. The following trials were performed during the kinetic study of an oxidation-reduction reaction:

$$2\,MnO_4^-(aq) + 5\,H_2C_2O_4(aq) + 6\,H^+(aq) \rightarrow 2\,Mn^{2+}(aq) + 10\,CO_2(g) + 8\,H_2O(l)$$

$[MnO_4^-]_{initial}$ (mol/L)	$[H_2C_2O_4]_{initial}$ (mol/L)	$[H^+]_{initial}$ (mol/L)	Initial Rate of Formation of Mn^{2+} (mol $L^{-1}s^{-1}$)
1.0×10^{-3}	1.0×10^{-3}	1.0	2.0×10^{-4}
2.0×10^{-3}	1.0×10^{-3}	1.0	8.0×10^{-4}
2.0×10^{-3}	2.0×10^{-3}	1.0	1.6×10^{-3}
2.0×10^{-3}	2.0×10^{-3}	2.0	1.6×10^{-3}

(a) Use the data in the table for the initial rates of formation of the manganese(II) ion to determine the rate law and the rate constant for the redox reaction.

(b) By what factor would the initial reaction rate change if the concentrations of all three reactants doubled?

(c) By what factor would the initial reaction rate change if the volume of the reaction system doubled due to the addition of distilled water?

4. The equation for a general reaction is: $2\,A(g) + 2\,B(g) \rightarrow C(g) + 2\,D(g)$. The initial rate of formation of C is determined in four trials with various initial concentrations of reactants as shown in the table.

Trial Number	Initial [A] (mol·L^{-1})	Initial [B] (mol·L^{-1})	Initial Reaction Rate (mol·L^{-1}·s^{-1})
1	0.100	0.100	4.00×10^{-5}
2	0.200	0.100	1.60×10^{-4}
3	0.100	0.200	4.00×10^{-5}
4	0.300	0.200	?

(a) Determine the rate law for the reaction.

(b) Determine the rate constant with units.

(c) Calculate the initial reaction rate for Trial 4.

5. The table below provides data obtained under lab conditions for the reaction:

$$2\ MnO_4^{2-} + H_3IO_6^{2-} \rightarrow 2\ MnO_4^- + IO_3^- + 3\ OH^-$$

The experimental trials involved measuring the initial rate of formation of the iodate (IO_3^-) ion with varying initial concentrations of reactants.

Experimental Trial	$[MnO_4^{2-}]_0$ (mol·L^{-1})	$[H_3IO_6^{2-}]_0$ (mol·L^{-1})	Initial Rate (M L^{-1}min^{-1})
1	1.6×10^{-4}	3.1×10^{-4}	2.6×10^{-6}
2	6.4×10^{-4}	3.1×10^{-4}	4.2×10^{-5}
3	1.6×10^{-4}	6.2×10^{-4}	2.6×10^{-6}
4	3.2×10^{-4}	3.1×10^{-4}	?
5	?	6.2×10^{-4}	2.3×10^{-5}

(a) Determine the rate law for the reaction.

(b) Calculate the rate constant with units.

(c) What is the initial rate of formation of IO_3^- ion for Trial 4?

(d) What is the required initial concentration of MnO_4^{2-} ion for Trial 5?

(e) What is the initial rate of formation of MnO_4^- ion for Trial 1?

6. The equation for the bromination of acetone in acidic solution is:

$$CH_3COCH_3(aq) + Br_2(aq) \rightarrow CH_3COCH_2Br(aq) + H^+(aq) + Br^-(aq)$$

The following data were collected in four trials by varying the concentration of reactants and measuring the initial rate of disappearance of aqueous bromine ($Br_2(aq)$).

Trial Number	$[CH_3COCH_3]_0$ (mol/L)	$[Br_2]_0$ (mol/L)	$[H^+]_0$ (mol/L)	Initial Rate (mol L^{-1}s^{-1})
1	0.30	0.050	0.050	5.7×10^{-5}
2	0.30	0.100	0.050	5.7×10^{-5}
3	0.30	0.100	0.100	1.4×10^{-4}
4	0.40	0.050	0.200	3.2×10^{-4}

Determine the rate law and the rate constant (with appropriate units) for the acidic bromination of acetone.

4.5 Integrated Rate Equations

Warm Up

Graph the following data using the grids provided.

Time (s)	Concentration (mol/L)	ln Concentration	1/Concentration (L/mol)
0	0.500		
10	0.197		
20	0.078		
30	0.031		
40	0.012		
50	0.005		

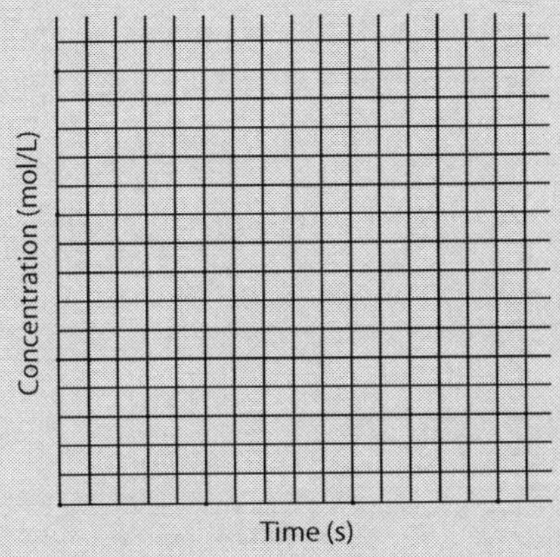

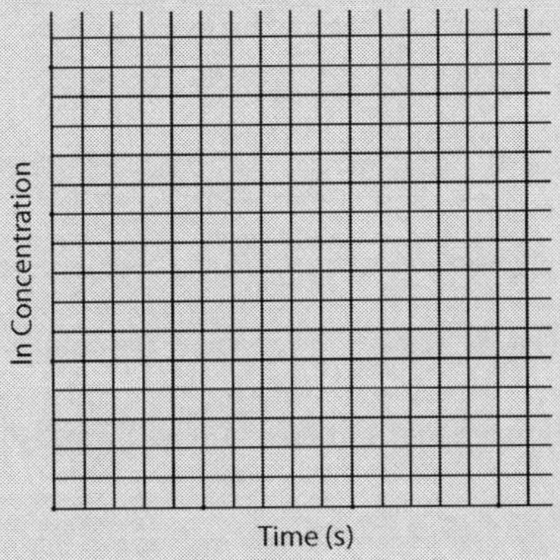

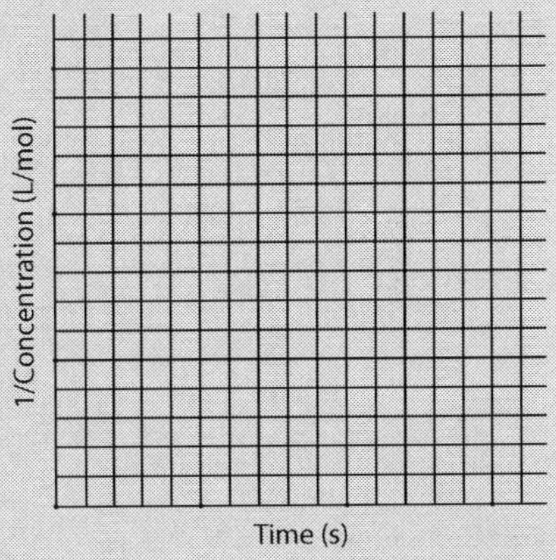

Before answering these questions, you may find it helpful to review the graphical relationships in your M4 Chemistry textbook.

1. Which set of data gives represents a direct relationship?

   ____

2. What type of relationship do the other sets of data represent?

   ____

3. Determine the equation for the straight-line graph.

Integrating Rate Laws — Relating Concentration to Time

In section 4.4, we learned how to determine the rate law for a chemical reaction by comparing experimentally determined initial rates with concentrations of reactants. Measuring the initial rate of a reaction involves determining small changes in the concentration of a reactant or product during a very short time interval. It can be difficult to obtain sufficiently precise experimental data for such small changes. An alternative is to use an **integrated rate law**, which expresses the *concentration of a species directly as a function of time*. For a *simple rate expression* (also called a *differential rate expression*), calculus provides the math to calculate a corresponding integrated rate law. In deducing the rate law from experimental data, we can analyze the integrated rate laws for zero-, first-, and second-order reactions to determine which equation fits the data.

Using Calculus to Derive Integrated Rate Equations

If you have taken a calculus course this year, you may already know how to find a derivative. A derivative function is an equation that defines a rate of change. In the kinetics unit, we determined the rate of change of some measurable property during a chemical reaction over a period of time (e.g., the change in concentration of a reactant or product over time). Solving for an antiderivative is the reverse operation of finding a derivative. For integration calculations, we determine antiderivatives over the endpoints of an interval. In kinetics, we consider the interval from time zero to a time, *t*. Over this interval, we are interested in how an initial concentration, *C* changes to a new concentration, *C*.

Some antiderivatives are fairly easy to express and others are more challenging. The following table shows three functions, $f(x)$, the antiderivatives of these functions, $F(x)$, and the integrals of these functions between two points, x_2 and x_1, where a is a constant.

Table 4.5.1 *Applying Calculus to Derive Integrated Rate Equations*

Function $f(x)$	Antiderivative $F(x)$	Integral $\int_{x_1}^{x_2} f(x)\,dx$
a	ax	$ax_2 - ax_1$
$1/x = x^{-1}$ $(x>0)$	$\ln x$	$(\ln x_2 - \ln x_1) = \ln (x_2/x_1)$
$1/x^2 = x^{-2}$	$-1/x = -x^{-1}$	$-(1/x_2 - 1/x_1)$

You will not be required to produce derivatives, antiderivatives, or integrals as part of the AP Chemistry course. However, the following discussion will help you understand the derivation of three important integrated rate equations in AP Chemistry.

First-Order Rate Laws

Dinitrogen pentoxide decomposes as follows: $N_2O_5(g) \rightarrow 2\ NO_2(g) + \frac{1}{2}\ O_2(g)$. From experimental data, scientists determined the rate law for this reaction follows first-order kinetics, expressed as follows:

$$\text{rate} = \frac{-\Delta[N_2O_5]}{\Delta t} = \frac{-d[N_2O_5]}{dt} = k[N_2O_5]$$

The negative sign indicates the decrease in reactant concentration. A derivative is a rate of change, hence we replace the symbol Δ, which means "change in," by *d*. Replacement of $[N_2O_5]$ with *C* (for concentration) gives the following equation for the change in concentration as a function of time:

First-order reaction: $$\frac{dC}{dt} = -kC$$

Multiplying both sides by *dt* and dividing both sides by *C* results in: $(1/C)dC = -kdt$

Referencing Table 4.5.1 shows that integration from an initial concentration C_0 at time = 0 to a concentration *C* at time = *t* appears as follows:

$$\int_{C_0}^{C} \frac{1}{C} dC = -k\int_0^t dt$$

This gives $\ln C - \ln C_0 = -kt$, which we can also express as

$$\ln\left(\frac{C}{C_0}\right) = -kt$$

The linear $y = mx + b$ equation of this first-order integrated rate equation becomes:

$$\ln C = -kt + \ln C_0$$

Integrated first-order rate equation: $\ln C = -kt + \ln C_0$ or $\ln\left(\frac{C}{C_0}\right) = -kt$

Sample Problem — Calculating the Time Required to Reach a Desired Concentration

Dinitrogen pentoxide is the unstable anhydride of nitric acid that decomposes by first-order kinetics into nitrogen dioxide and oxygen gas, as shown earlier in this section. The rate law is rate = $k[N_2O_5]$. The rate constant for the reaction is $6.22 \times 10^{-4}\ s^{-1}$ at 45°C. If the initial concentration of N_2O_5 is 0.500 mol/L, how long will it take for the concentration to drop to 0.0500 mol/L?

What to Think About	How to Do It
1. Determine the order for the reaction.	The question states that the reaction is first order. The exponent in the rate law ($r = k[N_2O_5]$) is a 1 and the units for the rate constant are also consistent with a first-order rate law. The units of the rate constant of first-order reactions are always the reciprocal of a unit of time (in this case the unit is s^{-1}).
2. Substitute into the integrated rate equation for a first-order reaction. Take care not to drop the negative sign. Be sure to substitute the values of C and C_0 correctly.	Since $\ln(C/C_0) = -kt$, $t = \frac{\ln(C/C_0)}{-k}$ $t = \frac{\ln(0.0500\ M/0.500\ M)}{-6.22 \times 10^{-4}\ s^{-1}} = 3.70 \times 10^3\ s$

Sample Problem — Calculating the Concentration of a Reactant After a Given Period of Time

If the initial concentration of N_2O_5 is 0.250 mol/L at 45°C, what is the concentration after exactly 1 h?

What to Think About	How to Do It
1. The previous example indicates that the decomposition reaction is first order. Use the integrated rate equation for a first-order reaction to solve for ln C.	$\ln C = -kt + \ln C_0$ $= -6.22 \times 10^{-4}\ s^{-1}(3600\ s) + \ln 0.250\ mol/L$ $= -3.62$
2. Use the inverse ln function, or e^x to determine the concentration. Take care not to drop the negative sign.	$C = \text{antiln } -3.62 = e^{-3.62}$ $= 0.0266\ mol/L$

Practice Problems — Relating Concentrations and Time in First-order reactions

1. What is the rate constant for a first-order reaction with an initial reactant concentration of 0.300 mol/L if, after 158 s, the concentration is 0.200 mol/L?

2. The reaction in question 1 occurs at the same temperature with an initial reactant concentration of 1.50 mol/L. What is the reactant's concentration 2.75 min later?

3. The reaction in question 1 reacts for 5.00 min at the same temperature until the reactant concentration drops to 0.0100 mol/L. What was the reactant's initial concentration?

Second-Order Rate Laws

Another oxide of nitrogen, nitrogen dioxide, decomposes as follows:

$$2\ NO_2(g) \rightarrow 2\ NO(g) + O_2(g)$$

From experimental data, scientists determined that this reaction is second order with respect to the concentration of NO_2. Hence the following is true:

$$\text{rate} = \frac{-d[NO_2]}{dt} = k[NO_2]^2$$

Replacing $[NO_2]$ with the more general symbol C:

$$\textbf{Second-order reaction: } \frac{dC}{dt} = -kC^2$$

Algebraic manipulation of the second-order rate expression results in

$$\frac{1}{C^2}dC = -kdt$$

Integrating from an initial concentration, C_0 at time = 0 to C at time = t gives:

$$\int_{C_0}^{C} \frac{1}{C^2}dC = -k\int_0^t dt$$

This becomes: $-1/C + 1/C_0 = -kt$ or in the format of the linear equation ($y = mx + b$): $1/C = kt + 1/C_0$.

$$\textbf{Integrated second-order rate equation: } \frac{1}{C} = kt + \frac{1}{C_0}$$

Sample Problem — Calculating Concentration after a Given Period of Time for a Second-Order Reaction

Nitrosyl chloride, NOCl, is a corrosive orange gas that intensely irritates membranes in the human body, including eyes and skin. It decomposes slowly to form the gases NO and Cl_2 by second-order reaction kinetics with a rate constant, $k = 0.020$ L/mol·s. Given an initial concentration of 0.450 mol/L, what concentration of NOCl will remain after 40.0 h of decomposition?

What to Think About	How to Do It
1. Determine the reaction order.	The reaction is second order as stated in the question. A second-order rate law is also consistent with the units of the rate constant. The units of the product of reciprocal molarity and reciprocal time indicate a second-order reaction.
2. Substitute into the integrated rate equation for a second-order reaction.	$1/C = kt + 1/C_0$ $1/C = 0.020 \text{ L mol}^{-1} \text{s}^{-1} \times (40.0 \text{ h} \times 3600 \text{ s}/1 \text{ h}) + 1/0.450 \text{ mol/L}$ $= 2882 \text{ L/mol}$
3. Apply algebra to solve for *C*.	Thus $C = (2882 \text{ L/mol})^{-1}$ $= 3.5 \times 10^{-4} \text{ mol/L}$

Practice Problems — Relating Concentrations and Time in Second-Order Reactions

1. Refer to the reaction in Sample Problem above and determine how long it will take for a sample of NOCl with an initial concentration of 0.038 mol/L to drop to 0.012 mol/L.

2. Pharmacokinetics is the study of how the body takes up, distributes, and eliminates drugs. The elimination of a newly designed Canadian drug from the body follows second-order kinetics. The drug is called Zippidy Eh. Its molar mass is 122.0 g/mol. The rate constant for the elimination process is 2.4 L mol^{-1} min^{-1}. If the initial dose of Zippidy Eh is 250 mg for a 70 kg patient with a blood volume of 4.8 L, what mass of the drug will remain 12 h after ingestion?

Zero-Order Rate Equations

Most reactions involving a single reactant follow either first- or second-order kinetics. However, zero-order kinetics with respect to a reactant are possible. In first- and second-order reactions, the rate of reaction is fastest at the beginning of the reaction when the concentration of the reactant is the greatest. In zero-order reactions, the reaction rate is constant throughout the reaction and is independent of the reaction concentration.

$$\textbf{Zero-order reaction: } \frac{dC}{dt} = kC^{0} = k(1) = k$$

For a zero-order reaction, the rate does not depend on concentration. Only temperature or the presence of a catalyst can affect the rate of a zero-order reaction.

$$\textbf{Integrated zero-order rate equation: } C = -kt + C_0$$

Zero-order reactions are common when reactions occur in the presence of a heterogeneous enzyme. Exposing the surface of the enzyme provides a lower activation energy pathway for the reaction. The reaction's rate depends on the enzyme's available surface area rather than the concentration of the reactant.

Graphical Method for Distinguishing Orders of Reactions

In the previous section, we used an algebraic method to determine reaction order using given initial rates and reactant concentrations. In the laboratory, initial rates are not easily determined. In fact, some kinetics experiments use the reciprocal of time as an indicator of initial reaction rate since these two values are directly proportional. One way to study a reaction's rate is by collecting changes in concentration values as a function of time. Graphing this data allows us to determine which of the integrated rate equations plots as a straight line.

First-order reactions are more common than zero- or second-order reactions. In a first-order reaction, a plot of C versus time looks like the graphs we studied in section 4.1. The tangent line is steepest at the beginning of the reaction when the rate is the greatest. Plotting ln C versus time gives a straight line with a negative slope. The absolute value of the slope is equal to the rate constant. The value of the *rate constant must always be positive*. The *y*-intercept is equal to ln C_0. The reciprocal of concentration versus time gives a parabolic shape with an upward curve (Figure 4.5.1).

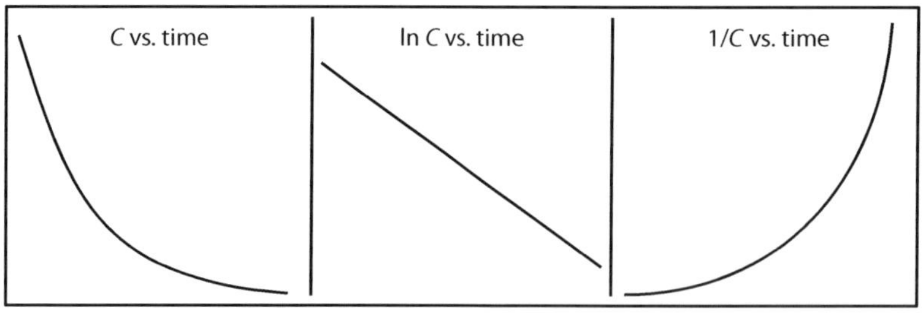

Figure 4.5.1 *Typical graphs for a first-order reaction*

A plot of C versus time for a second-order reaction produces a curve similar to that of a plot of C versus time for a first-order reaction. The ln C-versus-time plot of a second-order reaction produces a graph that is slightly less curved than the C-versus-time plot. Unlike the curve produced for a first-order reaction, a plot of the reciprocal of C versus time for second-order reactions gives a straight line with a positive slope. The slope of this line is equal to the rate constant. The *y*-intercept is equal to $1/C_0$ (Figure 4.5.2).

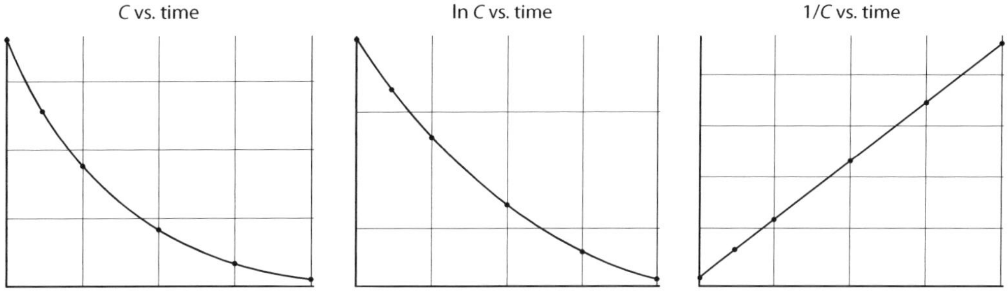

Figure 4.5.2 *Typical graphs for a second-order reaction*

The relationship between C and time for a zero-order reaction is simply a straight-line graph with a negative slope. The absolute value of the slope is equal to the rate constant for the reaction. For zero-order reactions, the ln C-versus-time relationship is a convex curve with increasingly steep negatively sloped tangents and the $1/C$-versus-time plot is a concave curve with increasingly steep positively sloped tangents (Figure 4.5.3).

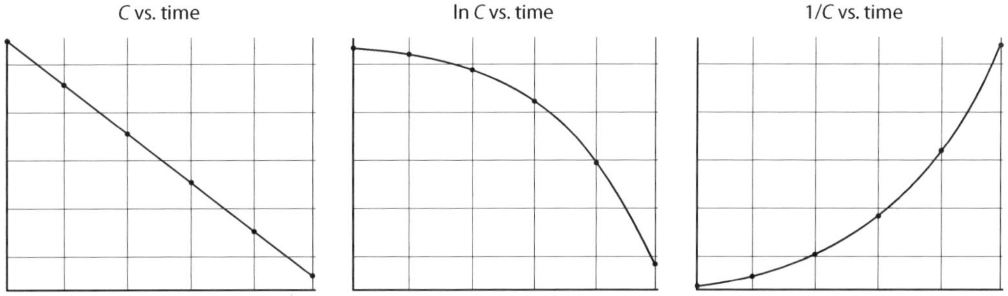

Figure 4.5.3 *Typical graphs for a zero-order reaction*

Straight-line integrated rate equations:

zero order: $C = -kt + C_0$

first order: $\ln C = -kt + \ln C_0$

second order: $\frac{1}{C} = kt + \frac{1}{C_0}$

Sample Problem — Graphical Analysis of Integrated Rate Equations

Nitrosyl bromide is a reddish brown gas that decomposes into nitrogen monoxide and bromine:

$$2\ NOBr(g) \rightarrow 2\ NO(g) + Br_2(g)$$

Complete the following table of experimental data for the decomposition. Plot three graphs to determine whether the reaction is zero, first, or second order with respect to NOBr. Write the rate law expression and determine the rate constant with units.

Time (s)	[NOBr] (mol/L)	ln [NOBr]	1/[NOBr] (L/mol)
0.00	0.0100		
2.00	0.0071		
4.00	0.0055		
6.00	0.0045		
8.00	0.0038		
10.00	0.0033		

Continued

Sample Problem (*Continued*)

What to Think About

1. Complete the data table for the missing columns.

How to Do It

Time (s)	ln [NOBr]	1/[NOBr] ($M^{-1}L$)
0.00	−4.61	100.
2.00	−4.95	141
4.00	−5.20	182
6.00	−5.40	222
8.00	−5.57	263
10.00	−5.71	303

2. Plot graphs of:
   [NOBr] vs. time
   ln [NOBr] vs. time
   1/[NOBr] vs. time

3. The [NOBr] vs. time graph is curved. This indicates the decomposition is not zero order.

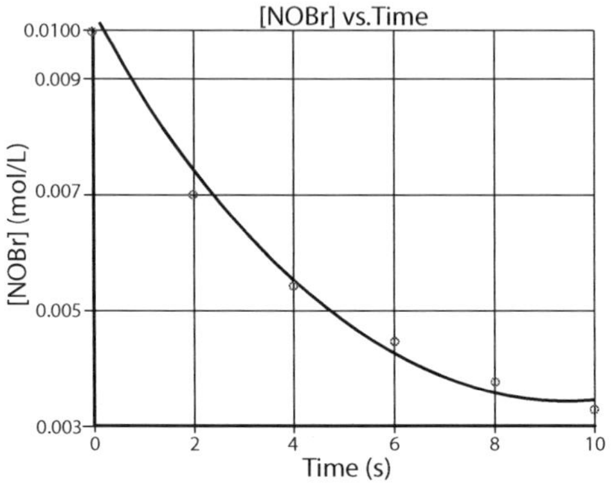

4. The ln [NOBr] vs. time graph is also curved, indicating the decomposition is not first order.

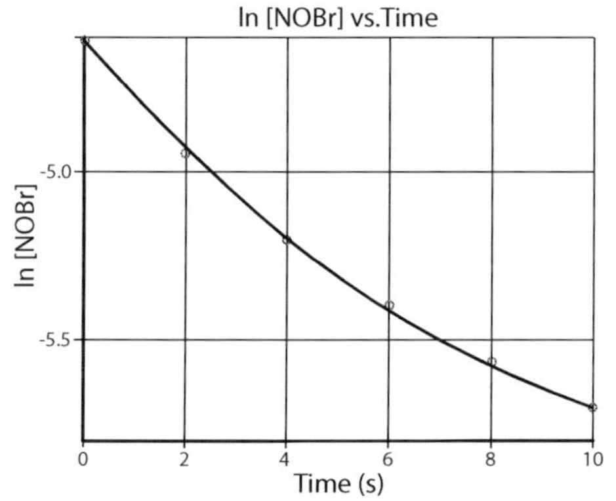

5. You may have predicted that the reciprocal plot would be a straight line by examining the changes every 2 s. Both [NOBr] and ln [NOBr] decrease most rapidly at the beginning of the reaction, while 1/[NOBr] increases by about 40 M^{-1} in each 2 s increment.

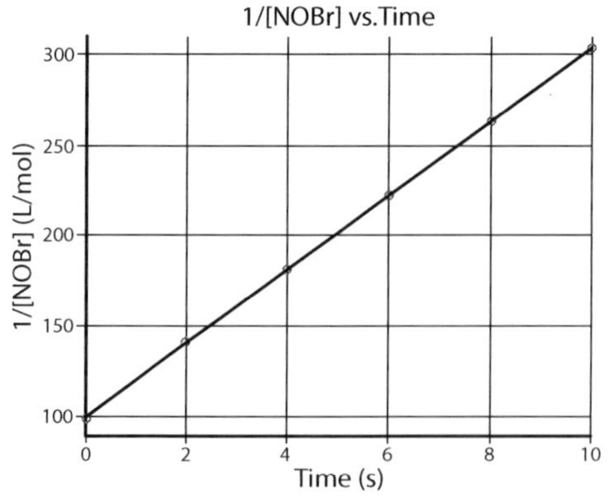

6. Determine the rate constant by finding the slope of the straight-line graph.

The 1/[NOBr] vs. time graph produces a straight line; hence, the decomposition is a second-order reaction.

rate = $k[NOBr]^2$

The straight-linegraph-shows a slope = k

= the rate constant

= 20.L/mol•s in denominator

Practice Problems — Graphic Analysis of Integrated Rate Equations

1. We can use **pseudo integrated rate analysis** when a reaction involves more than one reactant. We use a large excess of one of the reactants to manipulate the system so that the change in the concentration of the excess reactant is negligible. The value of the concentration of the excess reactant is subsumed into the rate constant because it barely changes and is therefore constant within the margin of error. We determine the order with respect to the species that is present in a very small concentration. We refer to the absolute value of the slope of the straight line plot as the **pseudo rate constant, *k′*** (*k* prime). We determine the actual rate constant by dividing *k′* by the [excess].
A student collected the following data during a laboratory study of the substitution reaction:
$(CH_3)_3CBr + OH^- \rightarrow (CH_3)_3COH + Br^-$ with a large excess of OH^-.

Time (s)	$[(CH_3)_3CBr]$ mol/L	ln $[(CH_3)_3CBr]$	$1/[(CH_3)_3CBr]$ L mol^{-1}s^{-1}
0	0.100		
30	0.074		
60	0.055		
90	0.041		

Draw graphs of $[(CH_3)_3CBr]$ vs. time, ln $[(CH_3)_3CBr]$ vs. time, and $1/[(CH_3)_3CBr]$ vs. time. Is the substitution reaction zero, first, or second order with respect to $(CH_3)_3CBr$? What is the value of the pseudo rate constant with units?

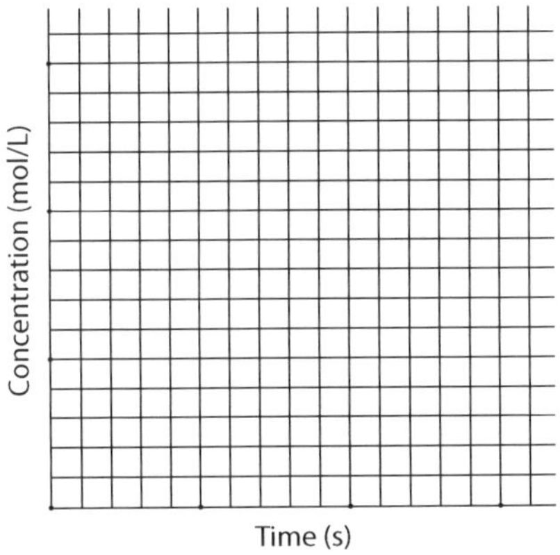

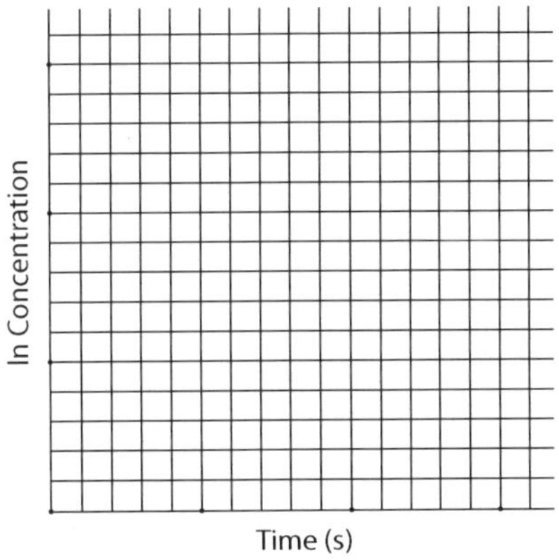

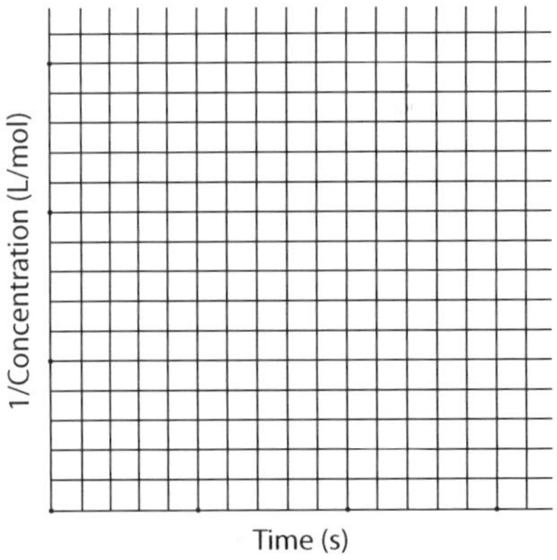

2. Nitrogen dioxide decomposes as indicated in the following equation:
$$2\ NO_2(g) \rightarrow 2\ NO(g) + O_2(g)$$
A student collected the following data for the decomposition at an elevated temperature.

Time (s)	$[NO_2]$ (mol/L)	ln $[NO_2]$	$1/[NO_2]$ (L/mol·s)
0	0.0100		
50.	0.0079		
100.	0.0065		
200.	0.0048		
300.	0.0038		
400.	0.0032		

(a) Draw three graphs and determine the rate law expression and the rate constant with units for the decomposition of nitrogen dioxide.

Continued

Practice Problems (*Continued*)

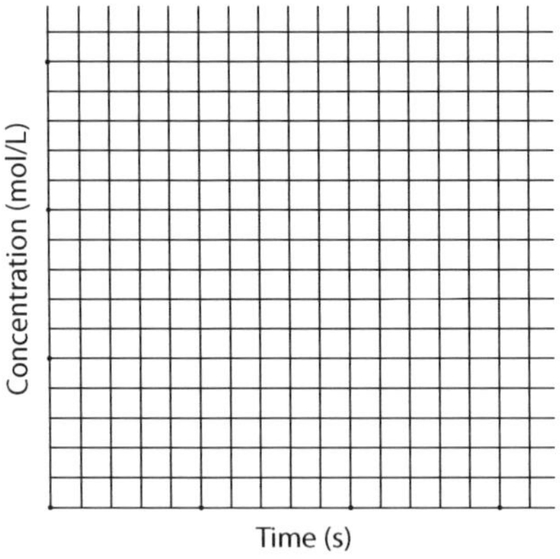

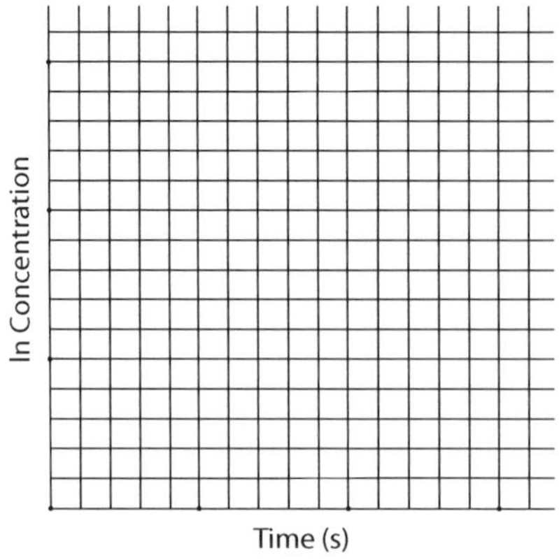

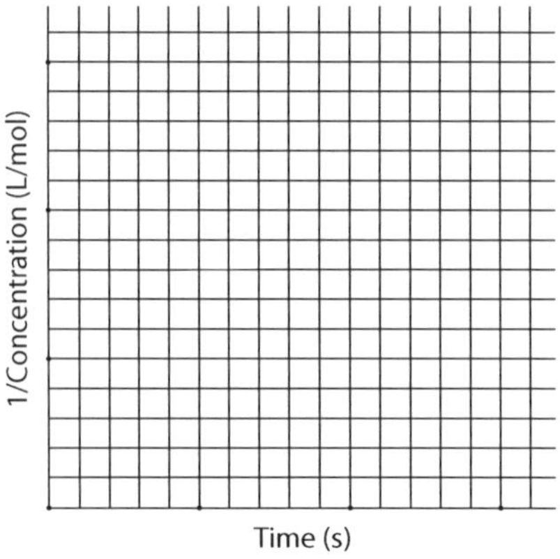

(b) How would the straight-line graph change (in general) if:
 (i) the initial concentration of the nitrogen dioxide were increased?

 (ii) the temperature of the decomposition were elevated?

Half-Life

The magnitude of the rate constant k is a good indication of the speed of a chemical reaction. The larger the magnitude of the rate constant, the greater the rate of a reaction. The *half-life of a reaction* is another useful measure of the rate of a reaction (Figure 4.5.4). You may have heard about half-lives in an earlier course in science, most likely associated with nuclear radiation.

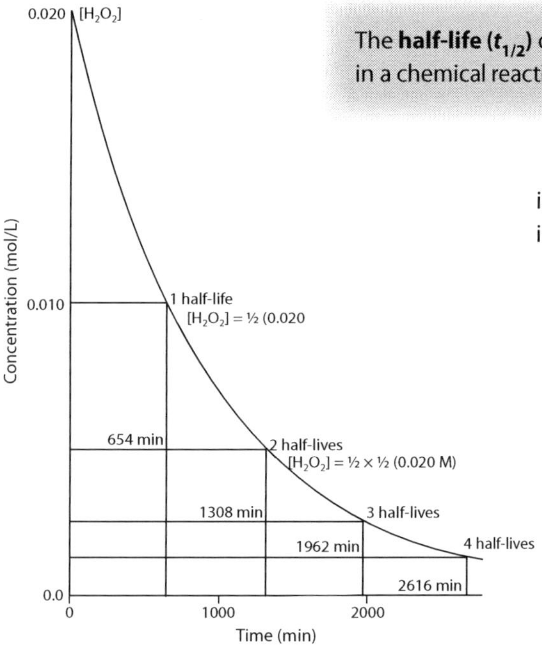

Figure 4.5.4 *A graph of the concentration of hydrogen peroxide against time shows the $[H_2O_2]$ dropping to one-half of its previous concentration every 654 min.*

The **half-life ($t_{1/2}$)** of a reaction is the time it takes for one-half of a reactant to be consumed in a chemical reaction.

To derive an equation for the half-life of a reaction, substitute $1/2C_0$ for C in the integrated rate equation and solve for time. For example, in a first-order integrated rate equation:

$\ln (1/2C_0) = -kt_{1/2} + \ln C_0$

Subtracting $\ln C_0$ from both sides of the equation gives:

$\ln (1/2C_0) - \ln C_0 = -kt_{1/2}$

Applying the logarithm quotient rule gives:

$\ln [1/2C_0/C_0] = -kt_{1/2}$

Cancelling C_0/C_0 gives:

$\ln (1/2) = -kt_{1/2}$

Finally, multiplying both sides by −1 gives:

$\ln 2 = kt_{1/2}$

For a first-order reaction: $t_{1/2} = \ln 2/k = 0.693/k$ and $k = \ln 2/t_{1/2} = 0.693/t_{1/2}$

Sample Problem — Half-life of a First-Order Reaction

The rate constant for the catalyzed isomerization of *cis*-2-butene gas to produce trans-2-butene gas is 0.00693 s^{-1}.

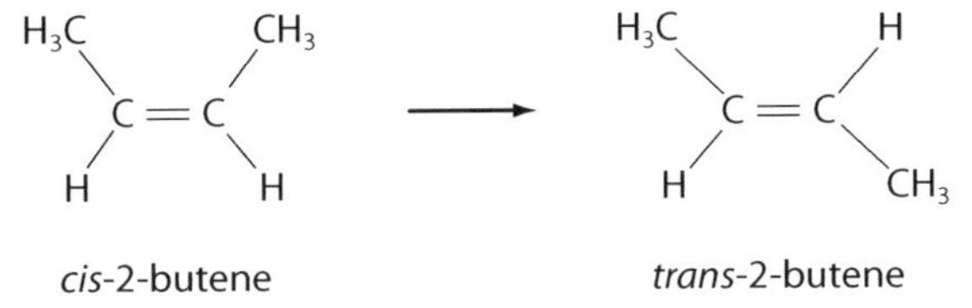

(a) What is the half-life of the reaction?
(b) What fraction of the original *cis*-2-butene sample remains 5.00 min after the reaction begins?
(c) If the original [*cis*-2-butene] were 3.45 mol/L, what concentration remains 7.00 min after the reaction begins?

What to Think About	How to Do It
1. Determine the order of the reaction so that you can apply the correct equations to calculate the half-life. A rate constant unit of reciprocal time is typical of a first-order reaction.	(a) For a first-order reaction: $t_{1/2} = \ln 2/k$ Thus $t_{1/2} = 0.693/0.00693\ s^{-1}$ $= 100.\ s$
2. Convert 5.00 min to seconds.	(b) 5.00 min x 60 s/1 min = 300. s This is equivalent to the time required for the reaction to go through three half-lives. The fraction of the original sample remaining after 3 half-lives is calculated by dividing by 2 three times: $1 \rightarrow 1/2 \rightarrow 1/4 \rightarrow 1/8$ remains
3. The time of 7.00 min does not divide by a whole number of half-lives. Using the integrated rate equation for first-order reactions, calculate the final concentration. The answer to (c) is slightly less than 1/16 (3.45 M) as it should be since 7.00 min is just over four half lives.	(c) $\ln C = -kt + \ln C_0$ $= -0.00693\ s^{-1}(7.00\ min \times 60\ s/1\ min) + \ln 3.45\ mol/L$ $= -0.00693\ s^{-1}(420.\ s) + 1.24$ $= -1.67$ Finally, $C = e^{-1.67} = 0.188\ mol/L$

Practice Problems — Half-Life of a First-Order Reaction

1. The rate constant for the first order conversion of cyclopropane to propene in a laboratory is $9.0 \times 10^{-4}\ min^{-1}$.
   (a) What is the half-life of the reaction?

   (b) Assuming the initial concentration of the cyclopropane is 1.50 mol/L, what concentration will remain after 51.2 h?

2. The half-life for the decomposition of N_2O_5 under laboratory conditions is 2.0 min.
   (a) What is the rate constant for the reaction under these conditions?

   (b) What is the concentration of N_2O_5 270 s after the reaction starts, assuming an initial concentration of 0.180 mol/L?

   (c) How much time does it take for the concentration of N_2O_5 to drop from 0.180 mol/L to 0.100 mol/L?

Second-Order Half-Life Equations

Second-order half-life equations are derived in a similar way. The second-order integrated rate equation is $1/C = kt + 1/C_0$, which can be rearranged to:

$$1/C - 1/C_0 = kt$$

Setting $t = t_{1/2}$ and $C = 1/2C_0$ gives:

$$2/C_0 - 1/C_0 = kt_{1/2}$$

Solving for $t_{1/2}$ gives:

$$t_{1/2} = 1/kC_0$$

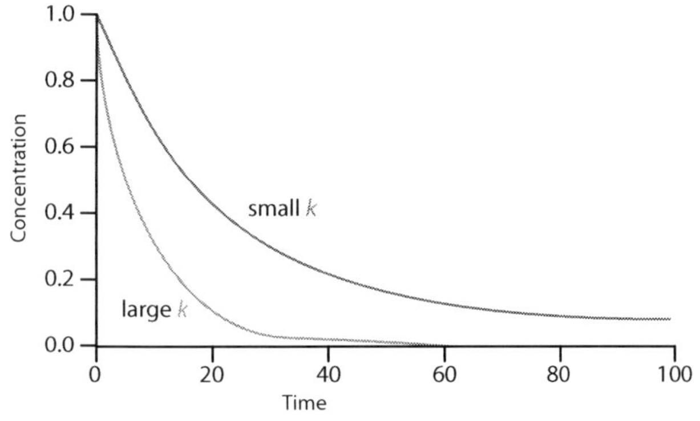

Figure 4.5.5 *Faster reactions have larger rate constants.*

For both first- and second-order reactions, $t_{1/2}$ is inversely proportional to k. This makes sense because the larger the value of k, the faster the reaction (Figure 4.5.5). The faster the reaction, the shorter the time required to consume half of the reactant.

The half-life for a second-order reaction is also inversely proportional to the initial concentration of the reactant. This means the smaller the C_0, the longer the $t_{1/2}$. Each successive half-life is double the length of the previous one.

For a *second-order reaction:* $t_{1/2} = \dfrac{1}{kC_0}$

Each successive $t_{1/2}$ is double the length of the previous $t_{1/2}$.

For a zero-order reaction, substituting $1/2C_0$ for C_0 and solving for t in the integrated rate equation demonstrates that the half-life is inversely proportional to k, but is directly related to the initial concentration of the reactant. As with first- and second-order reactions, a larger rate constant, k, means a faster reaction and a shorter half-life. A lower initial reactant concentration also leads to a shorter half-life. For zero-order reactions, each successive half-life is half the previous one (Figure 4.5.6).

For a *zero-order reaction*: $t_{1/2} = \dfrac{C_0}{2k}$

Each successive $t_{1/2}$ is half the length of the previous $t_{1/2}$.

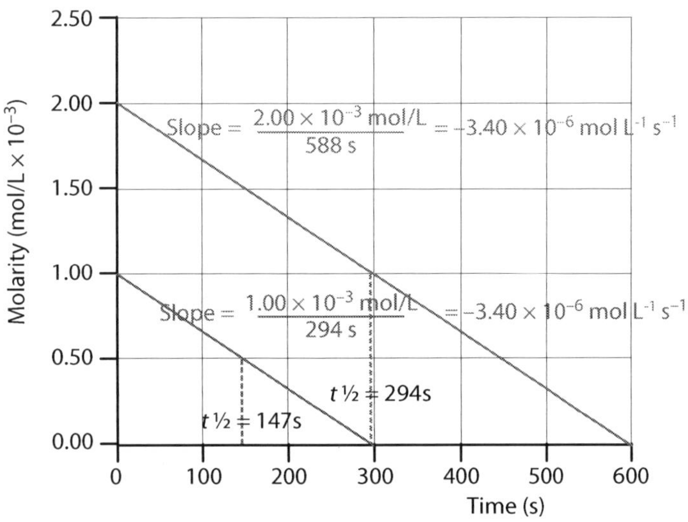

Figure 4.5.6 *A zero-order reaction gives a straight line with a negative slope when we plot concentration against time. A second plot shows that when we halve the reactant concentration, the half-life is also halved. The slope remains the same for both plots. The absolute value of the slope is equal to the rate constant k, which is the same for all reactant concentrations. (Note that the slope is also equal to the rate, which is constant for a zero-order reaction.)*

Sample Problem — Half-Life of a Second-Order Reaction

Earlier in this section, we determined that nitrosyl bromide, NOBr, decomposes via second-order kinetics with a rate constant of 20. L/mol·s under a particular set of laboratory conditions.

(a) What is the half-life for nitrosyl bromide?

(b) How long would it take the concentration of nitrosyl bromide to drop from 0.0100 mol/L to 0.0025 mol/L?

What to Think About

1. Determine the order of the reaction so that you can apply the correct equation to calculate the half-life. The units for the rate constant are (L/mol·s) and units of reciprocal molarity, reciprocal time are typical of a second-order reaction.

2. Remember that each successive half-life is twice the previous.

How to Do It

(a) For a second-order reaction:
$t_{1/2} = 1/kC_0$

$$t_{1/2} = \frac{1}{20.\ \cancel{L}/\cancel{mol}\cdot s(0.0100\ \cancel{mol}/\cancel{L})}$$

$= 1/0.20\ s^{-1} = 5.0\ s$

(b) Because 0.0025 mol/L is 1/4 of 0.0100 mol/L, 2 half-lives are required.

$5.0 + 2(5.0) = 5.0 + 10.0 = 15.0\ s$

Practice Problem — Half-life of Second and Zero-Order Reactions

1. The reaction $2\ HI(g) \rightarrow H_2(g) + I_2(g)$ has the rate law, rate = $k[HI]^2$, with $k = 0.0796\ L\ mol^{-1}s^{-1}$ at 500°C.

   (a) What is the half-life for this reaction when the initial concentration is 0.100 mol/L?

   (b) What is the concentration after 375 s if the initial concentration is 0.100 mol/L?

2. If the half-life of a reaction is independent of the initial concentration of the reactants, what do you know about the reaction?

Table 4.5.1 *Summary of Integrated Rate Laws and Half-Lives*

Order in C	Rate Law	Integrated Form $y = mx + b$	Rate Constant (k) Units	Straight Line Plot	Half-life $t_{1/2}$	Graph
Zero order (n=0)	rate = $kC^0 = k$	$C_t = -kt + C_0$	$\frac{\text{mol/L}}{\text{s}}$	C_t vs. t (slope = $-k$)	$t_{1/2} = \frac{C_0}{2k}$	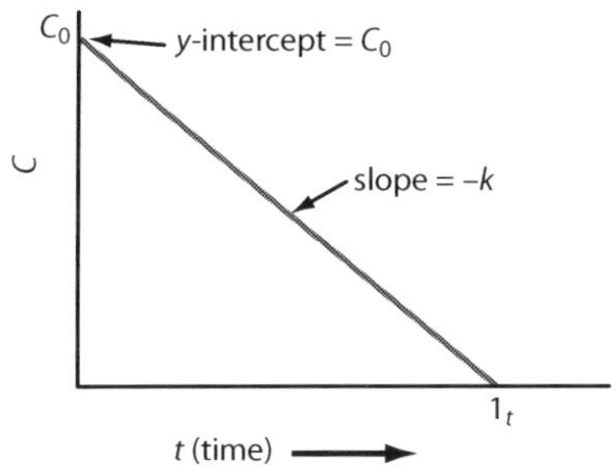
First order (n=1)	rate = kC^1	$\ln C_t = -kt + \ln C_0$	$\frac{1}{\text{s}}$	$\ln C_t$ vs. t (slope = $-k$)	$t_{1/2} = \frac{\ln 2}{k} = \frac{0.693}{k}$	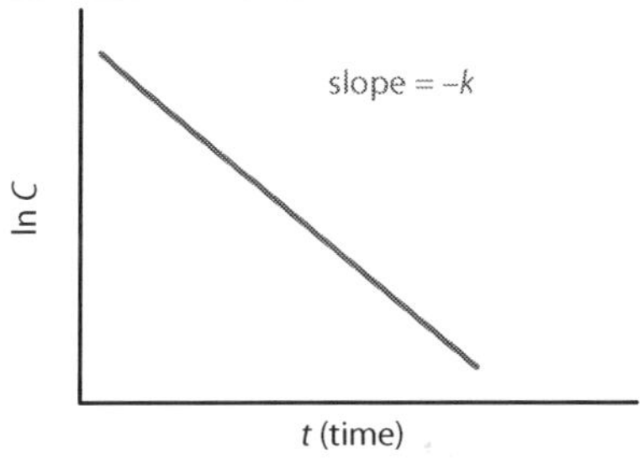
Second order (n=2)	rate = kC^2	$\frac{1}{C_t} = kt + \frac{1}{C_0}$	$\frac{1}{\text{mol/L}\cdot\text{s}}$	$\frac{1}{C_t}$ vs. t (slope = k)	$t_{1/2} = \frac{1}{kC_0}$	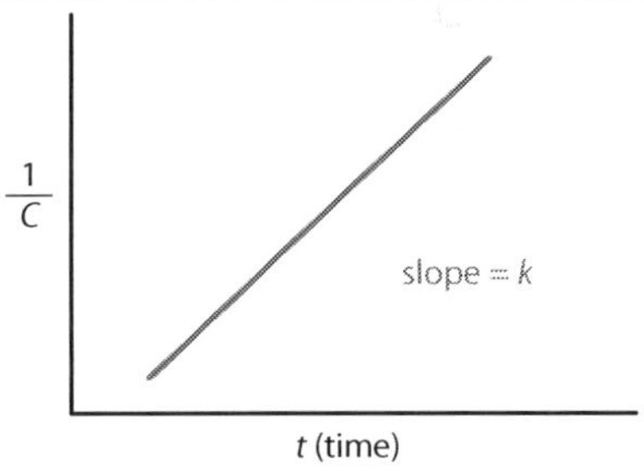
nth order	rate = kC^n	$\frac{1}{C^{(n-1)}} = (n-1)kt + \frac{1}{C_0^{(n-1)}}$	$\frac{1}{\text{mol/L}^{(n-1)}\cdot\text{s}}$	$\frac{1}{C_t^{(n-1)}}$ vs. t (slope = $(n-1)k$)	$t_{1/2} = \frac{2^{(n-1)}-1}{(n-1)kC_0^{(n-1)}}$	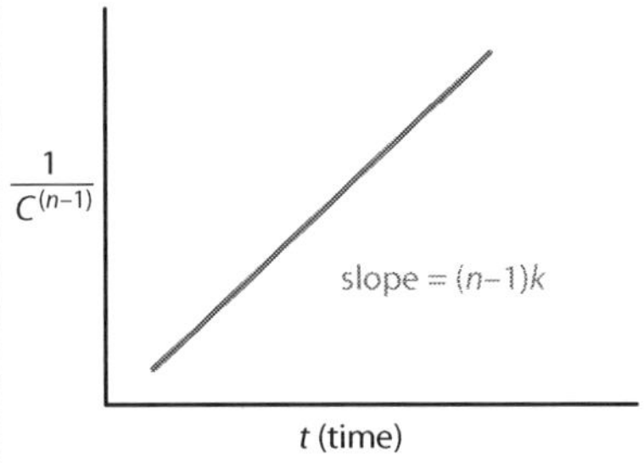

4.5 Review Questions

1. (a) What happens to each of the following as time passes for a first-order reaction?
   (i) rate of reaction

   (ii) rate constant

   (iii) half-life

   (b) Answer question (a) for a zero-order reaction.
   (i) rate of reaction

   (ii) rate constant

   (iii) half-life

   (c) Answer question (a) for a second-order reaction.
   (i) rate of reaction

   (ii) rate constant

   (iii) half-life

2. The rate constant of a first-order reaction is $4.03 \times 10^{-3}\ s^{-1}$. What concentration of reactant remains after 74.6 s assuming an initial concentration of 0.300 mol/L?

3. The reaction $2\ B \rightarrow C + A$ is a second-order reaction, and the rate constant is 0.15 L/mol·min. If the initial concentration of B is 2.00 mol/L, what is the concentration of B after 45 min?

4. A zero-order reaction has $k = 0.0025$ mol/L/s for the disappearance of A. What is the concentration of A after 35 s if the initial concentration is 0.50 mol/L?

5. In 17.5% w/w HCl, the complex ion $Ru(NH_3)_6^{3+}$ decomposes to a variety of products. The reaction is first order in $[Ru(NH_3)_6^{3+}]$ and has a half-life of 14 h at 25°C.
   (a) What is the rate constant for this reaction?

   (b) Under these conditions, how long will it take for the $[Ru(NH_3)_6^{3+}]$ to decrease to 6.25% of its initial value?

6. What is the rate constant in s^{-1} for a first-order reaction with an initial concentration of 0.600 mol/L if, after 142 s, the concentration is 0.444 mol/L?

7. What is the half-life in seconds for a second-order reaction with the rate constant $k = 2.74 \times 10^{-1}$ L $mol^{-1}s^{-1}$ if the initial reactant concentration is 0.500 mol/L?

8. Compare the two graphs shown here, focusing on lines (a), (b), and (c), which represent plots for various experimental trials run for the same first-order reaction under different conditions.

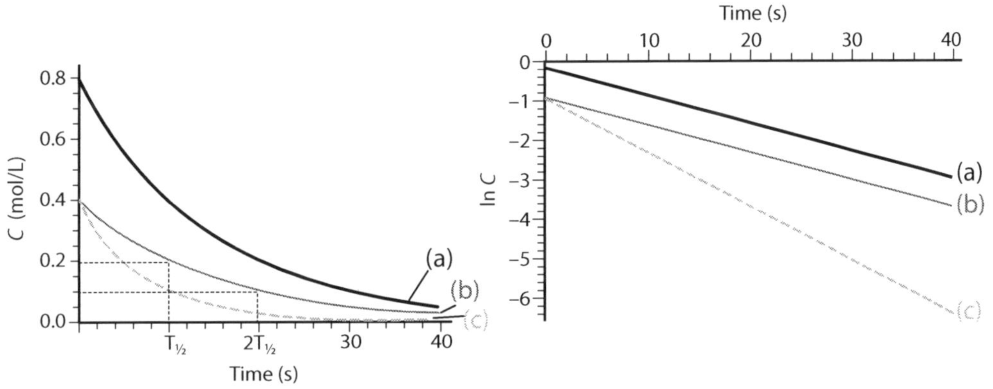

(a) What condition was changed from trial (a) to trial (b)?

(b) What effect did the change have? Explain your answer.

(c) What was not affected by the change? Justify your answer.

(d) What condition was changed from trial (b) to trial (c)? Be specific.

(e) Give two things about the reaction that this change impacted. Justify your answers.

9. Compare the two graphs shown here, focusing on lines (a), (b), and (c), which represent plots for the same second-order reaction under different conditions.

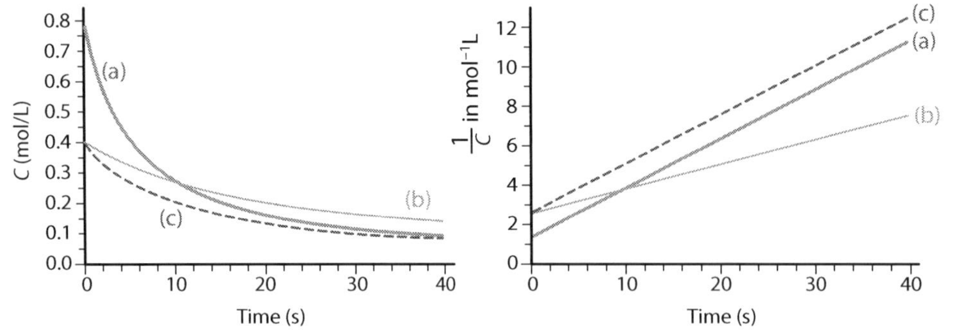

(a) What condition was changed from trial (a) to trial (b)?

(b) What effect did the change have? Explain your answer.

(c) What was not affected by the change? Justify your answer.

(d) What condition was changed from trial (b) to trial (c)? Be specific.

(e) Give two effects the change had on the reaction? Justify your answers.

10. The decomposition of aqueous sucrose to form the isomers glucose and fructose is a common organic reaction, which requires a strong acid catalyst: $C_{12}H_{22}O_{11}(aq) + H_2O(l) \rightarrow 2\,C_6H_{12}O_6(aq)$. The following data were collected during the process:

Time (min)	$[C_{12}H_{22}O_{11}]$ (mol/L)
0	0.316
39	0.274
80	0.238
140	0.190
210	0.146

Use the following grids to plot three separate graphs of $[C_{12}H_{22}O_{11}]$, ln $[C_{12}H_{22}O_{11}]$, and $1/[C_{12}H_{22}O_{11}]$ against time to determine the reaction order.

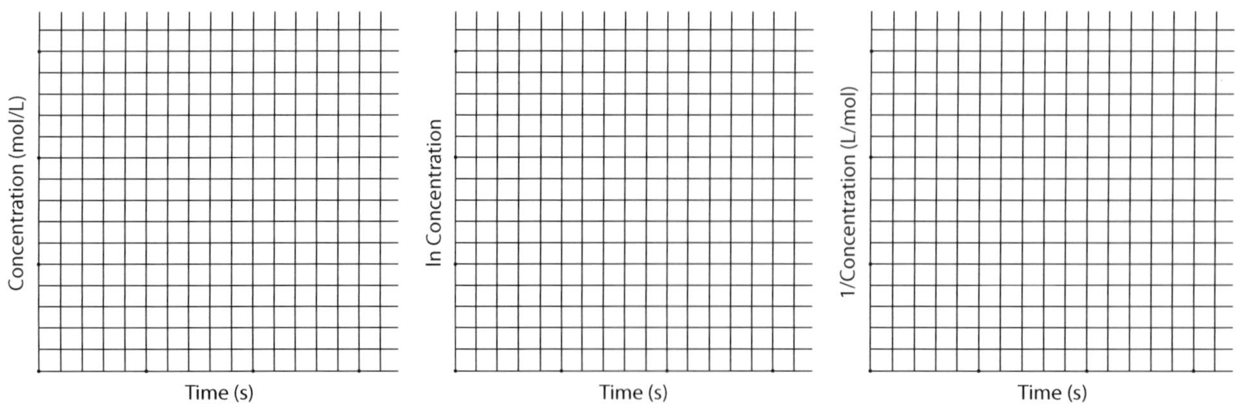

(a) Write the rate law expression in its general form (water should not be included).

(b) Determine the rate constant with units.

(c) Determine the half-life.

(d) If we performed a new trial with an initial concentration of sucrose of 0.400 mol/L, what concentration would remain after 4.00 h has passed?

11. Methyl isonitrile isomerizes to acetonitrile: $CH_3NC(g) \rightarrow CH_3CN(g)$ at 215°C.
The following data were collected during the process:

Time (s)	$[CH_3NC]$ (mol/L)
2000	0.0110
5000	0.0059
8000	0.0031
12000	0.0014
15000	0.0007

Use the following grids to plot three separate graphs of $[CH_3NC]$, ln $[CH_3NC]$, and $1/[CH_3NC]$ against time to determine the reaction order.

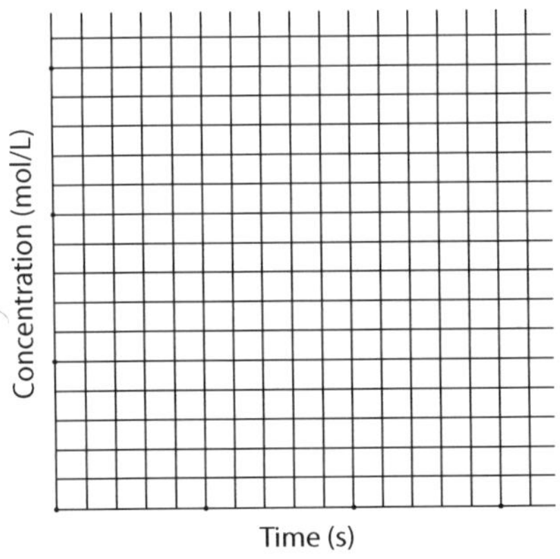

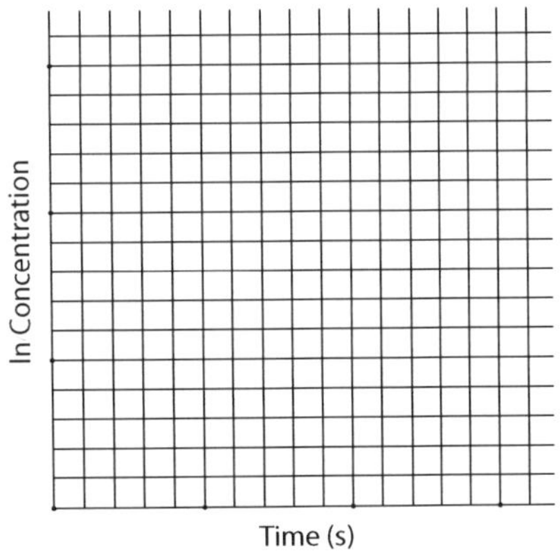

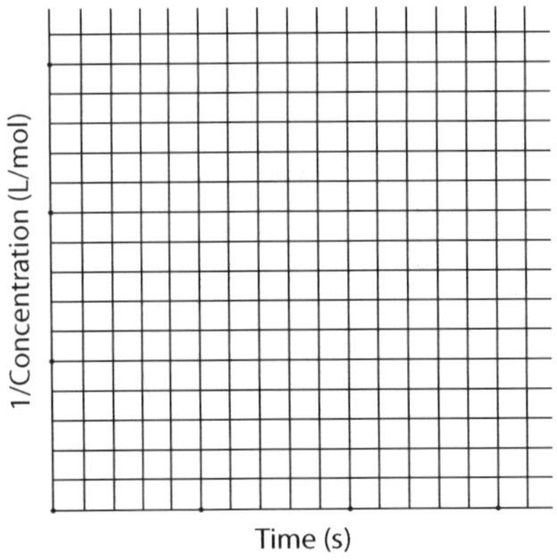

(a) Write the rate law expression in its general form.

(b) Determine the rate constant.

(c) Determine the half-life.

(d) Assuming the process continues, what concentration of methyl isonitrile would we expect after 5.00 h?

12. (a) What is the rate constant for a second-order reaction with an initial reactant concentration of 0.300 mol/L if after 158 s, the concentration is 0.200 mol/L?

(b) What is the half-life of this reaction?

13. Tritium decays by a first-order process that has a half-life of 12.5 y. How many years will it take to reduce the radioactivity of a tritium sample to 15% of its original value?

14. A zero-order reaction has a rate constant $k = 0.025$ mol/L/s for the disappearance of reactant, A.

(a) What is the half-life of this process?

(b) What will be the concentration of A after 15 s if the initial concentration is 0.50 mol/L?

15. The half-life is 22.7 s for the first-order conversion of cyclobutane to ethylene, $C_4H_8(g) \rightarrow 2\ C_2H_4(g)$, at a constant temperature. How much time, in seconds, does it take for the partial pressure of cyclobutane to decrease from 100.0 mmHg to 10.0 mmHg?

4.6 Reaction Mechanisms, Catalysis, and Rate Laws

Warm Up

Study the following series of molecular collisions representing the catalyzed decomposition of formic acid.

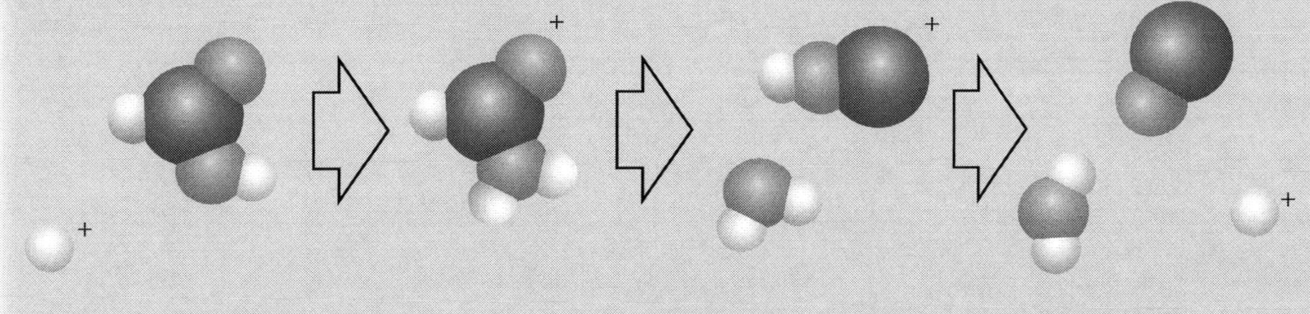

1. How many reactions are shown in the series above? ____________

2. In the format provided below question 3, write the balanced chemical equation for each reaction in the series. As it is a product of the overall series of collisions, the H_2O produced in the second step should *not* be shown as a reactant *or* product in the *third* step.

3. Algebraically sum the three equations to give the overall reaction. (Species that appear as reactants in one step and products in another should be cancelled.) What is the overall reaction once the three steps have been added together?

Step 1: →

Step 2: →

Step 3: →

Overall Reaction: →

Reaction Mechanisms

A balanced equation for a chemical reaction shows us what substances are present before and after the reaction. Unfortunately, it tells us nothing about the detailed steps occurring at the molecular level in between. Studies have shown that most reactions occur by a series of steps called the reaction mechanism. The individual steps in such a series are called **elementary processes.** These steps are themselves individual *balanced* chemical reactions that may be added together algebraically to give the overall balanced chemical equation.

A **reaction mechanism** is a series of steps that may be added together to give an overall chemical reaction.

In section 4.3 we learned that successful collisions require sufficient energy and appropriate orientation. As a consequence, the simultaneous collision of more than two reactant molecules with good geometry and E_a is highly unlikely. It's not surprising then that reactions having more than two reactant particles almost always involve more than one step in their reaction mechanism.

As mentioned above, each step in a reaction mechanism is called an elementary process. The **molecularity** of each elementary process is defined as the number of reactant species that must collide to produce the reaction indicated by that step. A reaction involving one molecule only is called a **unimolecular** step. A reaction involving the collision of two species is called a **bimolecular** step, and a reaction involving three species is called a **termolecular** step. Termolecular steps are extremely rare.

Quick Check

1. Why are termolecular steps extremely rare?

____

2. Indicate the molecularity of each of the following reactions.

   (a) $NO(g) + Br_2(g) \rightarrow NOBr_2(g)$ ____________________

   (b) $HCOOH(aq) \rightarrow H_2O(l) + CO(g)$ ____________________

   (c) $2\ NO(g) + Cl_2(g) \rightarrow 2\ NOCl(g)$ ____________________

3. An overall reaction is the sum of two or more elementary processes. Is each reaction above likely to be an elementary process or an overall reaction?

____

Species Identification: Intermediates and Catalysts

Since we can't actually *see* reacting particles colliding, flying apart, and reassembling, the mechanisms we use to describe chemical reactions are really just theoretical models. Chemists determine these models by altering the concentration of species involved in the mechanism and examining the effects these alterations produce. Computer models are also very useful in understanding mechanisms.

In any multi-step reaction mechanism the first collision, or decomposition of an energized reactant, always produces some product that is consumed in a later step of the mechanism. Such a species is called a reaction intermediate.

An **intermediate** is a species that is formed in one step and consumed in a subsequent step and so does not appear in the overall reaction.

As was described briefly in earlier sections, a catalyst functions by "providing an alternate, lower-energy pathway" for a reaction to follow. We now know this "alternate pathway" is actually a different reaction mechanism. In essence, most catalysts function by allowing the assembly of a different, lower-energy activated complex than would have formed if the catalyst was not present. Since catalysts are present before and after a reaction is complete, they must be used to facilitate the formation of the lower-energy activated complex in one step and then be reformed in some later step.

Catalysts in biological systems are referred to as **enzymes**. Enzymes are proteins that have an *activesite*. This active site is exposed to assist a biological reaction in one step of a mechanism so an *enzyme-substrate* complex can form. Once the substrate reacts, the complex comes apart and the enzyme is regenerated for use again (Figure 4.6.1).

A *catalyst* is consumed in one step and regenerated in a subsequent or later step.

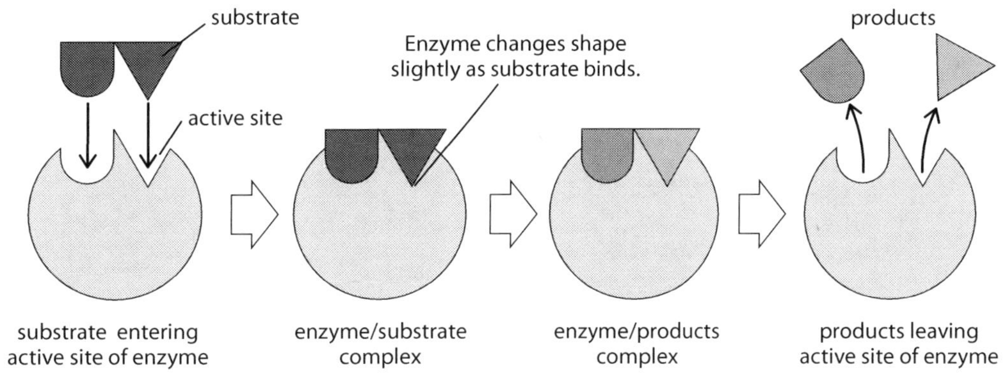

Figure 4.6.1 *Notice that the catalyst (in this case the enzyme) is consumed and then regenerated in its original form.*

Reaction Mechanisms and Potential Energy Diagrams

Despite the fact that many reactions involve only two reactant particles, studies show that the majority of chemical changes occur by mechanisms that involve at least two steps. Often one step is much slower than the other(s). The overall reaction rate cannot exceed the rate of the slowest elementary process. Because this slow step limits the overall reaction rate it is called the **rate-determining step**. A variety of conditions may cause a particular step to limit the overall reaction rate. These include the step having:

- complex collision geometry
- a high activation energy
- low concentrations of reactants
- a termolecular collision

A good analogy for this concept occurred back in the days before collating copy machines were available. In those days, teachers had to assemble pages of students' notes by hand and staple them together individually.

If several teachers were teaching the same course, they might get together with each taking on a portion of the job. One teacher would pull the pages off the copier and pass them to another who would assemble the pages in the correct order. Another would tap each pile on the table to make sure the edges were all aligned. Finally, a fourth teacher would staple the pile together. Which of these jobs would be the rate-determining step? Would it increase the rate of the job if a math teacher were asked to assist with passing the papers from the copier or tapping or stapling them? Clearly the assembler is the rate-determining step in such a job. Calling in a math teacher to assist with passing papers would have no effect on the overall rate at all. In fact, it might only serve to annoy the assembler.

As the analogy implies, adding reactants that appear in the non-rate-determining steps of a mechanism will have no effect on the reaction rate. To increase the rate of a reaction, it is necessary to increase the concentration of the reactants that appear in the rate-determining step.

The slowest elementary process in a reaction mechanism determines the overall reaction rate and is called the *rate-determining step*.

Each step in a reaction mechanism involves different chemical species with different bonding arrangements and hence different potential energies or enthalpies. Each step also has its own *rate constant* and its own *activation energy*, depending on the activated complex formed for that step. As a consequence, the potential energy diagram for a particular reaction will have the same number of *peaks,* as there are *steps* in the reaction mechanism.

Calculation of the activation energy for a multi-step reaction mechanism can be confusing. The activation energy for any particular step is simply the potential energy change from the reactants for an elementary process to the activated complex for that process. Consequently, the rate-determining step is the step with the highest activation energy. This value, however, is *not necessarily* the overall activation energy for the reaction. Rather, the overall activation energy is the difference between the potential energy of the activated complex with the highest energy and the potential energy of the reactants for the reaction as a whole.

> E_a for a reaction with a multi-step mechanism is equal to
>
> $$PE_{\text{highest energy activated complex}} - PE_{\text{reactants}}$$

As an example, consider the potential energy profile for the reaction in the Warm Up. Figures 4.6.2 and 4.6.3 are for the uncatalyzed reaction followed by the catalyzed reaction. In Figure 4.6.2, a methanoic acid molecule (HCOOH) is energized and forms an activated complex by shifting a hydrogen ion. The energized molecule then decomposes into water and carbon monoxide. This occurs in a single step.

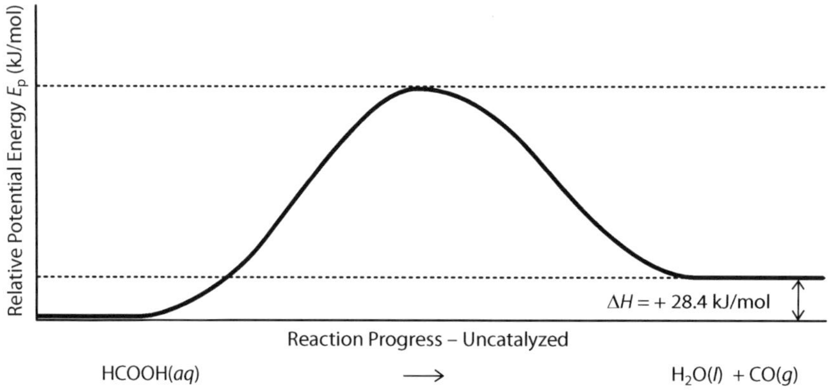

Figure 4.6.2 *A methanoic acid molecule (HCOOH) forms water and carbon monoxide in a single step.*

Notice that Figure 4.6.3 has three "peaks" corresponding to the three steps in the catalyzed reaction mechanism. The rate-determining step is the second one. This step would also determine E_a for the overall reaction. The enthalpy change or ΔH value is unaffected by catalysis as the reactants and products remain the same.

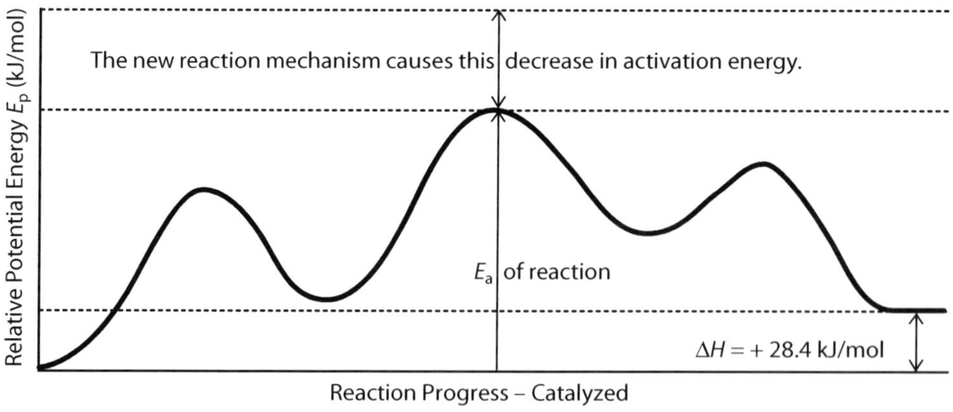

Figure 4.6.3 *This diagram shows the three peaks representing the three steps in a catalyzed reaction.*

Sample Problem — Identifying Intermediates and Catalysts in a Mechanism

Use the reaction mechanism produced in the Warm Up for this section to identify reaction intermediates and catalysts.

What to Think About

1. To describe the reaction mechanism, write three reactions for the reactants listed on the left side of each arrow to form the products on the right. As water was an overall product, do not include it as a reactant or product in step 3.

2. Sum the three steps algebraically to give the overall reaction. Cancel species appearing on both sides of the arrows. Identify species based on the definitions in the grey boxes above.

3. Intermediates appear as *products* first *(on the right side)* and as *reactants* later *(on the left side)*. Identify them by drawing a slash from the upper right to the lower left through intermediates.

4. Catalysts are consumed, so they appear as *reactants* first *(left)* and *products* later *(right)*, as they are regenerated. Identify catalysts by drawing a slash from the upper left to the lower right through them.

How to Do It

$$\cancel{H^+} + HCOOH \rightarrow \cancel{HCOOH_2^+}$$
$$\cancel{HCOOH_2^+} \rightarrow H_2O + \cancel{HCO^+}$$
$$\cancel{HCO^+} \rightarrow CO + \cancel{H^+}$$
$$HCOOH \rightarrow H_2O + CO$$

Intermediates include: $HCOOH_2^+$ and HCO^+ ions.

There is only one catalyst (as is typically the case). It is homogeneous and is in solution in this case. Specifically the catalyst is the H^+ ion.

Practice Problems — Identifying Intermediates and Catalysts in a Mechanism

For each of the following reaction mechanisms, determine the overall reaction and identify all catalysts and intermediates (some may not have catalysts). Then sketch a potential energy diagram for the reaction. Indicate E_a for the overall reaction. A numerical value is *not* expected.

1. $O_3(g) \rightarrow O_2(g) + O(g)$ (slow)

   $O(g) + O_3(g) \rightarrow 2\,O_2(g)$ (ΔH value for entire reaction = –284.6 kJ/mol)

2. Palladium catalyzes the hydrogenation of ethene (commonly called ethylene) in a reaction having a ΔH value of –136.9 kJ/mol. The mechanism is as follows.

$$H_2(g) + 2\,Pd(s) \rightleftharpoons 2\,Pd\text{-}H(s)$$
$$C_2H_4(g) + Pd\text{-}H(s) \rightarrow C_2H_5\text{-}Pd(s) \quad \text{(slowest step)}$$
$$C_2H_5\text{-}Pd(s) + Pd\text{-}H(s) \rightarrow C_2H_6(g) + 2\,Pd(s)$$

Continued

Practice Problems (*Continued*)

3. A "chain reaction" often involves *free radical* halogen or hydrogen atoms. These are atoms with an unpaired electron. Free radicals are high energy, unstable, and therefore very reactive. The formation of two free radical atoms in the first step of this mechanism makes the first step the rate-determining one. The first step in a chain mechanism is called the *initiation step*. The second step, however, has the highest energy activated complex. The overall reaction is slightly exothermic.

$Cl_2(g) \rightarrow Cl(g) + Cl(g)$		initiation step
$(CH_4(g) + Cl(g) \rightarrow CH_3Cl(g) + H(g) \times 2$		propagation steps
$H(g) + H(g) \rightarrow H_2(g)$		termination step

Heterogeneous Catalysts

Catalysts may be classified as one of two types, heterogeneous or homogeneous. **Heterogeneous catalysts** are those in which reactions are limited to their surface area only. Most heterogeneous catalysts are solids. The most common are transition metals such as platinum or nickel. Catalysts of this type undergo *adsorption*of reactants onto their surface. The catalyst energizes the reactants and holds them in a position that allows easy interaction between them and other reacting species. Figure 4.6.4 describes the function of a typical heterogeneous metal catalyst in an addition reaction involving ethene (ethylene), a component of natural gas and hydrogen.

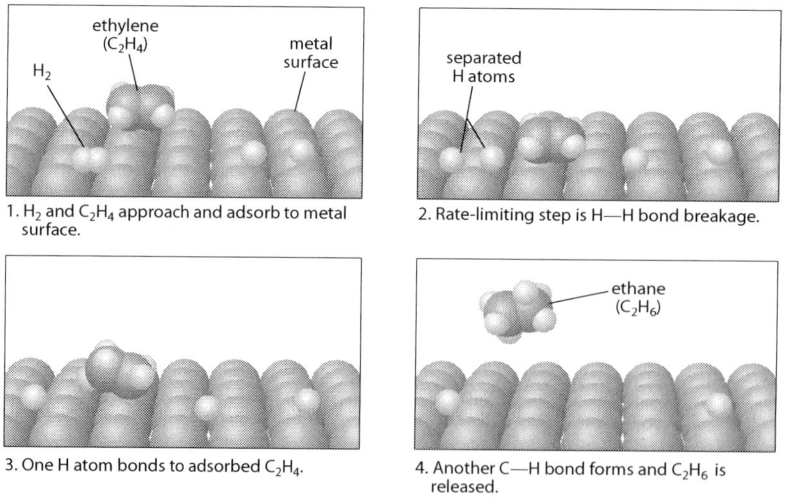

Figure 4.6.4 *This process reduces the double bond in $CH_2CH_2(g)$ to a single bond in $CH_3CH_3(g)$ by addition of $H_2(g)$*

Heterogeneous catalysis also occurs inside the exhaust system of our automobiles. A device called a **catalytic converter** activates several oxidation and/or reduction reactions. These transform harmful pollutants such as carbon monoxide, a variety of hydrocarbons, and nitrogen oxides into harmless carbon dioxide, water, and nitrogen gas. The converter contains a series of honeycomb-patterned channels lined with the catalyst, platinum (Figure 4.6.5). A number of other transition metals may function as catalysts in a catalytic converter.

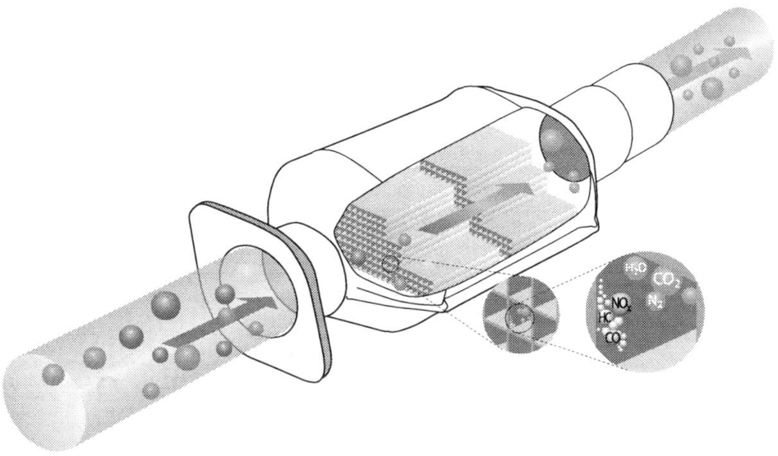

Figure 4.6.5 *Vehicleswithproperlyfunctioningcatalyticconvertersnearlyalways passemissionstests.*

Homogeneous Catalysts

Many reactions are catalyzed by the presence of an acid. In such a case, the hydrogen ions from the acid react with and somehow modify the structure of a reactant to make it more susceptible to reaction with another reagent. The decomposition of methanoic acid using an acid catalyst is shown in the Warm Up and the Sample Problem 4.6.1 in this section. Catalysts such as this, which exist in the same phase as the rest of the reaction system, are sometimes called **homogeneous catalysts**.

One of the most important catalysts in the world is the enzyme, *nitrogenase*. Nitrogenase catalyzes the life-sustaining process of nitrogen fixation. Microorganisms convert the nitrogen in animal waste and dead plants and animals into $N_2(g)$, which is returned to the atmosphere. For the food chain to be sustained, however, there must be a means of converting atmospheric nitrogen back into a form plants can use. This process is called *nitrogenfixation*. The fixing of nitrogen involves the high activation energy reduction of elemental nitrogen into ammonia. Sometimes atmospheric lightning can provide the energy. Bacteria that live in the root nodules of certain plants carry out most of the nitrogen fixation. These bacteria contain **metalloenzymes** that are particularly useful for catalyzing oxidation and in this case, reduction, reactions. Nitrogenase contains an iron-molybedenum-sulfur cofactor in its structure. A cofactor, sometimes called a coenzyme, is a secondary substance that is required for an enzyme to function properly.

Reaction Mechanisms and Rate Laws

A valid reaction mechanism for a particular chemical reaction must fit these criteria:

1. The elementary steps must algebraically sum to the overall balanced equation.
2. Each elementary step is most commonly unimolecular or bimolecular. The chances of more than two particles colliding at once with sufficient energy and proper geometry are infinitesimally small.
3. The reaction mechanism must correlate with the rate law. The steps involved in correlating a mechanism with a rate law are outlined below.

There are four steps involved in the deduction of a rate law from a reaction mechanism:

1. Locate the *rate-determining step*.

As indicated earlier in this section, the *rate-determining step* is the slowest elementary process in the reaction mechanism and determines the overall reaction rate. This step is labeled "slow" or "rate determining."

2. Write a temporary *rate law expression*.

The temporary rate law expression uses the reactants in the rate-determining step and their molecularity. The coefficients for each reactant (the reactant *molecularity*) become the exponents of that reactant's concentration in the temporary rate law (the *order* with respect to that reactant).

3. Write an *equilibrium expression* or a *"fast-forward reversible" expression*.

We will delve into the rate law expression for a fast-forward reversible equilibrium elementary step in more detail in section 2.5. The *double arrow* in the equation indicates that an elementary step is in equilibrium.

4. Use the expression to *substitute for appropriate species* in the temporary rate law.

As the final rate law is determined experimentally, it must ONLY contain reactant species (or in rare cases, a catalyst) that a chemist can manipulate directly. This means we must substitute actual reactants for intermediates or products that appear in the temporary rate law. We can algebraically manipulate the equilibrium expression to allow substitutions to occur.

Sample Problem — Deducing a Rate Law from a Mechanism

The reaction of nitrogen monoxide and chlorine gas occurs via the following two step mechanism:

fast-forward reversible: $NO(g) + Cl_2(g) \rightleftharpoons NOCl_2(g)$ (step 1)

slow: $NOCl_2(g) + NO(g) \rightarrow 2\ NOCl(g)$ (step 2)

overall reaction: $2\ NO(g) + Cl_2(g) \rightarrow 2\ NOCl(g)$

Determine the rate law for the overall reaction.

What to Think About

1. Step 2 in the given mechanism is rate determining and the coefficients of both species in this step are 1's. Consequently both of these species are first order in the *temporary rate law*.
2. Write an expression for the *equilibrium* or *fast-forward reversible* step. The first elementary step is an equilibrium, as indicated by the presence of the double arrow.

How to Do It

The temporary rate law based on the slow step in the given mechanism is

$$\text{rate} = k'[NOCl_2][NO]$$

Note: The rate constant is also temporary and so is shown as k' ("k prime").

The equilibrium expression for the reaction in the first elementary step is:

$$K_{eq} = \frac{[NOCl_2]}{[NO][Cl_2]}$$

According to the K_{eq} expression above,

$[NOCl_2] = K_{eq}[NO][Cl_2]$

Continued

Sample Problem (*Continued*)

3. Substitute the $[NOCl_2]$ in the temporary rate law since it is an intermediate and does not appear in the overall reaction. The product of two constants such as $k' \times K_{eq}$ is equal to a new constant, in this case, the overall rate constant, *k*.

Substitute this expression into the temporary rate law to give:
$rate = k'K_{eq}[NO][Cl_2][NO]$
This rate law simplifies to:
$rate = k[NO]^2[Cl_2]$

Practice Problems — Deducing a Rate Law from a Mechanism

1. The reaction of the iodide ion and the hypochlorite ion is an oxidation-reduction reaction occurring in basic solution:

$$I^-(aq) + OCl^-(aq) \rightarrow IO^-(aq) + Cl^-(aq) \quad (basic)$$

The three-step mechanism is represented as follows:

fast-forward reversible: $OCl^-(aq) + H_2O(l) \rightleftharpoons HOCl(aq) + OH^-(aq)$

rate-determining step: $I^-(aq) + HOCl(aq) \rightarrow HIO(aq) + Cl^-(aq)$

$HIO(aq) + OH^-(aq) \rightarrow H_2O(l) + IO^-(aq)$

(a) Show how the above steps combine mathematically to give the overall reaction. Identify all *intermediates* and *catalysts*. (Show work directly on the mechanism provided.)

(b) Show that the mechanism provided gives the rate law: $rate = k[I^-][OCl^-][OH^-]^{-1}$
(Note: Because this *redox* reaction is occurring in a basic solution, $[OH^-]$ can appear in the rate law expression.)

Continued

Practice Problems (*Continued*)

2. Although fractional orders are rare, they can occur. Consider the following overall equation for a substitution reaction to form carbon tetrachloride from chloroform:

$$Cl_2(g) + CHCl_3(g) \rightarrow CCl_4(g) + HCl(g)$$

Here are the three elementary steps in the mechanism:

fast-forward reversible reaction: $Cl_2(g) \rightleftharpoons 2\,Cl(g)$

slow reaction: $Cl(g) + CHCl_3(g) \rightarrow HCl(g) + CCl_3(g)$

fast reaction: $Cl(g) + CCl_3(g) \rightarrow CCl_4(g)$

(a) Show how the reactants and products of the elementary steps cancel to produce the overall reaction.

(b) Identify any *intermediates or catalysts.* (Show work for parts (a) and (b) on the steps provided above.)

(c) Determine the overall rate law for the reaction.

Equation Coefficients and Rate Law Exponents

It is impossible to deduce a reaction mechanism from an equation alone. The rate law provides guidance as to what occurs on the pathway between the reactants and products. It helps us determine what is formed and consumed during the mechanism for a reaction. Rate laws are determined experimentally. They relate the rate of a reaction to the concentration of the reactants. Rate laws help us determine whether the equation for an overall reaction represents an elementary process, and if it is not, rate laws help us deduce a reaction mechanism.

If the coefficients in an equation match the exponents in a rate law, the reaction *may* consist of *one step*. However, if they do *not*, there is no doubt that the reaction *must* consist of more than one step. Information such as this can be helpful in determining the relationship between a rate law and a reaction mechanism.

4.6 Activity: A Molecular View Of a Reaction Mechanism

Question

How can you determine the mechanism for a reaction given a "molecular view"?

Background

Two series of "snapshots" of a reacting system taken several microseconds apart are available for viewing. The first set is of an uncatalyzed reaction. The second set is of the same reaction, but it is catalyzed.

Uncatalyzed reaction: Reactants are B + G; Product is BG.

Snapshot 1

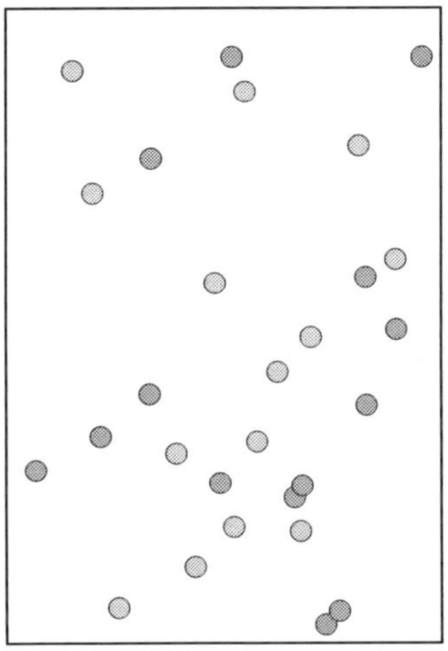

Snapshot 2

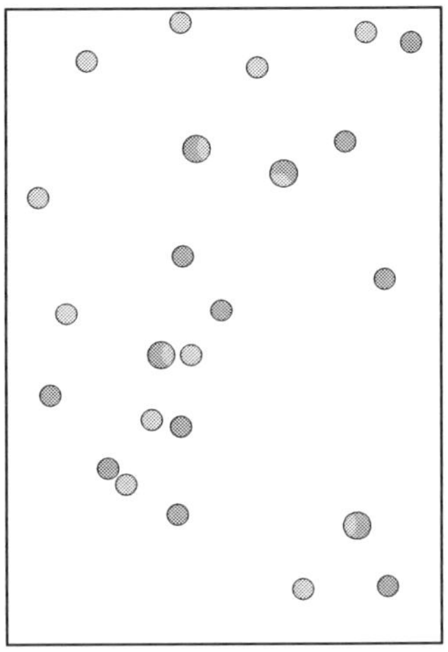

Snapshot 3

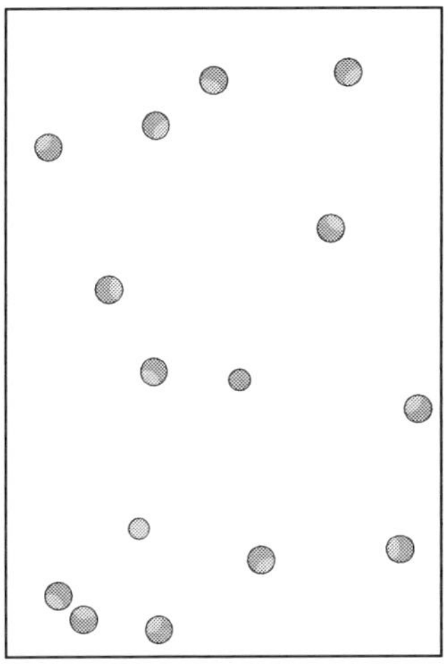

Catalyzed reaction: Reactants are the same as above. Catalyst R added.

Snapshot 1

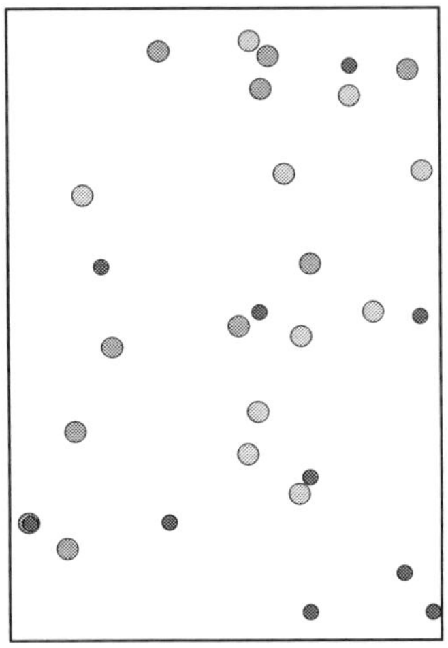

Snapshot 2

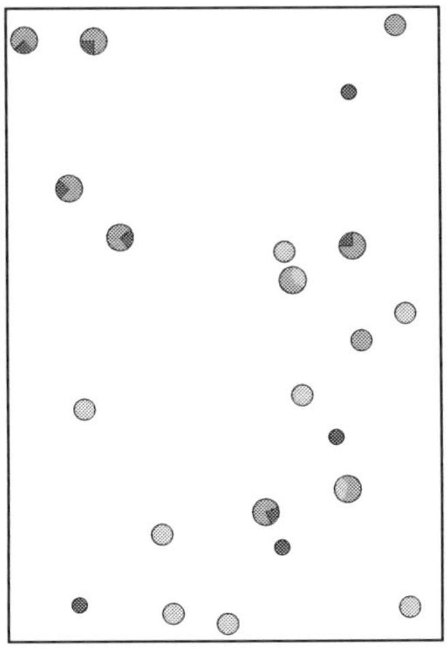

Snapshot 3

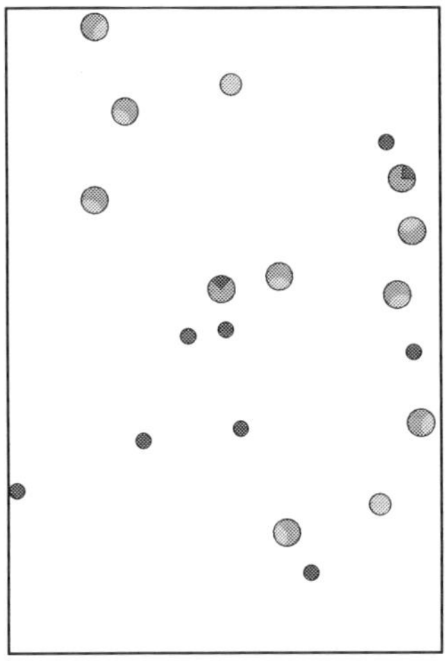

Procedure

1. Determine an equation that represents the uncatalyzed reaction.

2. Determine the reactions that represent the two-step mechanism for the catalyzed reaction.

   Step 1:

   Step 2:

   Overall Reaction:

Results and Discussion

1. Show how steps 1 and 2 sum to give the overall catalyzed reaction.

2. How does the overall reaction compare with the uncatalyzed reaction?

3. Identify the catalyst in the mechanism.

4. Identify any and all intermediates in the mechanism.

5. How would the time passed from snapshots 1 through 3 in the catalyzed series compare with the time for the uncatalyzed series?

6. Assume the second step in the catalyzed series is rate-determining. How would the time passed between snapshots 1 and 2 compare to the time passed between snapshots 2 and 3?

7. For the catalyzed reaction, how would the addition of more B affect the overall reaction rate? More G? Explain your answers.

4.6 Review Questions

1. What is a reaction mechanism?

2. What is a rate-determining step?

3. How do chemists determine reaction mechanisms?

4. Indicate whether each of the following reactions involves heterogeneous or homogeneous catalysis:

   (a) $H_2(g) + CH_2CH_2(g) \xrightarrow{Pt(s)} CH_3CH_3(g)$ hydrogenation of ethylene

   (b) Chlorofluorocarbons (CFCs) catalyze the conversion of ozone ($O_3(g)$) to oxygen gas (O_2).

   $2\,O_3(g) \xrightarrow{CFC(g)} 3\,O_2(g)$

   (c) Manganese(IV) oxide catalyzes the decomposition of hydrogen peroxide.

   $2\,H_2O_2(aq) \xrightarrow{MnO_2(s)} 2\,H_2O(l) + O_2(g)$

5. The oxygen produced by the decomposition of hydrogen peroxide may be used to clean a variety of items from contact lenses to dentures. The decomposition may be initiated by the addition of small disks. Study the following mechanism:

   1st: $H_2O_2(aq) + I^-(aq) \rightarrow H_2O(l) + IO^-(aq)$ slow

   2nd: $H_2O_2(aq) + IO^-(aq) \rightarrow H_2O(l) + O_2(g) + I^-(aq)$ fast

   Overall reaction:

   (a) Determine the overall reaction.

   (b) Identify any intermediate(s) present.

   (c) What is the material contained on the disks?

6. Examine the following potential energy diagram and use it to construct a reaction mechanism. Show each step and the overall reaction. Label the rate-determining step.

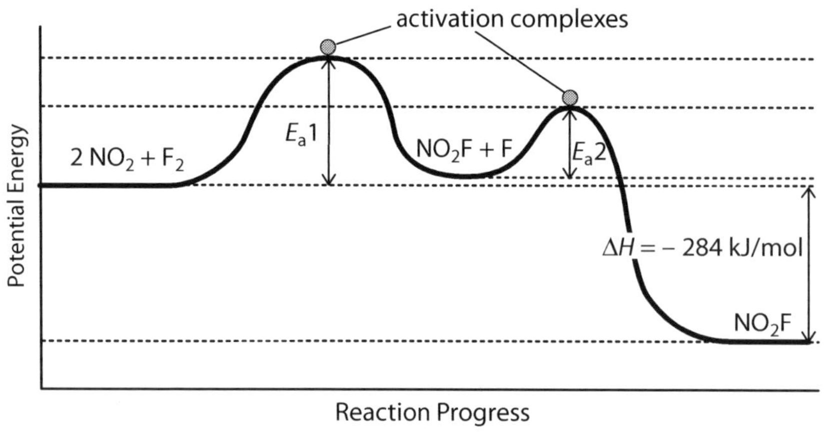

7. Look at the PE diagram shown here and answers the questions below. Write your answers at the end of each question.

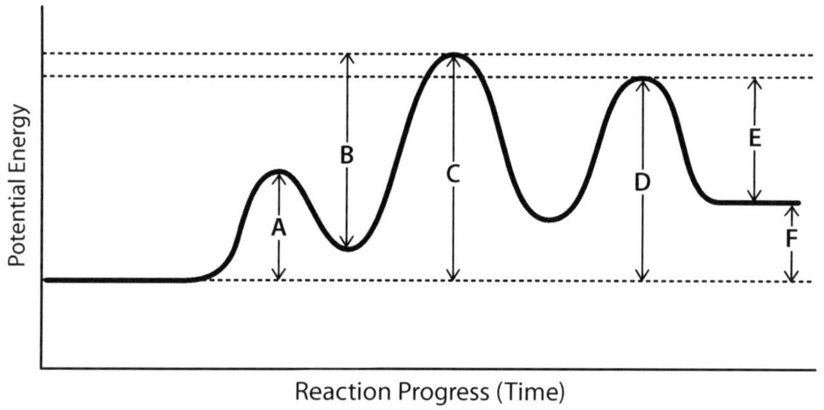

(a) How many steps are in the reaction represented by this potential energy profile?

(b) Which step is rate determining?

(c) What arrow represents E_a for the forward reaction?

(d) What arrow represents E_a for the rate-determining step?

(e) What arrow represents ΔH for the reaction?

(f) Is this an endo- or exothermic reaction?

8. The reaction, $CO(g) + NO_2(g) \rightarrow CO_2(g) + NO(g)$ may occur by either of the following two mechanisms:

Mechanism 1: Step 1: $2\ NO_2(g) \rightarrow NO_3(g) + NO(g)$ slow

Step 2: ______________________________ fast

Reaction:

Mechanism 2: Step 1: $2\ NO_2(g) \rightarrow N_2O_4(g)$ fast

Step 2: ______________________________ slow

Reaction:

(a) Fill the reaction in and use it to discern the missing step 2 for each mechanism.

(b) Experimental data shows that increasing the [CO] has *no effect* on the overall reaction rate. Based on this data, which mechanism must be correct?

9. Consider the reaction: $4\ HBr(g) + O_2(g) \rightarrow 2\ H_2O(g) + 2\ Br_2(g)$ + heat

(a) Does this reaction represent an elementary process? Explain

(b) Propose a reaction mechanism for the overall reaction, given the following clues: There are two intermediates in the reaction. The first to form is HOOBr(g) and the second is HOBr(g).

(c) Experimental data shows that a change in [HBr] has the same effect on the rate of the reaction as an identical change in $[O_2]$. What is the rate-determining step?

(d) Sketch a potential energy profile for the reaction. Recall that two identical steps involving the same potential bond energies will be shown as the *same step* in a potential energy diagram.

10. Sketch a potential energy diagram for the following reversible reaction:

$$\text{heat} + 2\,A + 2\,B \rightleftharpoons 3\,C$$

Be sure to label the axes. Indicate the following features on the diagram:

(a) reverse activation energy

(b) ΔH

(c) potential energy of activated complex

(d) use a dotted line to represent the pathway for a catalyzed reaction

11. Consider the following mechanism for a chemical reaction.

Step 1: $2\,NO(g) \rightleftharpoons N_2O_2(g)$ *fast-forward reversible*

Step 2: $N_2O_2(g) + O_2(g) \rightarrow 2\,NO_2(g)$ *slow*

(a) Determine the overall reaction. Indicate any catalysts or intermediates.

(b) Determine the rate law for the overall reaction.

12. A hypothetical reaction, $2\,A + B \rightarrow C + D$, has the rate law, rate = k [A][B].
Your teacher proposes the following three reaction mechanisms for the reaction. Which of these mechanisms is consistent with the rate law ? Consider and address each mechanism in turn and justify your choice.

Mechanism 1: $A + B \rightleftharpoons C + M$ *fast-forward reversible*
$M + A \rightarrow D$ *slow*

Mechanism 2: $B \rightleftharpoons M$ *fast-forward reversible*
$M + A \rightarrow C + X$ *slow*
$A + X \rightarrow D$ *fast*

Mechanism 3: $A + B \rightleftharpoons M$ *fast-forward reversible*
$M + A \rightarrow C + X$ *slow*
$X \rightarrow D$ *fast*

13. The reaction of NO and O_2 gases likely occurs according to the following mechanism.
Step 1: $NO(g) + O_2(g) \rightleftharpoons NO_3(g)$ *fast-forward reversible*
Step 2: $NO_3(g) + NO(g) \rightarrow 2\,NO_2(g)$ *slow*

(a) Show how the two steps combine to give the overall reaction.

(b) Determine the rate law for the overall reaction.

14. You propose the following three-step mechanism for a reaction. The second step is rate determining.

$NH_3(aq) + OBr^-(aq) \rightleftharpoons NH_2Br(aq) + OH^-(aq)$
$NH_2Br(aq) + NH_3(aq) \rightarrow N_2H_5^+(aq) + Br^-(aq)$
$N_2H_5^+(aq) + OH^-(aq) \rightarrow N_2H_4(aq) + H_2O(l)$

(a) Show how the three steps combine to give the overall reaction.

(b) Identify any catalysts and/or intermediates.

(c) Determine the rate law predicted by this mechanism.

Table A8 Thermodynamic Data at 25°C for Assorted Substances

Table A8-Inorganic *Thermodynamic data at 25°C for assorted inorganic substances.*

Substance	Enthalpy of formation ΔH_f^0, kJ/mol	Free energy of formation ΔG_f^0, kJ/mol	Entropy S^0, J/(K·mol)
Aluminum			
$Al(s)$	0	0	28.33
$Al^{3+}(aq)$	-524.7	-481.2	-321.7
$Al_2O_3(s)$	-1675.7	-1582.3	50.92
$Al(OH)_3(s)$	-1276	---	---
$AlCl_3(s)$	-704.2	-628.8	110.67
Antimony			
$SbH_3(g)$	145.11	147.75	232.78
$SbCl_3(g)$	-313.8	-301.2	337.80
$SbCl_5(g)$	-394.34	-334.29	401.94
Arsenic			
As(*s, gray*)	0	0	35.1
$As_2S_3(s)$	-169.0	-168.6	163.6
$AsO_4^{3-}(aq)$	-888.14	-648.41	-162.8
Barium			
$Ba(s)$	0	0	62.8
$Ba^{2+}(aq)$	-537.64	-560.77	9.6
$BaO(s)$	-553.5	-525.1	70.42
$BaCO_3(s)$	-1216.3	-1137.6	112.1
$BaCO_3(aq)$	-1214.78	-1088.59	-47.3
Boron			
$B(s)$	0	0	5.86
$B_2O_3(s)$	-1272.8	-1193.7	53.97
$BF_3(g)$	-1137.0	-1120.3	254.12
Bromine			
$Br_2(l)$	0	0	152.23
$Br_2(g)$	30.91	3.11	245.46
$Br(g)$	111.88	82.40	175.02
$Br^-(aq)$	-121.55	-103.96	82.4
$HBr(g)$	-36.40	-53.45	198.70
Calcium			
$Ca(s)$	0	0	41.42
$Ca(g)$	178.2	144.3	154.88
$Ca^{2+}(aq)$	-542.83	-553.58	-53.1
$CaO(s)$	-635.09	-604.03	39.79
$Ca(OH)_2(s)$	-986.09	-898.49	83.39
$Ca(OH)_2(aq)$	-1002.82	-868.07	-74.5

Table A8-Inorganic *Thermodynamic data at 25°C for assorted inorganic substances (continued).*

Substance	Enthalpy of formation ΔH_f^0, kJ/mol	Free energy of formation ΔG_f^0, kJ/mol	Entropy S^0, J/(K·mol)
$CaCO_3$(*s, calcite*)	-1206.9	-1128.8	92.9
$CaCO_3$(*s, aragonite*)	-1207.1	-1127.8	88.7
$CaCO_3$(*aq*)	-1219.97	-1081.39	-110.0
CaF_2(*s*)	-1219.6	-1167.3	68.87
CaF_2(*aq*)	-1208.09	-1111.15	-80.8
$CaCl_2$(*s*)	-795.8	-748.1	104.6
$CaCl_2$(*aq*)	-877.1	-816.0	59.8
$CaBr_2$(*s*)	-682.8	-663.6	130
CaC_2(*s*)	-59.8	-64.9	69.96
$CaSO_4$(*s*)	-1434.11	-1321.79	106.7
$CaSO_4$(*aq*)	-1452.10	-1298.10	-33.1
Carbon			
C(*s, graphite*)	0	0	5.740
C(*s, diamond*)	1.895	2.900	2.377
C(*g*)	716.68	671.26	158.10
CO(*g*)	-110.53	-137.17	197.67
CO_2(*g*)	-393.51	-394.36	213.74
CO_3^{2-}(*aq*)	-677.14	-527.81	-56.9
CCl_4(*l*)	-135.44	-65.21	216.40
CS_2(*l*)	89.70	65.27	153.34
HCN(*g*)	135.1	124.7	201.78
HCN(*l*)	108.87	124.97	112.84
Cerium			
Ce(*s*)	0	0	72.0
Ce^{3+}(*aq*)	-696.2	-672.0	-205
Ce^{4+}(*aq*)	-537.2	-503.8	-301
Chlorine			
Cl_2(*g*)	0	0	223.07
Cl(*g*)	121.68	105.68	165.20
Cl^-(*aq*)	-167.16	-131.23	56.5
HCl(*g*)	-92.31	-95.30	186.91
HCl(*aq*)	-167.16	-131.23	56.5
Copper			
Cu(*s*)	0	0	33.15
Cu^+(*aq*)	71.67	49.98	40.6
Cu^{2+}(*aq*)	64.77	65.49	-99.6
Cu_2O(*s*)	-168.6	-146.0	93.14
CuO(*s*)	-157.3	-129.7	42.63
$CuSO_4$(*s*)	-771.36	-661.8	109

Table A8-Inorganic *Thermodynamic data at 25°C for assorted inorganic substances (continued).*

Substance	Enthalpy of formation ΔH_f^0, kJ/mol	Free energy of formation ΔG_f^0, kJ/mol	Entropy S^0, J/(K·mol)
Fluorine			
$F_2(g)$	0	0	202.78
$F^-(aq)$	-332.63	-278.79	-13.8
$HF(g)$	-271.1	-273.2	173.78
$HF(aq)$	-332.36	-278.79	-13.8
Hydrogen			
$H_2(g)$	0	0	130.68
$H(g)$	217.97	203.25	114.71
$H^+(aq)$	0	0	0
$H_2O(l)$	-285.83	-237.13	69.91
$H_2O(g)$	-241.82	-228.57	188.83
$H_2O_2(l)$	-187.78	-120.35	109.6
$H_2O_2(aq)$	-191.17	-134.03	143.9
$D_2(g)$	0	0	144.96
$D_2O(l)$	-294.60	-243.44	75.94
$D_2O(g)$	-249.20	-234.54	198.34
Iodine			
$I_2(s)$	0	0	116.14
$I_2(g)$	62.44	19.33	260.69
$I^-(aq)$	-55.19	-51.57	111.3
$HI(g)$	26.48	1.70	206.59
Iron			
$Fe(s)$	0	0	27.28
$Fe^{2+}(aq)$	-89.1	-78.90	-137.7
$Fe^{3+}(aq)$	-48.5	-4.7	-315.9
Fe_3O_4(*s, magnetite*)	-1118.4	-1015.4	146.4
Fe_2O_3(*s, hematite*)	-824.2	-742.2	87.40
$FeS(s,\alpha)$	-100.0	-100.4	60.29
$FeS(aq)$	---	6.9	---
$FeS_2(s)$	-178.2	-166.9	52.93
Lead			
$Pb(s)$	0	0	64.81
$Pb^{2+}(aq)$	-1.7	-24.43	10.5
$PbO_2(s)$	-277.4	-217.33	68.6
$PbSO_4(s)$	-919.94	-813.14	148.57
$PbBr_2(s)$	-278.7	-261.92	161.5
$PbBr_2(aq)$	-244.8	-232.34	175.3
Magnesium			
$Mg(s)$	0	0	32.68

Table A8-Inorganic *Thermodynamic data at 25°C for assorted inorganic substances (continued).*

Substance	Enthalpy of formation ΔH_f^0, kJ/mol	Free energy of formation ΔG_f^0, kJ/mol	Entropy S^0, J/(K·mol)
$Mg(g)$	147.70	113.10	148.65
$Mg^{2+}(aq)$	-466.85	-454.8	-138.1
$MgO(s)$	-601.70	-569.43	26.94
$MgCO_3(s)$	-1095.8	-1012.1	65.7
$MgBr_2(s)$	-524.3	-503.8	117.2
Mercury			
$Hg(l)$	0	0	76.02
$Hg(g)$	61.32	31.82	174.96
$HgO(s)$	-90.83	-58.54	70.29
$Hg_2Cl_2(s)$	-265.22	-210.75	192.5
Nitrogen			
$N_2(g)$	0	0	191.61
$NO(g)$	90.25	86.55	210.76
$N_2O(g)$	82.05	104.20	219.85
$NO_2(g)$	33.18	51.31	240.06
$N_2O_4(g)$	9.16	97.89	304.29
$HNO_3(l)$	-174.10	-80.71	155.60
$HNO_3(aq)$	-207.36	-111.22	146.4
$NO_3^-(aq)$	-205.0	-108.74	146.4
$NH_3(g)$	-46.11	-16.45	192.45
$NH_3(aq)$	-80.29	-26.50	111.3
$NH_4^+(aq)$	-132.51	-79.31	113.4
$NH_2OH(s)$	-114.2	---	---
$HN_3(g)$	294.1	328.1	238.97
$N_2H_4(l)$	50.63	149.34	121.21
$NH_4NO_3(s)$	-365.56	-183.87	151.08
$NH_4Cl(s)$	-314.43	-202.87	94.6
$NH_4ClO_4(s)$	-295.31	-88.75	186.2
Oxygen			
$O_2(g)$	0	0	205.14
$O_3(g)$	142.7	163.2	238.93
$OH^-(aq)$	-229.99	-157.24	-10.75
Phosphorus			
$P(s, white)$	0	0	41.09
$P_4(g)$	58.91	24.44	279.98
$PH_3(g)$	5.4	13.4	210.23
$P_4O_{10}(s)$	-2984.0	-2697.0	228.86
$H_3PO_3(aq)$	-964.0	---	---
$H_3PO_4(l)$	-1266.9	---	---

Table A8-Inorganic *Thermodynamic data at 25°C for assorted inorganic substances (continued).*

Substance	Enthalpy of formation ΔH_f^0, kJ/mol	Free energy of formation ΔG_f^0, kJ/mol	Entropy S^0, J/(K·mol)
$H_3PO_4(aq)$	-277.4	-1018.7	---
$PCl_3(l)$	-319.7	-272.3	217.18
$PCl_3(g)$	-287.0	-267.8	311.78
$PCl_5(g)$	-374.9	-305.0	364.6
$PCl_5(s)$	-443.5	---	---
Potassium			
$K(s)$	0	0	64.18
$K(g)$	89.24	60.59	160.34
$K^+(aq)$	-252.38	-283.27	102.5
$KOH(s)$	-424.76	-379.08	78.9
$KOH(aq)$	-482.37	-440.50	91.6
$KF(s)$	-567.27	-537.75	66.57
$KCl(s)$	-436.75	-409.14	82.59
$KBr(s)$	-393.80	-380.66	95.90
$KI(s)$	-327.90	-324.89	106.32
$KClO_3(s)$	-397.73	-296.25	143.1
$KClO_4(s)$	-432.75	-303.09	151.0
$K_2S(s)$	-380.7	-364.0	105
$K_2S(aq)$	-471.5	-480.7	190.4
Silicon			
$Si(s)$	0	0	18.83
$SiO_2(s,\alpha)$	-910.94	-856.64	41.84
Silver			
$Ag(s)$	0	0	42.55
$Ag^+(aq)$	105.58	77.11	72.68
$Ag_2O(s)$	-31.05	-11.20	121.3
$AgBr(s)$	-100.37	-96.90	107.1
$AgBr(aq)$	-15.98	-26.86	155.2
$AgCl(s)$	-127.7	-109.79	96.2
$AgCl(aq)$	-61.58	-54.12	129.3
$AgI(s)$	-61.84	-66.19	115.5
$AgI(aq)$	50.38	25.52	184.1
$AgNO_3(s)$	-124.39	-33.41	140.92
Sodium			
$Na(s)$	0	0	51.21
$Na(g)$	107.32	76.76	153.71
$Na^+(aq)$	-240.12	-261.91	59.0
$NaOH(s)$	-425.61	-379.49	64.46
$NaOH(aq)$	-470.11	-419.15	48.1

Table A8-Inorganic *Thermodynamic data at 25°C for assorted inorganic substances (continued).*

Substance	Enthalpy of formation ΔH_f^0, kJ/mol	Free energy of formation ΔG_f^0, kJ/mol	Entropy S^0, J/(K·mol)
$NaCl(s)$	-411.15	-384.12	72.13
$NaBr(s)$	-361.06	-348.98	86.82
$NaI(s)$	-287.78	-286.06	98.53
Sulfur			
S(*s, rhombic*)	0	0	31.80
S(*s, monoclinic*)	0.33	0.1	32.6
$S^{2-}(aq)$	33.1	85.8	-14.6
$SO_2(g)$	-296.83	-300.19	248.22
$SO_3(g)$	-395.72	-371.06	256.76
$H_2SO_4(l)$	-813.99	-690.00	156.90
$H_2SO_4(aq)$	-909.27	-744.53	20.1
$SO_4^{2-}(aq)$	-909.27	-744.53	20.1
$H_2S(g)$	-20.63	-33.56	205.79
$H_2S(aq)$	-39.7	-27.83	121
$SF_6(g)$	-1209	-1105.3	291.82
Tin			
Sn(*s, white*)	0	0	51.55
Sn(*s, gray*)	-2.09	0.13	44.14
$SnO(s)$	-285.8	-256.9	56.5
$SnO_2(s)$	-580.7	-519.6	52.3
Zinc			
$Zn(s)$	0	0	41.63
$Zn^{2+}(aq)$	-153.89	-147.06	-112.1
$ZnO(s)$	-348.28	-318.30	43.64

Table A8-Organic *Thermodynamic data at 25°C for assorted organic substances.*

Substance	Enthalpy of combustion ΔH^0_c, kJ/mol	Enthalpy of formation ΔH^0_f, kJ/mol	Free energy of formation ΔG^0_f, kJ/mol	Entropy S^0, J/(K·mol)
Hydrocarbons				
$CH_4(g)$, *methane*	-890	-74.81	-50.72	186.26
$C_2H_2(g)$, *acethylene*	-1300	226.73	209.20	200.94
$C_2H_4(g)$, *ethylene*	-1411	52.26	68.15	219.56
$C_2H_6(g)$, *ethane*	-1560	-84.68	-32.82	229.60
$C_3H_6(g)$, *propylene*	-2058	20.42	62.78	266.6
$C_3H_6(g)$, *cyclopropane*	-2091	53.30	104.45	237.4
$C_3H_8(g)$, *propane*	-2220	-103.85	-23.49	270.2
$C_4H_{10}(g)$, *butane*	-2878	-126.15	-17.03	310.1
$C_5H_{12}(g)$, *pentane*	-3537	-146.44	-8.20	349
$C_6H_6(l)$, *benzene*	-3268	49.0	124.3	173.3
$C_6H_6(g)$	-3302	---	---	---
$C_7H_8(l)$, *toluene*	-3910	12.0	113.8	221.0
$C_7H_8(g)$	-3953	---	---	---
$C_6H_{12}(l)$, *cyclohexane*	-3920	-156.4	26.7	204.4
$C_6H_{12}(g)$	-3953	---	---	---
$C_8H_{18}(l)$, *octane*	-5471	-249.9	6.4	358
Alcohols, phenols				
$CH_3OH(l)$, *methanol*	-726	-238.86	-166.27	126.8
$CH_3OH(g)$	-764	-200.66	-161.96	239.81
$C_2H_5OH(l)$, *ethanol*	-1368	-277.69	-174.78	160.7
$C_2H_5OH(g)$	-1409	-235.10	-168.49	282.70
$C_6H_5OH(s)$, *phenol*	-3054	-164.6	-50.42	144.0

Table A8-Inorganic *Thermodynamic data at 25°C for assorted organic substances (continued).*

Substance	Enthalpy of combustion ΔH^0_c, kJ/mol	Enthalpy of formation ΔH^0_f, kJ/mol	Free energy of formation ΔG^0_f, kJ/mol	Entropy S^0, J/(K·mol)
Aldehydes, ketones				
HCHO (*g*), *formaldehyde*	-571	-108.57	-102.53	218.77
CH_3CHO (*l*), *acetaldehyde*	-1166	-192.30	-128.12	160.2
CH_3CHO (*g*)	-1192	-166.19	-128.86	250.3
CH_3COCH_3 (*l*), *acetone*	-1790	-248.1	-155.4	200
Carboxylic acids				
HCOOH (*l*), *formic acid*	-255	-424.72	-361.35	128.95
CH_3COOH (*l*), *acetic acid*	-875	-484.5	-389.9	159.8
CH_3COOH (*aq*)	---	-485.76	-396.46	86.6
$(COOH)_2$ (*s*), *oxalic acid*	-254	-827.2	-697.9	120
C_6H_5COOH (*s*), *benzoic acid*	-3227	-385.1	-245.3	167.6
Sugars				
$C_6H_{12}O_6$ (*s*), *glucose*	-2808	-1268	-910	212
$C_6H_{12}O_6$ (*aq*)	---	---	-917	---
$C_6H_{12}O_6$ (*s*), *fructose*	-2810	-1266	---	---
$C_{12}H_{22}O_{11}$ (*s*), *sucrose*	-5645	-2222	-1545	360
Nitrogen compounds				
$CO(NH_2)_2$ (*s*), *urea*	-632	-333.51	-197.33	104.60
$C_6H_5NH_2$ (*l*), *aniline*	-3395	31.6	149.1	191.3
NH_2CH_2COOH(*s*), *glycine*	-969	-532.9	-373.4	103.51
CH_3NH_2 (*g*), *methylamine*	-1085	-22.97	32.16	243.41

Answer Key

Chapter 3

Chapter 4

73603812R00100

Made in the USA
Columbia, SC
06 September 2019